CW00400534

# The Adventures of an Introvert:

## Ten Countries,
## Four Continents;
## Minimal Eye Contact

David R.Y.W. Chapman

Copyright © 2019 David R.Y.W. Chapman

All rights reserved.

ISBN: 9781712356098

To Mum, Dad, Carol, John, and all of the people that have supported me through this process and have inspired me to document my wonderful memories.

I hope that Jonah, Lyrah, Daniel, Jessica, Jeanette, and all of the young members of our family can one day experience as many thrilling adventures as I have; whether they occur at home or abroad. Without the social anxiety, of course.

# CONTENTS

# CHAPTER 1: A GRAND VOYAGE
## AN INTRODUCTION FROM THE UNITED KINGDOM
## OCTOBER 2008

I was feeling increasingly anxious about the journey that I was set to embark upon. I had spent the last thirty minutes finding excuses to delay leaving my home in Timperley. Was I in possession of the required documentation? Had I remembered to pack everything? This resulted in me repeatedly checking to see if I had accounted for every situation known to mankind.

After delaying my departure until the last possible moment before the risk of missing my train from Manchester Piccadilly had become too severe, I told myself: "No more excuses. I am setting off now."

Adrenaline was flowing through my body as I left home and I strode with purpose towards the station. I was proud of myself for undertaking this grand voyage...to Birmingham.

It seems laughable now but this modest journey was a significant moment in my life. Although the purpose of the trip was to attend a live sporting event, this would, unbeknown to me at the time, eventually lead to a life of travel. I had never been particularly interested in visiting other countries and I had not left the United Kingdom for nearly a decade.

During my childhood, I had been on numerous family holidays to places such as Hong Kong, Toronto and Florida. As much as I enjoyed those trips, I could not say that they inspired me to travel around the world. That would come much later; after my exotic adventure in Birmingham.

In order to explain the significance of my long weekend in the Midlands in 2008, it is necessary to describe what kind of person I was at the time. I was a very shy child during my school years and as much as I had tried to break free from this, personality traits can often be difficult to change.

There was a certain mentality that remained from my childhood years; social interaction was limited to the bare minimum necessary to function in society, the quietest route would always be taken and most importantly, eye contact was to be avoided at all times.

Trips to the supermarket often resulted in me darting down an aisle that did not contain any items that I required; all because I had spotted a childhood acquaintance browsing the shelves that I actually needed. This would not be due to any particular dislike of the individual in question but it was based on a strong desire to avoid awkward conversations with people with whom I was only relatively familiar with.

I remember queueing up to purchase a book at a Waterstones store in Manchester many years ago when I realised that the person behind the till was a former classmate of mine from my time at Altrincham Grammar School for Boys. Again, I did not dislike him but the prospect of having to engage in the awkward, 'So how are you doing?' type of smalltalk was simply too much for me.

I knew that there was another Waterstones within the Arndale Centre; therefore, I took the course of action that felt the most natural to me. I put the book down and headed over to the other store to purchase it from there instead.

I would always have at least one obsession in my life at any given time. This included wrestling and football during my younger days, in which I collected the toy figures of every wrestler on the WCW roster and I religiously completed the annual Panini football sticker album. Building a collection linked to my hobbies would be a pattern that has continued into adulthood.

I find that the act of collecting something provides a sense of order and structure but it also makes you feel that you are working towards a more significant goal. In some sense, this gives the most enjoyable aspects of your life an extra level of meaning.

Whatever the current obsession was, this would be the most important thing, perhaps the only thing, in my somewhat empty life. There was a time during my barren teenage years in which the on-field success of Manchester United Football Club dictated the level of my happiness. In this respect, I guess I was extremely fortunate that I did not follow my brother's lead by supporting Blackburn Rovers.

Although obsession is not normally considered to be a good thing, it is what has driven me to escape the life of a recluse. I used to collect football stickers; now I collect countries. It is a rather expensive hobby but it has provided me with the very best form of escapism; the literal one.

*   *   *

My trip to Birmingham was centred around what was my latest obsession;

the sport of mixed martial arts. My unhealthy interest in the sport was enough to draw me out of my comfort zone and encourage me to venture out to another city on my own.

My time in Birmingham was not particularly eventful. I attended the UFC Fight Club activities that were held on the day before *UFC 89: Bisping vs. Leben* and observed the strange spectacle of the half-naked competitors getting weighed on stage.

This gave the fans a chance to get close to the mixed martial artists and to feel like they were a part of the event. On this occasion, I had my photograph taken with heavyweight competitor Cheick Kongo and UFC president Dana White. In some ways, it was like a gathering of lost souls who had finally been given a feeling of membership; albeit, one that the UFC charged a fortune for.

Fortunately, the UFC does not operate in the same way as the fictional organisation that was featured in the film *Fight Club,* otherwise I would have just broken the first rule of its membership. At least, I hope that it does not operate like that.

On that Friday evening, I bought a pre-packed sandwich, a bottle of Coca-Cola and a tub of Ben & Jerry's cookie dough to take back to my single room in one of the many Travelodge establishments that can be found within the Second City. As sad as it sounds, I was content to have a quiet night by myself and devour a big tub of ice cream whilst the bars and nightclubs were full of drunken revellers.

My brother, John, and his friends Scott and Paul, travelled down from Manchester the following day and we all attended the live event that evening. The others joined in with the rest of the crowd of nine thousand by having a few beers but I managed to avoid the drinking throughout the duration of the show. Unfortunately, I was unable to escape the alcohol related activities for too long, as my brother and his friends decided to head out to a few bars after the show.

Thankfully, I survived this ordeal and I was able to catch the train home in the morning without suffering from any freshly acquired mental damage. During the journey back to Manchester, I pondered whether many of those in attendance the previous evening were able to remember any of the action. Perhaps they were in a worse shape than Chris Leben after his defeat to Michael Bisping in the main event.

*　　*　　*

Whilst my passion for mixed martial arts has diminished in recent years, to the extent that I do not even watch it on television anymore, I shall always be grateful for the sport. Attending the live events that the UFC put on in a variety of locations throughout the world led to my love of travelling and, more importantly, it ensured that I would not remain a recluse forever. In the years that followed my trip to Birmingham, I attended mixed martial arts shows in a number of countries in Europe, North America, Asia and Oceania.

I may not have set out to explore the world and learn about new cultures but the sport took me to places where it was impossible not to do so. It was during this period of my life that the feeling of 'wanderlust' set in. As many others before me can testify, once the travel bug gets a hold of you, there is no known cure.

A short train journey to Birmingham once felt like a big adventure and something to fret about. If you would have told me back then that I would one day travel on my own to far flung places like Malaysia, I would have scarcely believed you. I certainly would have dismissed the notion that I would then undertake a twelve hour round trip to Singapore just to spend four hours exploring the city-state.

The prospect of visiting a country such as Oman would have seemed laughable. After all, I am not even sure that I was aware of its existence before I had started travelling around the world. Being told that I would journey to microstates such as San Marino and Andorra, places that do not even have an airport, would have seemed like the set-up of a joke at my expense. However, these events all form part of my travel journey, which has taken me to over sixty countries in six continents.

I liken my style of travel to the experience of eating at an international buffet restaurant. I sample some of the most well-known delights of as many countries as possible, whilst making a mental note of any that I would like to return to for a more in-depth, higher quality experience.

Part of the travel experience is to savour the best bits from each place whilst also considering the less pleasant aspects on offer. I have spent a varying amount of time in each nation, ranging from just a few hours to a couple of weeks. However, each one has added to my insatiable appetite for roaming the planet.

A new perspective is gained through overseas adventure. A person tends to look at things differently in their own country once they have adopted the mindset of a tourist; travelling almost becomes a state of mind rather than a physical relocation.

My daily commute involves a journey from my current home in Wigan, through Manchester, the city that has been an ever-present in my life, and then on to Altrincham, where I attended school and spent so much of my time during my childhood. Even this mundane and uncomfortable journey can also be viewed as part of my travel experience.

Applying the mentality of a traveller to my commute has caused me to appreciate everyday sights that I had previously neglected. I had ignored the wonderful architecture and industrial heritage of Manchester but I now view this city with the fondness that it deserves.

I have also enjoyed other beautiful places within the United Kingdom; with some of the more obvious highlights being Westminster and the River Thames in London, Arthur's Seat and the Royal Mile in Edinburgh, and the city walls of York.

I feel blessed to have been born in a fairly prosperous and liberal country, from which I am able to fly in and out of with ease. I am fortunate to live in a time in which one can make arrangements to voyage across continents almost as easily as one can plan trips within Great Britain.

My travel story is not the classic tale of ditching the nine to five routine in order to go backpacking through remote parts of the world for months on end. Instead, I have gone on a series of short adventures whilst remaining in full time employment.

The cheap and frequent flights offered by budget airlines have enabled me to touch down in a vast array of European countries during long weekend breaks, whilst my burning desire to see the world has given me enough discipline to accumulate the savings required to visit more exotic locations.

This book does not attempt to offer the definitive guide to travelling off the beaten track but my adventures hopefully demonstrate how it is possible for a socially awkward introvert to explore as much of our planet as he or she desires. It also highlights the many contradictions and conflictions within my life.

For example, I am risk-averse to the extent that when I am editing an office document, I nearly always elect to use the 'copy' rather than the 'cut' function; despite requiring the latter rather than the former. I will then go back and delete the original text or data once my eyes have seen the proof that the information has indeed been copied. Yet I will happily throw caution to the wind by travelling halfway across the world on my own.

I am eager to look around and admire the world that I inhabit yet my eyes are so often facing towards the ground; partly due to a fear of standing in dog excrement but also because I am hiding from potential social interaction.

And then there is the elephant in the room; in this case, the elephant has been leaving a rather sizeable carbon footprint. My heart is filled with joy when I travel to places of natural beauty but by doing so, I am helping to endanger those very locations.

Many of my early trips abroad, as detailed in this book, were filled with rookie mistakes and cringe-worthy moments in foreign lands. I hope that others find as much amusement in my embarrassing anecdotes as I do. The following thirteen chapters should provide you with an insight into how travelling has opened my eyes to new cultures and given me a different perspective on every element of life. It has also given me more confidence, courage and purpose. However, I still hide from people in supermarkets.

# CHAPTER 2: BABY STEPS AND FAST FOOD
## DUBLIN, THE REPUBLIC OF IRELAND
### JANUARY 2009

It could hardly have been a gentler start to my global exploration; not that I was aware at the time that I would become such a frequent traveller. The short plane journey across the Irish Sea only took around forty five minutes, most of which was part of either the takeoff or landing process.

I would soon find out that the Emerald Isle is an easy place for an Englishman to adapt to. The only problem was that I was an Englishman that had lived such a sheltered life that at one point during my pitiful existence, I would class leaving the house to buy a microwavable pizza from the local Mini Market in Timperley as a big social event that I had to mentally prepare for.

Although Irish is still the official first language, English is the most widely spoken. Dublin in particular has a familiar feel to the United Kingdom. Even the name of the city itself derives from the old Irish words 'Dubh' and 'Lind,' which roughly translates to 'Black Pool.'

If I felt uneasy about exploring a foreign city, I just had to tell myself that I was in Blackpool. Traditional Irish music and dance remains popular throughout the city, perhaps for the benefit of tourists, so maybe I would be unable to convince myself that I was in the familiar seaside town in the North West of England after all.

My interest in attending live mixed martial arts events had now grown to the extent that I was willing to venture outside of British soil. Rather than an exotic adventure to sun kissed lands with free-spirited friends, it was a cold and wet few days in January that marked my first taste of this new life of travel. I was not travelling alone though, as I would be accompanied by a fellow sports enthusiast. My dad.

Three nights in Dublin with my father was not exactly a voyage of self-discovery, nor did it result in an awakening of a desire to visit every corner of the planet but it was certainly a step further than the local Mini Market.

Like most things in life, the desire to travel was something that developed over time. A toddler's first steps are neither the most well executed nor graceful but they are perhaps the most important. It is a learning process in which you have to have the odd stumble before you have mastered the art. It is also during this time that you learn about the world, as you are able to interact with a wider range of situations. I would compare this to the early days of travelling, during which you see things that you had never even considered and you gain a whole new outlook on life. Those three nights in Dublin were, in effect, my first steps.

I had recently graduated from university and I was struggling to get a job. The old joke that states that: 'I had considered becoming a history teacher until I realised that there was no future in it,' was starting to feel rather apt. I had been volunteering for the British Red Cross for the past four years but I was lacking both a career and a purpose in life. Therefore, a fresh perspective would be most welcome.

Dad's lack of experience with technology, and his deep mistrust of it, had forced me into taking the lead role in organising the trip and making the necessary online bookings. He held a firm belief that mobile phones and computers were ruining the world. Remarkably, he still operated his successful accountancy business without the aid of either of the aforementioned items. He instead relied on the old-fashioned method of pen and paper. And the occasional use of a calculator.

My childhood is full of memories of Dad working frantically on his typewriter and adding machine. Most of you are probably not even aware of what an adding machine is but if you do, then you will know all about the excessive rolls of paper that it churns out simply to carry out a basic task of addition.

Whatever scenario my brother and I invented when making the case for Dad to purchase a mobile phone, he would come back with a counter argument, usually along the lines of not wanting to be contacted. Even if the hypothetical scene that we had painted involved him breaking both of his legs and being miles away from anyone else, he would still contend that a mobile phone would not be of any use to him.

As for justifying his 'old-school' methods, he would point to the outcome of *Rocky IV* as proof that technology is often detrimental.

Despite it being a fictional film, Rocky Balboa's victory over Ivan Drago served as a cornerstone for his argument.

I did not have any experience of organising trips away from home, so I relied on the knowledge that my mum had booked several holiday packages through Expedia. I was fortunate that flights and hotels, like most things nowadays, can be arranged online. This was a deal-breaker. The prospect of having to make a telephone call to a stranger or visit a travel agent in person did not bear thinking about and would almost certainly have put an end to any budding travel aspirations.

Although I no longer worry about such things to the same extent, I must admit that the option to make an online booking still heavily influences my everyday decisions. My choice of restaurant will depend on whether I can make an online reservation or not. When there is a problem with my theatre tickets, I will trawl through the website in the desperate hope of finding a way of contacting the theatre company via email so that I do not have to go through the horror of calling the customer service line.

I purchased a package that included our flights and accommodation without much consideration for the location of our hotel. This turned out to be fine on this occasion but it would prove to be a costly mistake during a break in Spain a few years later. I will cover this in another chapter, so you will have to wait a little longer before having a laugh at my expense; at least in regard to that matter. I am sure that there are plenty of other ways in which I have embarrassed myself prior to that shambolic episode.

Air travel had changed considerably since I had last used it. We were now in the era of budget airlines. It felt strange to check in online and head straight to security with our hand luggage. It was most welcome though; the less that I had to interact with other human beings, the more I would enjoy the trip. Neither of us had flown in the last decade, therefore it stood to reason that there was a good chance that one of us would pack something that we should not.

As it turns out, Dad had a small pair of scissors confiscated during the security check at Manchester Airport. Not too bad going for a couple of hapless chaps who felt overwhelmed by the throngs of passengers being herded through this area.

This is probably the most unpleasant part of a journey through the airport. However, it does leave me with mixed emotions. On the one hand, I feel reassured when I see that security is being thorough. The negative aspect of this is that it makes me feel suspicious that all eyes are focused on my every move. This anxiety causes me to remove my jacket, my belt, any toiletries and electrical items almost immediately after joining a queue that I know will take over ten minutes to reach the front of.

Speaking of queues, we were surprised to see people lined up and waiting to board our plane that was not due to take off for another fifty minutes. The call to commence boarding had not even been made yet. Were people really this keen to get on board the aircraft? I surveyed the scene before inspecting my boarding pass. It was at this point that I realised what was happening.

Ryanair did not allocate seats at the time of our trip; hence, passengers resorted to queueing up as early as possible in order to guarantee that they were able to sit together in an area that they desired. With nothing better to do, we joined the rest of the desperate souls in the queue.

Once boarding began, it was like a free-for-all, with people as good as pushing each other out of the way in order to snare their chosen seats. Dad and I managed to claim two seats next to each other but as I placed our luggage in the overhead lockers, someone slammed their case into the side of my head in the midst of this chaotic scene.

Everything else about the aviation experience was focused on safety yet this ridiculous approach to seat allocation seriously risked the welfare of passengers and crew alike. I had not experienced anything like it. The most fitting comparison I can make is of the utter madness that I have become accustomed to seeing during news coverage of the Black Friday sales. I sincerely hoped that the Irish airline experience was not an indicator of what to expect in the country itself.

I readied myself for the flight. Since I had not been on a plane since my adolescent years, I was not sure what to expect. Would it be stressful, exciting or frightening? The engines began to rumble and the pilot informed us that we were about to take off. Here we go...here we still go. The taxi to the runway seemed to take an eternity.

We were now in position for takeoff and the engines really began to roar. Ok, *now* here we go.

"Would you like a sweet?" Dad asked.

After accepting the fruit chew, I applied my gorilla grip to both armrests and I pressed myself back against my seat so hard that I almost became part of its fabric.

Some find takeoff to be an exhilarating experience. However, I just felt slightly uneasy as we swung in one direction then another in order to follow our flight path away from the airport. This sensation has remained with me even after the countless flights that I have taken in the following years.

It is not a surprise, given that I have never enjoyed any of the rollercoaster rides that I have been on. That is unless you count The Caterpillar. I do not even like it when I am a passenger in a car moving at speed whilst the windows are open; the toddler analogy probably seems more appropriate to all of you now.

We were up in the air and the plane was feeling steadier. Now we could relax. Around twenty minutes later, the pilot's voice was being played over the sound system once again, "Cabin crew prepare for landing."

That was quick. I wondered if all flights would be this straightforward. Thankfully, the descent and landing did not make me feel as uncomfortable as the take off had done. Perhaps I had not yet seen enough episodes of *Air Crash Investigation*.

Nowadays, I have a slight worry every time that I can hear the landing gear dropping in to place. Has the gear become jammed like on that flight that was featured in the programme that I saw the other week? Was that gust of wind an indication that the plane would be unable to stay on course for the runway? I have never really had anything worse than a bit of a bumpy landing but these thoughts tend to pop into my mind at the worst possible time.

*     *     *

Dad and I were now in Ireland. Dublin International Airport would provide the setting for my first adult experience of border control. The long queues have never bothered me as I have always accepted that this process is not something that should be rushed and I would want the officers in charge to do a thorough job.

I find it quite amusing that I show this understanding whilst holding a fairly liberal view on immigration issues, yet some individuals who are more hostile towards people moving between countries show a considerable impatience when held up at passport control. Perhaps they only think that stringent checks at the border should be carried out on people other than themselves.

We took a taxi to our hotel, which belonged to the Jurys Inn chain. It had never crossed my mind to research cheaper ways to reach the city centre and it would not be given consideration for a few more trips to come. Our overpriced taxi did not take too long to reach our hotel and, thankfully, Dad engaged in enough conversation with the driver that it allowed me to stay quiet for the entirety of the journey.

Dad was more than happy to chat about some of his favourite topics, such as the global financial crisis and various inept governments, whilst the driver informed him of the high unemployment in the country. That was a bullet dodged. If I had been forced to join in such conversations that may well have been enough to have put me off travelling for good.

Checking in to the hotel was straightforward, with the simple task of providing the name that the room was booked under being something that even a socially inept person like me could handle with ease.

We were soon in the room where we would spend the next three nights. I gave myself a pat on the back. I felt pleased with myself that I had managed to book a flight to the correct city and I had selected a hotel that was not falling apart. Even better, I had chosen a room with twin beds rather than a double. It felt like an outstanding achievement.

The room was surprisingly nice and we would go on to have a pleasant stay here. Generally speaking, I enjoy spending time in hotels. They not only provide somewhere to sleep for the night, I find that they also represent something more significant. As a guest of the hotel, one is able to truly relax and make the most of the facilities on offer, safe in the knowledge that there is no housework to do. Another positive is that hotel rooms, like the one that we were now stood in, are invariably tidier and much nicer in appearance than my bedroom has ever been.

The change of scenery is usually most welcome, which was certainly the case at the time of our trip to Dublin. My shyness would invariably lead to a repetitive life back in Timperley; I would only venture out of the house when it was absolutely necessary to do so. Therefore, three nights in a Jurys Inn was a bit of an adventure for me.

It was late Thursday afternoon and time to leave the hotel to explore what Dublin had to offer. The only problem was that I had absolutely no idea what Dublin did have to offer. Even my recently acquired history degree had not provided me with enough desire to carry out any research prior to our trip.

My lack of interest in travelling must have been evident to the hotel receptionist, of whom I asked the naïve question: "What is there to see in Dublin?"

The man behind the desk replied: "Well, there is plenty to see sir."

He may have rolled his eyes at me before reeling off a list of historical sites but I would not have noticed this as I was too busy avoiding any prolonged eye contact.

It turns out that the hotel was situated by the bank of the River Liffey and just a ten minute walk to O'Connell Street, the main thoroughfare of the city. Once we had exited the hotel, I could not remember anything else he had said, therefore our options were pretty limited. The river that divides the city was right in front of us, so I took a few photos. One of me stood in front of the river. Another of Dad stood in front of the river. One of me stood in front of the hotel. Another of Dad stood in front of the hotel. With the river ticked off, we were down to one place of interest that we knew of.

We set off for O'Connell Street with the knowledge that we would soon have seen everything on our extensive list of attractions. It was a simple walk along one long road to our destination. If we were more knowledgeable about the city, we would have known that there were a number of historic sites that were littered along our route.

We could have visited The Custom House, which was built in the eighteenth century for the purpose of collecting custom duties. We could have taken a tour around a replica of the *Jeanie Johnston* ship that successfully transported thousands of Irish emigrants to North America during the Great Famine. In truth, we were oblivious to the attractions around us as we made our way towards the heart of the city.

After walking for ten minutes, we eventually reached our destination. We turned right onto O'Connell Street without giving much more than a passing glance at the bridge to our left. O'Connell Bridge has a history going back to the eighteenth century but perhaps the most interesting fact about it is that its width is greater than its length. I think that we would have walked over the bridge and had a closer look if I had been aware of that quirky nugget of information.

The first thing that we saw on O'Connell Street was, unsurprisingly, a statue of Daniel O'Connell. Often referred to as 'The Liberator,' he was a key figure in restoring the rights of Catholics and, through his pioneering form of peaceful protest, he pushed for the repeal of the Acts of Union that had tied Ireland to Great Britain.

More radical figures would take over the mantle in what became an increasingly violent fight for independence, eventually resulting in both the Irish War of Independence and the Irish Civil War. A century after his death, the country officially became known as the Republic of Ireland and it was no longer ruled by the British monarchy.

The Spire of Dublin, or the 'Monument of Light,' is the most eye-catching structure of O'Connell Street and it is one of the most recognisable landmarks within the city. With a height of just under four hundred feet, it is hard to miss. With our heads tilted back and our eyes looking up towards the sky, we examined what appeared to be a giant lead pencil. It is easy to see why it has received a mixed reception since it was unveiled in 2003. When standing up close, you can see the intricate artwork around the base of the spire but from afar it just looks like a giant pole.

The Spire was a replacement for Nelson's Pillar, which once towered above what used to be called Sackville Street. The granite column was erected at the start of the nineteenth century, when Ireland was part of the

United Kingdom. It was built to commemorate Horatio Nelson after his success at the Battle of Trafalgar but the sight of an Englishman looking down on the local population was soon resented by many.

The pillar survived one attempt to blow it up during the Easter Rising but succumbed to that very fate in 1966. There is an element of irony attached to the fact that the Irish architect Francis Johnston heavily contributed to the final design of the pillar that was destroyed for symbolising British Imperialism, whilst its replacement was the creation of an English based architectural firm.

It was notable how many monuments there were that lined O'Connell Street. Aside from the aforementioned O'Connell Monument, there were statues that honoured other historical Irishmen such as Charles Stewart Parnell and Sir John Gray.

I did not have a clue whom any of them were but I figured that they must have been important for them to be immortalised in this way. I took pictures of them all with the intention of researching their importance at a later date. History lessons could wait; for now I just felt content that they at least made for pretty photographs and provided further proof that I had indeed visited Ireland.

The other striking thing about O'Connell Street was the number of fast food restaurants that could be found on either side of the street. This was by far the highest concentration of burger and fried chicken shops that I had ever seen in one place. I was astonished by how many different food outlets there were that were basically selling the same thing. How could any of them make a profit when there was such intense competition? I pondered this for a minute before realising that all of this thought of food had made me hungry.

We were now faced with the decision of which of these fine establishments to enter. Following a long discussion with Dad, we decided to sample some of the local cuisine. McDonald's, of course. After consuming this traditional Irish dinner, I decided to be brave and use the McToilet. This was a big mistake.

I had barely opened the door to the bathroom, let alone the cubicle, when I realised that I could not possibly spend more than three seconds there due to the horrendous smell. In order to avoid a conversation about toilets and bodily functions with Dad, I pretended that I had relieved myself and left the restaurant with a dire need to pass urine.

After dinner, we wandered into the cinema, where we watched a largely unremarkable film called *The Spirit*, which featured Gabriel Macht, Samuel L. Jackson, Eva Mendes and Scarlett Johansson. It did, however, serve its purpose of keeping us occupied for a couple of hours before we returned to our hotel.

It is quite sad when I look back and I realise that we were almost willing the time away during an evening in a lively city like Dublin. It was only the first night and we did not have any sightseeing left on our agenda. This did not really matter to us at the time, as we had mixed martial arts related events to keep us busy over the next couple of days. After all, this is what we had come to Dublin for. Sightseeing was just something to occupy the time between these sporting activities.

Judging by the price of the cinema tickets and fast food that we had consumed, it was perhaps for the best that we did not visit many attractions. The Republic of Ireland is in the European Union, so the Euro is the currency in use. As we would find out, one tends to need a fair amount of Euros for a visit to the Emerald Isle, as everything seems to be so expensive compared to back home in Britain.

And our trip was taken long before there had been any serious mention of Brexit. I dread to think how expensive everything would seem now. Sorry, I was hoping to make it further into the book without bringing up the dreaded 'B' word.

*   *   *

Watching a series of men standing on the stage of what was then called the O2 Arena with only their underpants on was the most significant event on Friday. This was not some erotic performance that we were attending; we were observing the weigh-ins for the following night's mixed martial arts show, which had been given the title of *UFC 93: Franklin vs. Henderson.*

As each competitor took to the scales, they appeared to be more nervous than someone that was getting weighed during their weekly Slimming World class. The relief of hitting their target weight was palpable; after all, they had spent the last couple of days jeopardising their health by trying to temporarily lose as much weight as possible. The Slimming World analogy again springs to mind.

I spotted one of the referees that would be officiating the following evening's proceedings sat a few rows in front of us and I deliberated whether I should approach him for a photograph. In the end, I did just that, which goes to show how deep my sporting obsession had become.

In normal circumstances, I would have done anything to avoid engaging in conversation with a stranger. Dan Miragliotta kindly posed for a photograph with me before doing the same for Dad. He was practically twice the size of me; and he was only one of the referees!

I had heard that Michael Bisping, Britain's most successful mixed martial artist, was making an appearance in one of the city's many pubs.

Apparently, there are around seven hundred and fifty pubs in Dublin. This seemed a lot to me but I was shocked to find out that there are over three and a half thousand within London.

The fact that the United Kingdom is the only country to consume more Guinness than the Republic of Ireland was also surprising but it really should not have been, given how much larger the population of the former is compared to the latter.

The British fighter's attendance had been arranged by the UFC Fight Club, which was an online community of fans of the sport. Dad and I had arrived early and we had ordered a couple of pints of the drink that was famous throughout the world for its black colour and full bodied flavour. Coca-Cola rather than Guinness, of course. We had even failed to embrace Irish culture, and flavour, whilst sat in a pub that was selling pints of the famous stout to more or less everyone other than the two of us.

Bisping soon arrived and sat down with his small entourage. After ten minutes of deliberation, I finally plucked up the courage to approach him. At that very moment, the food that he had ordered was being brought to his table. This was a case of bad timing, as it probably appeared that I was being rude by interrupting him at this point in time.

His response confirmed my suspicions: "Come on, I'm just about to eat."

Almost instantly, he forgave my poorly timed request and kindly posed for a photograph.

With that image successfully captured, we were left with two choices; stay and have some Irish stew and Guinness, or leave. Of course, we chose the latter. We had not touched a drop of Guinness and we would not even consume any alcohol at all during our stay in the Irish capital. A decade on, I have certainly acquired a taste for stout, so I imagine that I will consume a few pints upon my next visit to the city.

In the evening, we had some more fast food before going to see a stand-up comic performing at a nearby venue called The Sugar Club. Of course, even this revolved around the world of mixed martial arts; he was also one of the UFC's commentators for Saturday night's show.

If you have seen Joe Rogan perform, then you will know that his act is full of jokes about sex, drugs and a variety of generally rude subjects laced with profanity. His routine was certainly funny. Dad and I, however, have the classic middle class father and son relationship in which everything in our power is done to avoid talking about the type of subject matter that was discussed on stage that evening.

During my adolescent years, I would frantically try and find topics of conversation to occupy us for a minute or two whenever a sex scene popped up during a film that we were watching together on television. Therefore, spending a couple of hours sat next to each other whilst listening to a comedian joke about the strangest pornography that he had encountered on the internet was somewhat awkward. I enjoyed the show and I am sure that Dad also had a fun evening. Neither of us, however, would dare talk about it afterwards.

Instead, we mulled over the misfortune of the warm up act, who had to perform in front of a crowd that was already restless after being informed that Joe was running considerably late.

"The poor guy stood no chance," I remarked.

He tried his best to appease the hostile punters with his off-the-cuff, extended routine but his shaky voice portrayed an air of desperation mixed in with despair.

Following the conclusion of the show, I was pleased to have had my picture taken with Joe Rogan and fellow mixed martial arts personality Eddie Bravo. Even if the first attempt resulted in Dad taking a picture of himself due to him pointing the camera in the wrong direction.

We watched some television upon our return to our hotel room, tuning in to one of the numerous news channels. As it turns out, the world's attention was gripped by a couple of events that had taken place, or were due to take place, in a country that has strong historical links to Ireland.

The United States of America was preparing for the inauguration of Barack Obama, who was set to become its first black president. Washington D.C. had been planning this historic event since his election victory in November but another prominent news story involved something that had occurred without such prior warning.

Shortly after taking off from La Guardia Airport in New York, US Airways Flight 1549 faced a danger that could not have been predicted. Multiple bird strikes had caused both engines to fail, leaving the aircraft in an extremely perilous position. Remarkably, pilots Chesley Sullenberger, affectionately known as 'Sully,' and Jeffrey Skiles managed to glide the aircraft to a relatively safe landing in the Hudson River.

Incredibly, there were not any fatalities amongst the one hundred and fifty five people on board. The pilots were hailed as American heroes and a Hollywood movie called *Sully: Miracle on the Hudson,* starring Tom Hanks, soon followed. Understandably, these two events dominated the news coverage for the duration of our trip.

Here we were, cooped up inside of our hotel room, watching the same news reports being looped every hour whilst everyone else was partying away in this most vibrant of cities. Ireland's population has the youngest average age within the European Union and Dublin is one of the most popular locations in Europe for stag and hen weekends.

I can understand why this is the case, as the city seems so full of life and merriment; which is precisely why it was not our cup of tea. Incidentally, a cup of tea was our choice of nightcap, as this held more appeal to us than any of the whisky, stout and beer that was being served in the pubs of Dublin.

\*　　\*　　\*

*UFC 93: Franklin vs. Henderson* was held on Saturday evening. After spending most of the day aimlessly walking around the city and frequenting another fast food restaurant on O'Connell street, we headed towards the O2 Arena at around five in the evening. I spent the next few hours dehydrated in order to minimise the risk of needing the toilet halfway through the show.

This was not because I was worried about missing any of the action; rather, this was due to the ghastly thought of having to carry out some bodily functions whilst many of the other nine thousand people in attendance were crammed into a public bathroom with me.

We began the short walk back to the hotel following the conclusion of Dan Henderson's victory over Rich Franklin. I had made the ever-so-sensible decision of only wearing a T-shirt and jeans on this cold winter's night.

"Are you not cold?" Dad asked.

He seemed amused by the fact that had I spent the entirety of the ten minute walk with my body shivering and my teeth chattering.

\*　　\*　　\*

The return journey home the next day was relatively straightforward. We took another expensive taxi back to the airport before we travelled home on one of the many daily flights from Dublin to Manchester. The trip had been a success; neither of us had come to any harm and we had not missed any of the mixed martial arts related activities.

My thoughts were still focused on sporting events rather than sightseeing though. It would take a few more trips before I realised that I enjoyed the experience of exploring new places more than watching the shows themselves. The historic sites of Dublin Castle, Temple Bar and St. Patrick's Cathedral would have to wait until my next visit. As would Irish stew and Guinness. For now, I was simply content to have survived my first travel adventure.

# CHAPTER 3: ENGLISH IGNORANCE AND MANIACAL GERMAN DRIVERS
## COLOGNE, GERMANY
### JUNE 2009

"Cologne? Isn't that a type of perfume? Just kidding. I have actually been to Cologne many years ago. Yes, it will be a good trip".

That was Dad's reaction to my suggestion that we should follow up our trip to Dublin with a long weekend in Germany, in order to attend another mixed martial arts show. This was not surprising, given that it is a place that is synonymous with perfume, since Johann Maria Farina created 'Eau de Cologne' at the start of the eighteenth century.

This particular scent was so successful that the term, shortened to 'Cologne' in America, is widely used as a general reference to this type of perfume. Like many other people around the world, I had previously associated the word 'Cologne' with the perfume rather than Germany's fourth largest city.

Five months after our Irish adventure, we were preparing for the next trip abroad. Cologne, or Köln as it is known in German, may have been the destination this time around but it would not have mattered where the show was being held, as our only consideration was whether it was close enough to travel to. It turns out that we were lucky that the city chosen to host *UFC 99: The Comeback* was one of the most splendid in all of Germany.

There is a current trend for celebrities to appear in programmes in which they travel around with their parents for comedic effect. I, on the other hand, found myself travelling with a parent for a very different reason. I had a happy childhood but I had lived quite a sheltered life up to this point. During my school years, I would keep my head down and hope to make it through each day without incident. I never had anything particularly bad nor good happen to me; I more or less went unnoticed, which was exactly how I liked it.

Following the conclusion of the school day, my antisocial instincts would kick in, as I would wait for around forty five minutes for the Metrolink tram station in Altrincham to quieten down before making my way back to Timperley. Evenings would be spent in the sanctuary of my family home, watching whatever sport I could find on television.

I did not go to parties or socialise on the streets as many others did; instead, I enjoyed the safety and tranquillity of home and I was happy to spend time in my own company. Whilst I was content with this way of life, it did not prepare me for the wider world that I would need to engage in during adulthood.

The idea of travelling alone was unthinkable and I was not close enough to my friends to be able to convince them to accompany me on such a trip, so I turned to my parents. My father was the natural choice as he was a fellow sports enthusiast but my mother would soon join me on many of my trips. I was able to form an unlikely but effective travel duo with either parent but solo journeys were simply out of the question at this stage.

We had hardly carried out in-depth research on the tourist sites of Cologne but we had at least made some effort to improve on our feeble showing in Dublin. I was impressed with the images that I had seen of the famous Kölner Dom and the Hohenzollern Bridge. At least I would show some enthusiasm for sightseeing this time around.

Despite my inexperience, I was not deterred by the prospect of having to catch a connecting flight in order to reach our destination. After a one hour flight to Amsterdam, we found ourselves with three times that amount of time to kill in Schiphol Airport.

During the course of our journey, I had discovered that Manchester United had accepted a world record transfer bid from Real Madrid to sell their reigning FIFA World Player of the Year, Cristiano Ronaldo. The Spanish club were willing to pay a staggering eighty million pounds for his services. Whilst this has proven to be a sound financial investment by the Madrid based football club, it highlighted how ludicrous the world of football had become.

Footballers were now getting paid hundreds of thousands of pounds a week and mind boggling transfer fees like this one were becoming the norm. I was disappointed that United were losing their best player but Dad, being a staunch 'Anyone But United' man, was absolutely delighted.

We decided to eat at the food court but I immediately wished that we had spent a little longer searching for another option. This meant that I was now faced with one of the many social scenarios that I was slightly uncomfortable with. I would not only have to tell a Dutch stranger which food choices that I wished to make but I would also have to confirm this with another stranger further along the counter and hand over the correct amount of foreign currency.

Perhaps this was my final challenge before I could be sure that I was ready for a trip to a city in continental Europe. Against all odds, I passed this test without suffering any public humiliation. Bring on Germany!

I had read about a rather interesting fact regarding Cologne Bonn Airport prior to embarking on our trip; it was formerly one of NASA's Transoceanic Abort Landing sites. This meant that it could have been used in the event of an aborted launch, due to its long runway and because the airport had the personnel and equipment to deal with such a scenario.

It was not the only commercial airport to be granted this status; Morocco, Senegal, and The Gambia all had similar arrangements in place. Incidentally, the Royal Air Force station in Fairford, Gloucestershire was the only one in the United Kingdom. I had visions of a space rocket roaring past our aircraft on the way to the airport but the now defunct system was never used during its existence.

*   *   *

As it had taken around five hours to reach Cologne, the twenty minute taxi journey to our Radisson Blu hotel in the city centre seemed to fly by. And with the speed that the vehicle was travelling at, it almost felt like we were about to take off for our third flight of the day. This should not have been such a surprise, as we were now in a country that does not have a speed limit on many roads.

Indeed, the mere suggestion of introducing more widespread speed limits within Germany has been enough to draw intense criticism and ridicule. At least there was no danger of having to make small talk with the driver. I think I was quite happy with this trade off, even if it meant an increased chance of perishing in a head on collision.

The lady behind the hotel reception spoke fluent English, as had the taxi driver when he had informed us of our inflated fare. It served to highlight how fortunate I am that English is so widely spoken around the world and how lazy this could make me and my fellow English speaking tourists become. Wherever you travel in the world, there will more than likely be enough locals who speak English that it is possible to roam around the city without even uttering a single word of the native language.

My father and I had become the latest in a long line of Brits to have stumbled into this shameful ignorance. The only defence that I can put forward is that the German language can seem particularly daunting to foreigners.

The average German sentence seems to be so much longer than the English equivalent and some German words contain so many letters that they must have been the creation of either a comedian or a sadist. At the time of our visit, the longest word in the German language had a scarcely believable sixty three letters in it.

Rindfleischetikettierungsüberwachungsaufgabenübertragungsgesetz was a compound word that roughly translated to 'law delegating beef label monitoring' but it became obsolete in 2013. Officially, this was due to changes in European Union regulations about the testing of cattle but I suspect that it was actually because the authorities realised that this word came about because somebody fell asleep on a keyboard.

To compound matters, no pun intended, Dad was showcasing another classic British trait that was sure to test the patience of our hosts; speaking extremely slowly and loudly, as if to indicate 'do you understand me?' with every sentence.

The receptionist may well have had a better understanding of English than either one of us but she remained professional and did not show any sign of being offended by Dad saying: "CHAPMAN...ROOM FOR TWO...THREE NIGHTS."

She simply smiled and gave a warm reply of: "Ok Sir, we have located the booking. Here is your room key. The room is located on the second floor, which is accessible by either the lift or staircase behind you. The Wi-Fi password is listed on the back of the confirmation printout that I have just handed you."

It was Dad's turn once again: "OK...THANK YOU...GOODNIGHT".

I gave a rueful smile, coupled with a nod of acknowledgment towards the receptionist before we headed up towards our room.

Whichever country in the world that you are in, there is a good chance that the hotels will have at least one English language news channel available for guests to watch. This establishment was no exception. News coverage for that evening focused on events that were having an effect on the entire world. For example, a global swine flu epidemic had been declared by the World Health Organization on that very day.

The world was also in the grip of economic turmoil; with Brazil, Chile and Bulgaria recently joining many other countries in announcing that they had entered into a recession. On a more positive note, it was estimated that the worst of the economic crisis had passed and that these countries would soon come out of recession. With these cheery news stories fresh in our minds, we attempted to get some much needed shut-eye.

*     *     *

After a pleasant night's sleep in our hotel room, it was time for to head down for breakfast. What local delights would we plump for? Cornflakes for Dad and a bowl of Frosties for myself. It would be another few trips before I became adventurous enough to try unfamiliar foods. This would one day become a big part of my enjoyment of travelling but I was not ready for this yet.

Our itinerary was once again dictated by the order of events put on by the UFC. Another afternoon of watching half naked men standing on stage getting weighed awaited us. Before any of that, we headed out to explore Cologne, armed with the limited research that I had undertaken.

Considering that the green man icon was on display as we crossed the road, we felt shocked and angered when a car started to turn right around the corner and only stopped when it was yards from hitting us.

"Idiot," we both muttered.

Then the same thing happened at the next crossing.

"Is everyone in Germany undecided on whether to kill us?" I pondered.

When this happened for a third time a few minutes later, we knew that this must be normal practice here. We stood back and observed the scene for a while. It became apparent that cars turning right are permitted to do so even if the green man is on display. The cars are only required to stop if there are people crossing their path.

I expressed my concerns to Dad: "I don't think I like this system. You cannot be confident of crossing the road without a car ploughing into you."

Dad added that, "It's asking for trouble."

As it turns out, this system is used throughout much of continental Europe when there is a turn right signal rather than a red light. The driver turning right has to make way for pedestrians before using their judgement to decide whether it is safe to proceed. This is exactly what terrifies me. I never relish relying on other people's judgement; certainly not when the other person's decision could result in me being run over by a Mercedes or a BMW.

I want to walk across the road with peace of mind rather than a faint hope that a reckless person will restrain themselves from chancing his or her luck. Regardless of this, according to European Commission statistics, Germany had less pedestrian fatalities in relation to the size of their relative population than the United Kingdom did in the decade up to and including 2006.

We soon arrived at the first tourist attraction of our trip. The Hohenzollern Bridge was inaugurated in 1911 by Kaiser Wilhelm II, who is one of the four Prussian Kings and German Emperors that are honoured in the form of statues at either entrance point of the bridge. Most of the bridge seemed to be taken up by the three railway tracks that run through its centre.

Indeed, it is the most used railway bridge in Germany, with the city of Cologne being one of the busiest rail hubs in all of Europe. Three must be a popular number, given that each railway track has three iron arches above it that run the entire length of the bridge.

The Hohenzollern Bridge somehow survived all Allied attempts to destroy it by airstrike during the Second World War. In the end, it was the Nazis who eventually blew it up in an attempt to stop the advancing Allied forces from reaching the city.

If the bridge had not been restored, this vital transport link across the Rhine River would not exist and we would not have been treated to such a visual delight. More importantly, our already small list of attractions to visit would have been further diminished.

It was every bit as impressive as the images on the internet had indicated. The sun was out in full force and the blue sky contained very few clouds, so the skyline looked strikingly beautiful behind the historic bridge. Kölner Dom was an imposing building that dominated the view that we were being treated to.

In order to reach the cathedral, we would have to complete our relaxing stroll across the bridge.

"It is around four hundred metres long," I informed Dad.

I immediately regretted this comment, as he responded by saying: "I may run the length of it and see how fast I can do this."

I started to feel nervous. If anyone else had said this, I would have dismissed it as a joke but Dad was an athlete who had competed in events across Britain for over forty years. It was fairly common for him to take up an opportunity to sprint in an unconventional location. I prayed that this was not going to be such an occasion.

"The pathway is quite narrow so it could be difficult to avoid other pedestrians," I cautioned. I held little hope but this turned out to be one of the few times that Dad resisted such a temptation.

As we crossed the bridge at a sensible pace, we noticed something that I had never seen or heard of before. There were a series of padlocks that were attached to the railings that ran along the bridge and that separated the pedestrian footpath from the railway tracks. This made me curious as to why they had been placed there.

On inspection, it became clear why they had been affixed to the railings. There were the names of two people and a date written on each padlock; mostly a man and a woman's names. The logical conclusion was that they must be the names of lovers.

I was indeed correct. I would later look online and read about how it had become popular for these 'lovers' locks' to be affixed to bridges all over the world. The key would then be thrown into the river to symbolise how the love between the couple would last forever. I was not sure if I found this to be romantic or unsightly.

City councils tend to think the latter and end up removing the locks, often due to the sheer weight of them warping the integrity of the railings. I would go on to make a 'lovers' lock' with my future wife a few years later, so I guess I am in not in any position to criticise them. In any case, I somehow resisted the temptation to attach a lock adorned with the words: 'Barry and David. Father and son since 1984.'

The enormous size of the thirteenth century cathedral became more apparent once we were stood in its shadow. It is the largest Gothic cathedral in Northern Europe and it certainly felt like it. The historical and architectural value of the building was undeniable, making it clear why it has long been the symbol of the city and it is now the country's most visited attraction.

As soon as we had stepped inside, a clergyman gestured for me to remove my baseball cap. Although I had not intended any disrespect, it was a gentle reminder that places such as this were primarily sites of worship rather than just tourist attractions for the likes of myself to rummage around in.

After removing my headwear, Dad and I struggled to put into words our admiration for the building.

"Big, " Dad remarked.

"Very big," I replied.

We did, however, manage to acknowledge how it was remarkable to think that construction began several centuries ago and had stood proudly for all of this time, although much of its construction actually took place during the nineteenth century.

The sense of history appealed to me. I wondered how many people had passed through the huge doors of the main entrance and how many people had experienced significant moments within its walls. This is part of what I love about travelling; you get to acquire a feel for history in an interactive format rather than just reading about it in a book.

Whilst we admired the stained glass windows and Gothic architecture, there were a couple of notable features that we were unaware of at the time. The shiny gold reliquary behind the high altar is known as 'The Shrine of the Three Kings' and it is said to contain the bones of the Three Wise Men that visited Jesus. Regardless of whether I believed in God or not, the interesting history associated with it would have garnered my attention if I had been aware of its existence.

The cathedral also housed, what was at the time of our visit, the largest swinging bell in the world. Petersglocke, or Saint Peter's Bell as it is known in English, has a diameter of over three metres and weighs a whopping twenty four thousand kilograms. For what it is worth, it has since been surpassed in size by the bell of the People's Salvation Cathedral in Bucharest.

We left the cathedral and decided to take some pictures of the gigantic building that we had just been exploring. I soon realised that I would need to stand quite far away to capture it in all its glory. We ended up walking to the very edge of the square and stood at the furthest possible point from the dome. I could still not fit it all in one shot. Photography was not something I had taken seriously before but now I was cursing the fact that I could not snap the image that I desired.

I crouched down on one knee in the hope that this perspective would bring me some joy. I could still not quite capture the whole thing. The limitations of using an old camera that my mum had given to me were quickly becoming apparent. After settling for a photo of only three quarters of the building, I vowed to improve my photography skills and equipment before returning to the cathedral at some point in the future.

It was time for the weigh-ins for Saturday night's UFC show, so we headed back across to the other side of the Rhine, towards the Lanxess Arena. I always enjoyed attending these Friday festivities but when I think about what they involve, I am not sure why this was the case. A bunch of grown men and women, dressed in awful and unimaginative Tapout clothing, cheering vociferously as over twenty drawn-out competitors took it in turn to strip off and stand on the scales. The crowd would roar with approval every time that a fighter's weight was read out.

However strange this was, I guess that the energy from the crowd, combined with seeing the competitors up close and ready for action, helped build up my excitement for the following night's show. This was all part of the successful strategy of fan engagement that the UFC executes so well.

Getting the chance to meet the competitors was another key part of this. On this occasion, we met middleweight competitor Amir Sadollah and the legendary cutmen, Jacob 'Stitch' Duran and Leon Tabbs. All three were friendly and kindly obliged our requests for photographs.

With our first full day in Cologne was drawing to a close, we grabbed some dinner at a fast food outlet before retiring to our hotel room for the night. It had been a successful and thoroughly enjoyable day, in which we had seen the two most significant landmarks of the city.

The thought of walking around in a foreign country no longer seemed quite so daunting and my appreciation of historical sites was gradually being awoken. I just hoped that I would not be awoken in the middle of the night by Dad's snoring.

*   *   *

Having consumed some more cereal for breakfast, it was time to head back into the city centre. The arena doors opened at around five in the evening, so we had most of the day to wander around at our leisure. There was, however, a meet and greet with British fighter Michael Bisping scheduled for around mid-day.

We had already met him in Dublin but given that we had little else to do, we decided to attend. Besides, at least we could apologise for interrupting his meal last time around. There was little chance of the same thing happening again, as the event was due to take place inside a video game store called GameStop. Whilst we were in the queue to meet him, Bisping called out to us and indicated that we could skip the line.

Once at the front, he extended a warm greeting to Dad: "Hello there, you didn't have to queue up. How are you doing, Sir?"

I had not expected our previous encounter to have left such a positive and memorable impression.

He continued: "Your son has been working hard and he'll do well in his next fight."

He was not talking about me or my brother, so it was clearly a case of mistaken identity.

I had no idea which fighter's father he thought Dad was but we were in too deep now. We had to carry on with the pretence.

Dad eventually switched the conversation to his athletic endeavours and challenged Bisping: "I am going to see which one of us is the first to becomes a world champion. I aim to win a gold medal at the World Championships in athletics for my age group before you win the UFC title."

Bisping seemed surprised: "I did not know that you competed in athletics."

I think that it was at this point that he realised that Dad was not who he thought he was but, like ourselves, he was in too deep to own up to the error.

"Well, it was nice seeing you," he said as he shook our hands to communicate that it was time for the next person in the queue to come forward. We left the store, pleased with the outcome. We had managed to skip the queue without intentionally deceiving anyone and, by accident rather than design, we had experienced our most interesting conversation with a mixed martial artist to date.

Dad was confident that he would win the bet; he would be competing in the over sixty five age group from the following year whilst Bisping seemed quite far away from World Championship level. In a shocking turn of events, it was the professional mixed martial artist who won the challenge against the veteran amateur athlete, as he claimed the UFC Middleweight title in 2016.

Most of the stores along the main shopping street, Schildergasse, belonged to global brands, so there was not too much of interest for us. Nevertheless, it was pleasant to amble around in the summer sun with the knowledge that it would be another couple of days before I would be back at work.

I had recently started a job as a receptionist at a veterinary practice, which was an odd fit for me considering that I not only hated speaking to strangers on the phone but I am allergic to cat and dog hair. Having to take an antihistamine every day in the hope that it could stave off my allergies whilst I swept up cat and dog hair was hardly ideal.

The job was not particularly unpleasant but I was clearly unsuitable for the role. I had no history of pet ownership, so I did not understand much of the relevant terminology. For this reason, I once allocated a standard fifteen minute appointment for a spay procedure. If I was a dog that was due to be neutered, I would sincerely hope that the surgeons would spend more than a quarter of an hour attending to me.

I also had to carry dead animals and place them in the outdoor freezer, where they would be stored until they could be collected the next day. The first time I did this, I was not even aware of what I was holding; I just knew that whatever was in the bag was heavy. It was only afterwards that a colleague explained to me that I had just thrown a dead dog into what I had thought was a skip.

I was always on edge for the entirety of my shift, waiting for the phone to ring and having to deal with a situation that I was ill-equipped to handle. Even if I had been tempted to phone in sick, this would have involved having an awkward conversation over the telephone; which was precisely the thing that I was hoping avoid.

For this very reason, I have only ever called in sick a couple of times during my years of employment at various companies. I have to be almost on my death bed to face the horror of making that phone call.

My employment situation at the time also involved working at a newsagents and volunteering for the British Red Cross. This hectic schedule meant that I was even more grateful for a few days abroad. My job choices probably seemed somewhat strange considering that I had graduated from university with a history degree and I had recently become a qualified gym instructor.

However, I was content to simply drift through life, seeing what came my way rather than chasing any particular career path. I guess that my approach to the world of employment was a good indicator of my laid back way of life. Whether this is too laid back for my own good is a matter of opinion.

The shops were starting to close but I had just enough time to fit in one more embarrassing moment. I saw an employee pushing a glass door from the bottom so that it swing upwards in the manner that you would open a garage door.

Usually, this would have been enough to discourage a couple of cautious individuals like ourselves. I remember one occasion in which a neighbour, who transported traffic lights for a living, had left a traffic light on the red setting whilst it rested on the back of his truck that was parked in front of his house all night. As ridiculous as it sounds, it took nearly five minutes before Dad and I made the decision to drive past the truck.

Against all my instincts, I decided to check out what was behind this unusual entrance.

As I brushed past the shop worker, she shouted, "Hey!" and gave me an incredulous look that said: "What on earth are you doing?! Are you stupid? We are obviously closed! Get out!" Or whatever the German translation of that is.

She did not need to utter any more words. I sheepishly made a hasty exit and waited for the earth to swallow me up; I was left disappointed. I had done so well up until this point but I had now managed to make a complete fool of myself within the space of a few seconds. On that note, we decided to head to the Lanxess Arena for the show.

As we had not yet eaten, we would need to purchase some food from the concourse within the arena. Giant hot dogs dressed with fried onions, mustard and tomato ketchup were consumed with glee. It was probably for the best that we did not know what ingredients were used to make the hot dogs though.

This type of cheap sausage usually consists of a meat emulsion of pork and beef trimmings, which is a nice way of saying all of the bits that are not good enough to be consumed as they are. Mechanically separated chicken is often added to the mix before the final product is cooked. One hotdog may well consist of the lowest quality parts of an unfathomable amount of different animals and three or more different species. Despite all of this, they usually taste pretty good.

Although they were hardly the traditional sausages that Germany is famed for, at least we had eaten something vaguely resembling such cuisine. It was a bit of a stretch, but we could tell people that we had tried some sausage based food in Germany.

Just like I had done in Ireland, I decided against having a drink to accompany my meal, so that I could avoid using the bathroom for the next few hours. The crowd of over twelve thousand seemed to either enjoy the show or they were just having a great time getting intoxicated on a Saturday night. Either way, they made a lot of noise and were on their feet for much of the proceedings. I enjoyed my evening, which is strange considering how much I dislike large crowds of rowdy, drunk people.

Following Rich Franklin's victory over Wanderlei Silva in the main event, it was nice to get some fresh air as we walked back to the hotel. It had been a good few days spent overseas. We had seen some historic sites that filled us with awe, the weather had been kind and we had managed to keep the number of embarrassing moments to a minimum.

We eloquently summarised what we had seen of the city before going to bed: "It has been a nice trip, hasn't it?" I asked Dad.

"Yes, very nice," he replied.

"The cathedral was very big and impressive," I continued.

"Yes, very nice. It was huge," Dad remarked.

"Goodnight Dad," I said as I switched off the lights.

"Goodnight, son."

\*　　\*　　\*

After breakfast the next morning, we found ourselves with a few more hours to kill. As our flight home was scheduled for the early evening, we went for another stroll around sunny Cologne. Our final morning seemed to be over in the blink of an eye, as it was soon time for lunch.

Feeling slightly more adventurous, we sat down in the outdoor area of a pub. Unfortunately, it was not a traditional German establishment and they only served Italian food. Still, we enjoyed our pasta and Coca-Cola whilst sat in the sun.

There was a large group of British men sat nearby that, judging by their luggage, were also preparing to travel home. They appeared to have been on a stag weekend and were using their last few hours of their trip to introduce some more alcohol into their bloodstream, or as one of them stated: "There's still time to get completely leathered."

Although my initial reaction was to question whether it was embarrassing that I was sat having a soft drink with my dad rather than downing pints of beer with 'the lads,' I quickly realised that I would much sooner be where I was than mixing with the leery group that was sat next to us.

Perhaps, this was a sign that I was becoming more mature with age. Like many teenagers, I had often been embarrassed to be seen in my parents' company. If I had spotted a school friend whilst out with one of my parents, I would resort to my favoured technique of putting my head down and avoiding eye contact. Although this would not stop them noticing me, at least I would not notice them noticing me.

Sometimes I would even physically hide by darting into a shop when I found myself in such a situation. As I have grown older, I have realised just how silly all of that was. Of course it is actually nice to spend some quality time with a family member. Why should I feel embarrassed about that?

Following our lunchtime meal, we headed to the airport, ready for our flight home. I should have said our flights home, since we were flying indirectly via Amsterdam again. Once at Schiphol airport, we found ourselves with a couple of hours of free time before our onwards journey to Manchester. We decided to buy some souvenirs. Obviously, tacky souvenirs depicting Dutch stereotypes that were made in China would be the best gifts to bring back from our trip to Germany.

I purchased a big bag of sweets that came in packaging adorned with a cow pattern design and brought them in to work upon my return for my colleagues at the veterinary practice to share between themselves. They politely thanked me, even though they were almost certainly bemused by my choice of gift. Regardless, continental Europe had been conquered. This left me pondering, "Where next?"

# CHAPTER 4: HOSTILE GREETINGS AND POLITE MUGGINGS
## LAS VEGAS AND THE GRAND CANYON, THE UNITED STATES OF AMERICA
## NOVEMBER 2009

I had enjoyed a couple of family holidays to Florida when I was younger and I have memories of theme parks and attractions that felt like they belonged in a fantasy land. It was now time to visit another man-made entertainment zone in the United States of America.

This place, however, was certainly designed for adults, rather than children, to experience their wildest desires. The majority of the action happens on the Strip, which is a four mile section of Las Vegas Boulevard that is actually located just south of the city limits.

This area had been unremarkable until the big casino and hotel resorts started opening along this stretch. During the latter part of the twentieth century, hotels were built with increasing frequency and size, with each new resort introducing its own gimmick in an attempt to outdo their competitors. Bigger and better seemed to be the mantra.

I was excited to see the huge complexes and their signature features, such as the rollercoaster affixed to the outer building of New York, New York or the fountain shows regularly held outside of the Bellagio. Before that became a reality, I was faced with something that I had not experienced for over ten years; a long haul flight.

After taking some short plane journeys with budget airlines on my previous couple of trips, Dad and I were now faced with the airport check in and bag drop process. We arrived at the airport and checked the screens which indicated which check-in desks were allocated for our flight. We should have known that they were the counters with the longest queues.

Our time queueing up was spent observing the misfortunes of others ahead of us in the line. We watched people frantically removing items from their luggage before trying to rearrange the contents so that their cases somehow weighed less.

Others just argued the toss with the airline workers. One or two just accepted their fate and paid the applicable fees for exceeding the weight allowance. My first thought was to scoff at their poor preparation. They may have had months to plan their trip yet they still managed to get it all wrong.

Then it dawned on me that the people behind us in the queue would soon be entertaining themselves by watching Dad and I attempt to negotiate this process without incident. I started to worry that maybe I had also exceeded the luggage allowance. In reality, this would have been extremely unlikely, considering I was only taking a tiny suitcase that was packed with the bare essentials.

This did not stop me from feeling nervous when the airline employee asked me: "Have you packed your bag yourself, Sir?"

Of course, this was a routine enquiry that they ask every passenger but I always feel guilty in this type of situation. I am the kind of person that panics when I walk past a police car, even though I am such a square that I do not even cross the road unless the green man is on display.

I gave a tense reply of "yes," before a series of "no" responses to the standard "does your luggage contain...?" set of questions.

I imagine the nature of my responses were similar to those of a suspect in a murder enquiry who had been hauled in for questioning. Except that I was more nervous.

Our suitcases were so far below the weight limit that I began to worry that suspicion would fall upon us for packing so little. To my relief, our cases were added to the conveyor belt and we were handed our boarding passes rather than being detained by security.

Our flight was significantly longer than the previous couple of trips we had taken. What would we do to occupy ourselves for twelve hours? Whatever the answer was, we would have to find out in separate compartments. On different floors. We were travelling on a gigantic Airbus 380, which has two floors for passengers, in addition to the cargo deck below. I had never imagined being on a different floor to someone I was travelling with on a plane.

After experiencing the no-frills approach of budget airlines, it felt as if we were being treated like royalty; food and drink that you do not have to pay extra for and personal entertainment screens to watch films on. Aided by intermittent napping, the time passed by quicker than expected.

*   *   *

The bright lights of Las Vegas were soon within sight as we began our descent. I naively thought that it would not be long before we were on the Strip. I say naively because I had not considered the soul-destroying process of clearing the immigration checks that one faces when landing at an airport in the United States of America.

Having submitted our ESTAs online, we assumed that passport control would be fairly straightforward. After being reunited following the flight, however, we were met with a horrendously long queue at McCarran International Airport.

We were not in any particular rush, so we were not too disheartened at this point. Half an hour later, we realised that this was going to take longer than we had anticipated. We had hardly moved in the last thirty minutes. On the one hand, this is reassuring as it shows that the border force is thorough. Unfortunately, the agonising wait to get to the front of the queue is then followed by the misery of being interrogated by an immigration officer.

Now at the front of the queue, we were feeling good to have finally reached this point.

Dad greeted the border official with a warm, "Hi, how are you doing?"

This was met with a stern, "Hello, Sir," which told us that we were not going to receive any friendly American hospitality just yet.

"Look into the camera. Place your thumbs on the scanner. Now do the same with the four fingers of your left hand and then do the same with your right."

My overactive mind began to worry that the heavily moustached officer was trying to trip me up by quickly reeling off a list of instructions in the hope that I would make an error. Somehow, I managed to hold it together long enough to follow these three basic steps.

After we had submitted our biometric data, we were grilled by the official: "What is the purpose of your visit? Have you been to the States before? How long will you be staying?"

The questions were not out of the ordinary, but his stony stare indicated that he was more than ready to throw us into an interrogation room at any given moment. I just hoped that Dad would not make an inappropriate joke about carrying a bomb or being a terrorist.

After all, we were entering a highly patriotic country that has a history of casting suspicion on outsiders. To the extent that school children are instructed to recite the Pledge of Allegiance every day. This is something that most people would probably expect to occur within the dictatorial regime of North Korea rather than in a country that has given itself the title of 'Leader of the Free World.'

With a nod of his head, the officer eventually signaled that we were cleared to enter the United States of America. It was a relief to have cleared immigration, retrieved our luggage and left the terminal. Travelling through an American airport is often such a miserable affair; to such a degree that something has felt wrong on the rare occasions when a member of staff has smiled and spoken to me like a human being. I sincerely hope that these individuals did not face any disciplinary action for failing to tow the line.

Our night time taxi journey to our hotel on the Strip was pretty straightforward and it provided Dad and I with a glimpse of some of the bright lights that we would become accustomed to over the next ten nights. Another thing that we would have to get used to awaited us as soon as we arrived at the Mandalay Bay resort; I am referring to the incessant American tipping culture that seems so strange to us Brits.

This started as soon as we stepped outside of the taxi. Having rounded up the fare to give the driver a tip, our luggage was snatched from us within seconds and placed on to a trolley, which was then pushed through the main entrance and taken to the reception area. This was all most unnecessary. Our suitcases were tiny in comparison to most of the other guests and we only had to travel about twenty yards.

"I guess we will have to give him a tip, " I suggested.

"We know that we are in America now," Dad replied, as he thumbed through his wallet for the smallest note that he could find.

Five dollars was this man's reward for forcibly removing our luggage from our grasp and unnecessarily transporting it a few short steps away. I had felt as if I was being viewed as a potential criminal upon arrival at the airport but now I most certainly felt like I was being seen as a potential crime victim. An easy mark for a mugging. Albeit, a very polite one.

The check-in process made us realise just how big the resort is, as our hotel room was just one of over thirty two hundred that were located within the main tower. The receptionist informed us that the resort contained a 135,000 square foot casino, a two million square foot convention centre, an aquarium and a man-made beach. Even the twelve thousand capacity arena that we would watch *UFC 106: Ortiz vs. Griffin II* in was part of the complex.

As we walked to one of the twenty four elevators, or lifts as they are known to us Brits, we noticed how striking the gold décor of every facet of the lobby was. The elevators even had mini television screens showing adverts for upcoming events.

Our luggage was now, of course, on a different trolley and we were being accompanied by another member of staff who was no doubt eyeing up a potential tip. The porter pushed the trolley along to our room on the twentieth storey of this huge building and placed the cases on the floor.

He stood there in anticipation of his financial reward and after an awkward few seconds, Dad begrudgingly obliged by again paying for a service that we did not even want. It is not that we are mean and do not like to tip but like many Brits, we find it unpleasant how tipping is forced upon you in an almost dishonest manner.

In restaurants or other service outlets, a price is advertised that will be far less than what the customer is expected to pay. I consider myself a fairly generous tipper but the way that an extra fifteen to twenty per cent is added to the bill as a compulsory charge seems disingenuous.

Surely a tip is a nod of approval to the staff and it should be seen as a nice gesture from the customer. I understand that the staff are relying on this as a means of income but it would seem more appropriate for the business to pay their employees more, so that any tips should be a bonus on top of their salary.

This is all tied in to the state of workers' rights in the United States. Although conditions are much better than in most areas of the world, the minimum wage is relatively low in comparison to the economic power of the country and there is an absence of a federal law requiring companies to offer paid holidays or parental leave. Regardless, Dad and I tipped the workers wherever we went during our trip.

The welcome magazine that greeted us listed lots of entertainment venues in the area and featured a range of stories, such as the recent success of British singer Jay Sean and his hit song "Down." The previous month, he had become the first urban act from the United Kingdom to top the *Billboard* Hot 100 singles chart, finally bringing an end to the mind-numbing reign of "I Gotta Feeling" by the Black Eyed Peas.

I have always said that I find it strange that many people feel proud to have been born in a particular country but seeing a Brit bring down this highly irritating American group almost tempted me to reconsider my stance.

*   *   *

I slept well in our room that, like everything else in Vegas, was far bigger than was necessary. On waking up in this city of entertainment, I did what most warm-blooded males in their twenties would do. I got the ironing board out and removed the creases from all my clothing whilst overlooking the Strip. I believe that this is the kind of activity people have in mind when they say the clichéd line of 'what happens in Vegas, stays in Vegas.'

With this first act of hedonism complete, we headed down to the breakfast room, which was huge of course. It had to be for them to feed the sheer amount of people. After all, the number of guests staying in this one building exceeds the population of many small towns.

A few tables away from us were some mixed martial artists who were staying at the hotel before their bouts at the weekend. We did not bother them, as it would be rude to interrupt their meal. Just ask Michael Bisping. Plus, we would have plenty of opportunities to meet them at the various autograph signings that were scheduled throughout the week.

The signings were all very strange affairs for me. We would spend an eternity queueing up to meet each competitor before awkwardly exchanging a couple of lines of conversation and having our photo taken with them whilst they did the 'I am clenching my fist to show you that I am a fighter' pose.

We would spend hours repeating this process throughout the week, which is odd considering how I would normally do anything in my power to avoid situations that involve making smalltalk and mixing with large crowds of people.

Over the course of our trip, we had our photograph taken with over twenty different fighters, which felt rather exciting at the time. The photos all looked the same though; just swap the fighter clenching his fist for the camera and you have more or less the same image.

In any case, we felt pleased that we were able to meet the likes of Frank Mir, Jon Fitch, Robbie Lawler and many more. This was in addition to attending an autograph signing with the legendary Randy Couture the day before we had departed Manchester. I may not be interested in the sport anymore but Las Vegas is certainly a fight fan's dream destination.

One of the signings was held at a place that is held sacred in the United States of America; a Hooters bar and restaurant. I had heard this chain mentioned in various American television shows such as *Married with Children,* so I had a pretty good idea of what to expect.

Sure enough, it was a place that appeared to be designed to appease the desires of the average Neanderthal. The waitresses were top-heavy and scantily clad; all of whom were undoubtedly selected for the job based on their employment experience and skill set. Customers could watch live sport on the big TV screens, eat heart attack-inducing food and ogle at women dressed in hot pants and a skintight vest.

The fact that the signings were being held there unfortunately confirmed something that I had been trying my best not to acknowledge; the target audience of the sport of mixed martial arts largely consisted of the same clientele that frequented establishments like Hooters.

I would spend the next few years trying to distance myself from this crowd before I eventually stopped watching the sport altogether. Dad had a different mindset, as he proudly wore his array of MMA T-shirts at every opportunity.

I was somewhat conflicted; on the one hand, I was willing to fly to the other side of the world to follow the sport but I was almost embarrassed to be associated with the hoards of fans dressed in ugly and unimaginative Tapout or Affliction gear. Most fans were eager to display their affiliation with the sport in the form of a skull and crossbones inspired badge of honour but this was certainly part of the culture that made me cringe.

After enjoying a breakfast of croissants and cereal, whilst convincing myself that I had done the right thing by leaving the fighters in peace, it was time to go out and explore this fantasy land. Dad and I noticed that there was a sign for a monorail on the first floor of our hotel. Upon inspection, it was apparent that this connected the Mandalay Bay to the Luxor hotel and casino.

This did not appear to be very far on the map, prompting my dad to remark that: "The strip may be longer than we thought. Either that or everybody in Vegas is really lazy."

We boarded the interesting looking vehicle and gently glided over the busy street below. Although the distance travelled was not great, it did cut out a couple of large intersections that were teeming with so many people that they felt like tourist attractions in their own right. There were grand escalators that took you up to the bridges above the street, where huge screens played a mixture of music videos and advertisements as one crossed to the other side.

For some reason, the memory of Jordin Spark's music video for the song "Battlefield" being played on the big screens has stuck with me. I am not sure exactly why I remember this generic music video so vividly but I suspect that it has more to do with the size of the screens against the backdrop of glitzy Las Vegas rather than the video itself.

It also shows how people can form strong associations between music and events in their life, and that one can be taken back to a certain moment in their life just by hearing a song that is being played.

These walkways were effectively retail space for independent vendors, who capitalised on the heavy footfall. Perhaps they were chasing 'The American Dream.' Or maybe they were just trying to pay their monthly bills. One dishevelled man remarked that I looked like B.J. Penn. I was not sure how to take this comment, as he is a legendary mixed martial artist but he is also a chubby-cheeked balding fellow. Dad seemed more impressed by this than I was, which convinced me to take the positives from this comment.

A few days into the trip, one young man approached me on one of the walkways and asked me if I liked hip-hop music. I nodded and carried on walking, with the hope that he would not follow

"Here, take my CD and give it a listen. I'm an aspiring artist hoping to start a career," he suggested.

With the CD having been placed in my hand by the man, I naively replied: "Good luck, I'll listen to it and look out for your songs," before walking away.

He followed me and said: "I'm going to need paying for that CD."

I quickly handed it back and made a sharp exit. I never found out if he realised his ambition and whether I missed out on a rare and valuable demo tape from a future superstar. I have not lost any sleep contemplating that possibility though.

After disembarking the monorail at the Luxor, we took a moment to admire this Egyptian themed complex. Each resort seemed to require their own gimmick to make it stand out from the plethora of competitors that lined the Strip. The Luxor was a pyramid shaped building with a large sphinx design at the front. Later on, we would discover that a brightly coloured beam is projected from the top of the pyramid into the Las Vegas sky each night. We ventured inside and were slightly surprised by what we encountered.

Rather than being faced with a replica of a tomb or a mini version of the Nile river, we were now stood in front of a large, middle-aged man dressed as Santa Claus. Thanksgiving had taken place a few days earlier, so the Christmas marketing machine was now in full swing.

Children were queueing up to see Mr. Kringle, who was surrounded by all manner of festive decorations. The entire lobby looked like it belonged in the North Pole, which was all very pleasant but not necessarily what one expects to see when entering an Egyptian pyramid.

I was just thankful that we had not visited a month earlier, as Americans have a reputation for pushing the boat out for Halloween. Indeed, it is estimated that the average American spends somewhere in the region of eighty to ninety dollars on this holiday season, with billions spent by the country as a whole.

I can only imagine how tacky and over the top a place like the Luxor would look like during that time of year. At least the reindeers and elves had a certain charm to them; I am not sure that I would say the same if they were replaced by skeletons and vampires.

We walked through the casino, where we were immediately accosted by a slick looking employee.

"Hi guys, can I take a couple of minutes of your time to talk to you about a wonderful offer that I am going to make exclusively for you?" he asked.

"Nope," I responded.

The trouble was that my answer was only articulated in my own head and that Dad had already begun listening to the man's sales pitch.

"So guys, if you book a room here within the next twelve months, I can give you two nights of a five night stay free of charge and a hundred dollars to spend in the casino. What do you think?"

Obviously, this was a standard Vegas ploy to get customers to spend money in their casinos. If the resorts are willing to give away free rooms in order to entice people to gamble, it shows you where the biggest profits are made. The design of the casinos themselves hinted at this, as you will be hard pressed to find a window or a clock that would indicate to the gambler how long they have been throwing their money away.

Members of staff will ply you with free food and drink in order to keep you inserting coins into the slot machines. Gambling was clearly where the profit was. Unfortunately for this man, he had approached the only two tourists in town that had absolutely no intention of placing a single bet. After informing him of this, we soon moved on.

With the sun beating down, we began walking along the Strip, popping in to most hotels to explore their unique selling points. Over the next ten days, we would see the lion enclosure within the MGM Grand, witness the famed fountain show at the Bellagio, and watch the rollercoaster whizzing people around the outside of the New York, New York building.

We did not go for a ride on this or the 'Big Shot' at the top of the Stratosphere, which was the world's highest amusement ride at the time. I suspect that Dad would have gone on both rides if he was on his own but even the thought of this made me feel uneasy.

We witnessed the gondolas transporting tourists along the canals around the Venetian resort and stood beneath the replica of the Eiffel Tower that belonged to the Paris hotel.

Dad suggested that: "We don't need to go to Venice or Paris now, as we have seen the attractions of those cities, right here in Vegas."

This was not a sentiment that I agreed with but I could see how he was impressed by the outlandishness of it all.

We must have walked virtually the entire four mile length of the Strip every day that we were there. We would head out after breakfast to try to find new things to see. The hope was that this would pass enough time until we sat down for lunch, which usually consisted of fine dining at Wendy's or another similar establishment.

We would then repeat this process until we reached a respectable time to head back to the hotel. We soon realised that, despite the plethora of attractions along the Strip, there is only so much that you can do in Las Vegas when you do not gamble or drink alcohol.

In hindsight, it would have made more sense for us to have only booked a four or five night trip or arranged a few entertainment shows to frame our visit around. In the absence of such events, we found ourselves traipsing up and down the Strip, day after day, hoping to find something that we had not already seen. At least we were blessed with warm and dry weather on every day of our trip.

To be fair, we would always discover a new attraction to explore but there were times that I felt like Bill Murray in *Groundhog Day*.

A common occurrence during our countless walks up and down the Strip was the bombardment of flyers that were advertising various escort services to keep you 'entertained' in your hotel room. The bemusing thing about this was that the flyers were being handed out to any and all passers-by. The distributors were clearly being paid a pittance and were desperate to get rid of their stock of leaflets, since they did not care if they were given to elderly couples or young parents pushing their prams.

This resulted in Dad and I changing the topic of conversation whenever we passed the distributors and having to pretend that neither of us had seen them. Anything to avoid a father and son conversation about sex.

After our daily Vegas trek, we would usually find a fast food restaurant to have dinner in before returning to the hotel. Once we were back at the Mandalay Bay, it felt like we had a city within a city to explore. The aquarium was pretty similar to any other that I had previously been to but it felt remarkable that this was located within our hotel complex.

I felt the same about the arena in which we watched *UFC 106: Ortiz vs. Griffin II*. It looked like any other that we had visited but I had to occasionally remind myself that we were, along with twelve thousand others, still within the hotel resort. For those that are interested, Forrest Griffin defeated Tito Ortiz in the main event.

\*　　\*　　\*

As the order of events of our time in Vegas has become rather jumbled, I will cover the rest of the mixed martial arts events in this paragraph. A few days before the UFC show, we attended another event, this time put on by the WEC, which was owned by the same parent company, Zuffa. The show was held at the Pearl of the Palms, inside the Palms Casino Resort, which was located a short distance away from the Strip. This tiny arena was where we saw Jose Aldo defeat Mike Brown for the World Featherweight title in the main event of *WEC 44: Brown vs. Aldo*.

One of our most frequently visited areas of the hotel was the convenience store in the lobby. Each evening, we would buy a few snacks and soft drinks before retiring to our room at about eight o'clock. We would then watch television whilst devouring our cookies and bags of crisps, or potato chips as they are known in America. As much as I enjoyed a three hour marathon of the U.S. version of *The Office*, I could not help but think that we were missing out on the true Las Vegas experience.

In addition to the monorail, there was also a shopping mall known as Mandalay Place, that connected the Luxor to the Mandalay Bay. We had dinner one night at the imaginatively titled Burger Bar within the mall. It is apparently one of the best places to sample a burger in Vegas. As junk food was becoming synonymous with our trip to the United States, we thought that we may as well try one of the more reputable restaurants of this kind.

After we had been shown to our table, we were presented with menus that listed countless varieties of burgers and an equally vast range of customisable options. Dad went for a pretty safe choice of a regular cheeseburger topped with salad.

"You can't beat the classics," he remarked.

I plumped for a buffalo burger, which was described as lean and low in calories.

"Why bother about calories when you are ordering a burger?" Dad asked.

He had a point. A burger is not going to be a healthy meal. A meal in Vegas is not likely to be healthy. A meal in the U.S.A. in general is not often healthy. This is obviously an exaggeration that plays up to stereotypes about Americans and their food but it must be said that the large portion sizes of unhealthy food seems unwise, given that the United States has had a notably high obesity rate for decades.

Before our meals were brought to the table, our drinks were presented to us. I had ordered a Pepsi. Or at least that is what I thought that I had ordered. I took a sip and grimaced as I realised that it was laced with a rather unpleasant tasting vodka.

"Is everything OK, Sir?" asked the waiter.

This would be the moment that any normal person would alert him to the mix up.

However, I simply replied: "Yep, everything is fine. It is a nice drink."

I would sooner pay three times as much for a drink that repulsed me than go through the few seconds of awkward social interaction in which I would have to tell a stranger that the drink that they had served me was not what I wanted.

I was once again travelling down the path of least resistance. Route 66 may be the most iconic road in the United States of America but I was remaining faithful to the path that I was so familiar with.

An example of my unwavering devotion to this comes from a tale from my former workplace. A colleague mistakenly addressed me as Paul but instead of correcting her, I just acknowledged her as normal.

For the next six months, she would say, "Hi Paul" or, "Good morning Paul," every time that our paths crossed.

Each time that I went along with this pretence it made it more difficult to correct her without sounding like a weirdo, so I just smiled and returned the greeting. It was only when someone else called me David within earshot of her, that the situation reached its inevitably awkward conclusion.

"So...your name is David?" she asked, with a sense of bewilderment.

"Yes," I replied tentatively.

I could not think of anything else to say that would not sound completely ridiculous.

Her response of, "Oh...err....ok," indicated that she was going to make further enquiries but decided to abandon this idea, possibly fearing that I was a psychopath.

I was probably one of the few people in Vegas that was disappointed to find alcohol in my drink. We were certainly in the minority of people who did not indulge in the most prevalent vices of mankind. The alcoholic drink that I had ordered by mistake was the only one that either of us had on the trip and we did not gamble, smoke, drink coffee or take any other drugs. Unless you include my asthma inhalers. Despite enjoying our time in 'Sin City,' I would often think to myself: "What on earth are we doing here?"

\*     \*     \*

Towards the end of the trip, I discovered that the state of Nevada has some of the most permissive gun control laws in the entire country.

Nevada residents and visitors from states that have similar laws are allowed to carry a weapon on their person. Sales of shotguns, rifles and semi-automatic weapons are permitted, with no mandatory waiting period.

Although there are some cursory background checks carried out, you are not going to be denied a permit or sale unless you have a history of violent convictions or documented mental health problems.

What was even more worrying was the revelation that Nevada is an 'open carry' state, meaning that people can walk around with their gun on display. The one condition is that it is either in a holster or it is 'readily accessible.' The casinos can have their own rules about carrying weapons but ultimately they are not enforceable due to state law. It seems ludicrous to think that someone can walk along the Strip with their gun openly on their person.

After all, casinos are places in which people experience the emotional rollercoaster of gambling whilst being plied with alcohol. Guns, alcohol, gambling and a general loss of inhibitions certainly sounds like a recipe for disaster.

Getting shot here could lead to a couple of rather dreadful outcomes; we could either perish from our injuries or be charged thousands of dollars for healthcare. There is not an equivalent of the National Health Service in the United States, therefore you can be hit with a huge hospital bill if your insurance documents are not in order.

I crossed my fingers that I had ticked all of the correct boxes on my insurance questionnaire and tried not to think about getting shot. One of the real positives about travelling to other countries is that it makes one truly appreciate the NHS back in the United Kingdom.

I was starting to feel unsafe whilst wandering around this fantasy land where people showcase the wild side of their nature. A decade on and I would probably feel even more apprehensive if I returned. The current president seems to consistently stoke the flame of hatred, primarily aimed at immigrants and ethnic minorities, which could spell danger for someone with a complexion like mine.

Unbelievably, there has been an average of one mass shooting per day in 2019. Whatever the statistics were in the years leading up to our trip, it was a good job that I did not research gun crime in the United States beforehand, as I may have had second thoughts about visiting the country.

\*   \*   \*

As many other tourists do, we ventured outside of the state of Nevada by signing up for an organised tour of the Grand Canyon. One of the world's most breathtaking sights lies just over two hundred and fifty miles away in the state of Arizona. Unfortunately, we had to be up bright and early at six in the morning on the day of our tour.

As a pink jeep approached our hotel, I confidently proclaimed, "That will be our guide."

Bearing in mind that our tour operator was called 'Pink Jeep Tours,' this was hardly the boldest of predictions. Our guide stepped out of the vehicle and introduced himself as Shirley. Bleary eyed, we set off on our journey to see one of the wonders of the world.

Less than an hour into our journey, we arrived at our first stop of the tour. Situated on the Colorado River, at the border between Nevada and Arizona, the Hoover Dam has become a major tourist attraction. Around a million people a year flock to see this architectural and engineering triumph. In truth, it is not the prettiest thing that you will ever see but it is mightily impressive when you observe the surroundings and consider the significance of its construction.

Shirley gave us a brief overview of the history of the dam: "Construction began in 1931 and took about five years to complete. There was a long running debate over what the name of the dam should be. 'Boulder Dam' was the alternative title that was given the most consideration but in 1947 it was officially named after former President, Herbert Hoover. Thousands of workers contributed to the construction of the dam, with over a hundred of them losing their lives in the process."

I must admit that my knowledge of American history was fairly limited at this stage, so all of this information was new to me. Both the scale of the project and the loss of life took me by surprise. I had not truly considered this when we had signed up for the tour, as I had simply viewed the dam as a place that we were required to visit as part of our itinerary.

Shirley then explained that: "This innovative concrete arch-gravity dam was designed to provide hydroelectric power, to prevent a section of the Colorado River from flooding and to offer a supply of water primarily for Nevada, Arizona and California."

I took a few photographs before realising that I was unable to capture the scale and ingenuity of it all. As with many places, the best images are captured by your eyes and that committing them to memory is wiser than trying to take the perfect photograph. It was a nice bonus to have visited such a place, considering that we had only been bothered about exploring the Grand Canyon.

Just under four hours later, we were taking in the awe-inspiring view whilst standing at the top of the canyon. It was even more incredible to consider that there was an almost infinite amount of alternative angles from which to admire the Colorado River hundreds of metres below and the land that it has carved through over the course of millions of years. After all, the length of the Grand Canyon is more or less the same distance as the route that we had taken from Las Vegas.

The Grand Canyon National Park is just one of sixty one in the United States. Unfortunately, the current presidential regime has ordered the largest reduction of public land protections in American history. This is a source of worry for many who regard the national parks as the most treasured possession of the entire country.

Many of them occupy vast areas of land. Remarkably, Yellowstone National Park is larger than the states of Rhode Island and Delaware combined. Whilst the United States does not have the same level of documented man-made history as European countries, it is the incredible landscape and the wildlife within it that is revered by so many.

The Grand Canyon is one such example and I felt blessed to be in its presence. The remarkable force of nature is undeniable once you are presented with evidence of its consequences. It was clear that the feeling of 'wanderlust' was starting to take hold of me.

I took dozens of photographs but none of them could even come close to capturing the sheer magnitude of the canyon. Dad and I had our photograph taken at the edge of the rim before Shirley suggested that we should climb onto a ledge and pose for a photo to impress our friends back home. This would involve stepping over a small gap in order to reach the ledge. I politely declined, as I did not fancy falling hundreds of metres towards a certain death.

Before I knew it, Dad was already on the ledge beckoning me to join him. I once again declined, leaving Shirley to take my place. This meant that we ended up with a photo of Dad and our tour guide standing precariously close to the edge of the canyon. Furthermore, Shirley played up to the situation by pretending to lose his balance and fall backwards whilst I snapped the image.

As humorous as Shirley's actions may have been, the number of deaths resulting from attempting to take a risky photograph at sites such as the Grand Canyon is on the rise. The need to share photos of ourselves in unique and dangerous situations can lead to a potentially deadly game of one-upmanship.

I recently read about a study that was carried out in India which found that over two hundred and fifty people died whilst taking 'extreme selfies' during a six year period. Fortunately, Dad and Shirley did not suffer a similar fate.

I had visions of death as we began the next activity of our tour. A helicopter ride over the canyon offered panoramic views of the stunning scenery below before landing yards away from the Colorado River. Prior to even getting on the aircraft, Dad nearly came face to face with the Grim Reaper.

This is probably a bit of an exaggeration, as he simply lost his footing when trying to board the helicopter and ended up on his backside. The chances of being dissected by the propeller blade or being thrown off the edge of the rim were minimal. Dad may have died from embarrassment though.

The views provided by our helicopter ride were as breathtaking as advertised. All we could see was rugged yet beautiful scenery in every direction. The ride was thrilling, although I suspect that I may not experience this again.

Whilst travelling via aircraft is statistically very safe, I have reservations about helicopters and other light aircraft. I seem to be reading reports of accidents involving such aircraft on a relatively regular basis, yet there only seems to be a few crashes involving commercial airliners each year.

I recently read a headline stating that in terms of crashes per flight time, helicopters have a thirty five per cent higher rate than the overall score for aircraft. I do not have the appetite to research this grim topic any further, so I may be doing helicopters a disservice. Either way, the seed of doubt has been planted.

It was interesting to see the view from the river bank, as all of the images that I had seen prior to the trip were taken from the edge of the rim, hundreds of metres above. A new perspective can be achieved during travel, and not just in a physical sense. For example, Shirley informed us that Native Americans inhabited the land thousands of years before the area became a tourist attraction.

The Grand Canyon is considered a sacred site to many tribes, so the influx of people resulting from mass tourism has created issues.

Shirley explained that: "A responsible guide will not only inform you of the history of the landscape but will educate you on Native American culture and stress the importance of respecting the boundaries of sacred sites."

We were then introduced to a group of Native Americans, who showed us a replica of a small settlement and performed a traditional song and dance. It felt somewhat sad that these proud people were now reduced to staging this show for tourists, many of whom resembled the European colonists that invaded their land in the first place.

At least it encouraged visitors to take a moment to reflect on this subject. I had not even considered Native American history when planning our trip but in the following years I have begun to appreciate the plight of the indigenous people of the countries that I have visited.

The trip back to the hotel seemed to go pretty quick. I always feel better travelling back from a trip, as I now have the knowledge that I have successfully completed the task at hand and I am able to reflect on the day's events. We said farewell to Shirley and thanked him, both personally and monetarily, for his knowledgeable and engaging tour.

Dad and I agreed that our Vegas trip would not have been complete without our trip to the Grand Canyon.

"The scale of it was mind-blowing. What did you think?" I asked Dad.

"It was certainly big," was the initial, understated response.

After pausing for a moment, he continued by stating that: "The contrast between artificial Las Vegas and the natural beauty of the Grand Canyon is remarkable."

\*   \*   \*

The final day of our time in Vegas was once again spent walking up and down the Strip. This time we were on the lookout for souvenirs. Of course, we ended up with a bag full of tacky, mass-produced items but this did not seem too inappropriate considering everything about Vegas is artificial anyway.

My mum and my brother both ended up with useless tat that ended up in a drawer before too long. Once you start buying souvenirs for people, you feel obligated to purchase a gift for everyone you know, even if it is a terrible present for someone that you have only seen a handful of times.

This was the case with the Chinese doctor that I had started dating. Vivian ended up with a Hello Kitty teddy that was wearing a Las Vegas T-shirt. Our brief relationship ended a few months later, which probably had more to do with a lack of compatibility rather than the hideous teddy that I brought back from America.

This should have become apparent to me as soon as she practically forced me to watch one of the films from the terrible *Twilight* series. Vivian said that I reminded her of one of the central character's love interests, called Jacob. I think that this was intended to be a compliment, although tellingly, she followed this up by saying, "I prefer Edward though."

Dad and I decided to visit Fremont Street during our final night. The taxi driver who had picked us up from the airport when we had first arrived had enthused about it: "You have to check out Fremont Street. That's 'Old Vegas.' Sinatra. Elvis. Even the film *Casino* was based on events there. Gangsters in 'Old Vegas.' The big hotels along the Strip did not even exist when those guys were in their heyday."

My initial impression of Fremont Street was that it was pretty similar to the newer area of Vegas that we had frequented for the last ten days, only on a smaller scale. However, I quite liked the look of the older casinos and restaurants. They had more character than the behemoth structures that have superseded them.

Some of the iconic buildings like the Golden Nugget and the Four Queens were still standing, which I imagine added to the sense of nostalgia for older visitors. The huge neon cowboy shaped sign known as 'Vegas Vic' was still present too. This was one of the many famous sights of the part of Vegas that was once the most glamorous area within this city of entertainment. Hugely popular films such as *Viva Las Vegas* and *Diamonds Are Forever* were filmed here during its glory days.

McDonald's was once again the restaurant of choice for us that evening.

"At least we can say that we have eaten American food every day," Dad joked.

Or at least I think that he was joking. After all, McDonald's is an American institution that can count the current president as a regular customer.

The global franchise is often held up as the poster boy for the sinister tactics of global companies operating in a capitalist society. The company has been accused of offering extremely unhealthy food, targeting children with the toys that come with their Happy Meals, and exploiting their staff. McDonald's will not be too concerned by any of this, as they can rely on lazy customers like us to frequent their restaurants for a quick meal.

The 2016 film *The Founder*, starring Michael Keaton, tells the story of the company's early history, beginning with the opening of a restaurant in California in 1940. With the set up of the kitchen mimicking an assembly line and food being pre-cooked and kept warm, Richard and Maurice McDonald had created the formula for what would later be known as 'fast food.'

Soon, a franchise system was set up and restaurants were introduced in a number of locations. Eventually, the brothers were bought out. They were allowed to keep the original restaurant but the newly formed McDonald's Corporation forced them to remove their own name from the business and opened a franchise directly opposite it. Ultimately, this put the brothers out of business.

After finishing what seemed like our one hundredth burger of the trip, we took our drinks outside to witness one of the must-see events that regularly takes place on Fremont Street. Or rather, it takes place above Fremont Street. Each evening, there is a six minute light show that plays on what is marketed as the world's largest video screen

We stood under part of the four hundred and sixty metre long canopy whilst a dazzling display of colourful images and lights took place on the screen. This was accompanied by music from the likes of The Who blasting out from the ultra powerful sound system.

This is a central attraction of the 'Fremont Street Experience,' which was created to bring the crowds back to the old part of town. It was very impressive and it was just the type of thing that I associated with the razzmatazz of Las Vegas. I looked around and saw people lined up all along the street with their heads tilted back and their eyes fixed on the show above.

Apparently, the original plan was to have a floating parade suspended from the canopy. This was eventually scrapped in favour of the light show. Considering how difficult it would have been to be able to see the floats up there, I think that they made the right decision.

I tried to say something to Dad but he could not hear my words over the booming music. Although I do not usually like being in a place so loud that you are unable to hear the person next to you, this somehow added to the experience. Like everyone around us, we just stood quietly and took it all in.

With everyone looking up and admiring something so flash and expensive, it was easy to overlook a less fortunate situation below. There was a homeless man outside McDonald's asking for change so that he could buy some food. We gave him a couple of dollars as we made our way out of Fremont Street but we probably should have been more generous, considering that this was less than what we had been handing out in tips during the previous few days.

It seemed symbolic that tourists like ourselves were so busy looking up at the attractions above that we did not notice the suffering below. Or, perhaps, we chose to ignore it. I did not dwell on this too much but several years later this would become an increasingly common sight that would play on my mind.

I occasionally take bags full of food to Manchester and hand out the contents to homeless people but this barely scratches the surface of the problem. On a personal level, it presents me with an internal conflict; the desire to make a small gesture that benefits other human beings versus my strong instinct to avoid any social interaction that makes me uncomfortable.

On the first occasion that I did this, it took me an eternity to finally pluck up the courage to approach someone, which seems ludicrous given our respective situations. What eventually prompted me to act was the sight of a homeless man sprinting down the street as if his life depended on it. It turns out that he had spotted someone throwing some food away in a bin, which prompted him to run over to retrieve it. Having witnessed that scene, I realised just how silly I had been to show such hesitation.

\*   \*   \*

After checking out of the Mandalay Bay on our final day of the trip, we left our luggage in the huge storage room in the bowels of the building and set off on what felt like our one thousandth walk up and down the Strip. It would seem strange once our daily routine no longer involved walking past this almost endless row of gigantic entertainment complexes. Incidentally, we still had time for one more square shaped burger at Wendy's before returning to Mandalay Bay to catch a taxi to the airport.

We returned to the storage bunker with the worry that our luggage would be lost forever amongst the sea of suitcases. As I began to ponder if we could cope without our possessions, an heroic hotel employee, against all odds, emerged with both of our cases in hand. This was a situation in which we were more than happy to provide a tip. We had asked to use this service, we had benefitted from it and we were pleased with the outcome. Therefore, this felt like a genuine gesture rather than a polite mugging.

It was time to once again face the horror of an American airport. Making our way through security was even more tense than usual. As is the norm in America, we had to remove our shoes. I began to wonder if they would request that I remove my epidermis as well as my shoes, but thankfully this was not the case.

Aside from contracting influenza and consequently having to tell Mike, my boss at the newsagent that I was working at, that I would need a few extra days off work due to illness, our journey home passed without incident.

My travel aspirations were now expanding. We had survived a trip to another continent, so there was no limit to my global ambition; apart from relying on the UFC event schedule to tell me where to go next.

# CHAPTER 5: A HALF-NAKED PHOTO SHOOT IN THE ARABIAN DESERT
## ABU DHABI, THE UNITED ARAB EMIRATES
### APRIL 2010

Shortly after the pilot had informed us that we were flying over Iraq, our plane suddenly dropped what seemed like a thousand feet. I pinned myself back against my seat and gripped the armrests as tightly as the laws of physics would allow. Up until this point, I had been thankful of how smooth the flight had been but an announcement from the cockpit confirmed that we had encountered some unexpected turbulence. I hate the sensation that it causes, so this huge drop in altitude was deeply unsettling.

I calmed myself down by using some sensible rationale: "It is just a change in the airflow. Probably a pocket of unstable air pressure. Remember that it is extremely unlikely to cause any damage to the aircraft. It is unsettling but you will be ok. After all, the chance of being involved in a plane crash is about one in five million. Or perhaps even greater."

We then endured an even more severe drop.

"Ok, we're dead. And they will have to retrieve my body from a plane wreckage in a country that is being ravaged by war."

The fact that you are reading this has probably alerted you to the fact that the British authorities did not need to send a specialist team to search for my body in Iraq. Instead, the rest of the journey was a rather gentle affair. Indeed, apart from the two plunges of doom, the flight was very pleasant.

The latest Hollywood movies were available on our personal

entertainment screens as we sat back in our spacious and comfortable seats. The cabin crew provided an abundance of drinks to accompany the food that was considerably more tolerable than what is usually served at thirty five thousand feet. This luxury was not surprising, given that we were travelling to the United Arab Emirates with one of its flag carrying airlines.

*       *       *

Around seven hours after departing Manchester, our Etihad flight touched down in Abu Dhabi. The reason that Dad and I were once again travelling overseas was, predictably, to attend a mixed martial arts show. *UFC 112: Invincible* was the name of the event on this occasion, which seemed fitting, considering that we had somehow survived two death-defying plunges during our flight.

I had grown up with an image of the Middle East as a land of eternal conflict. If a younger version of myself had been told that I would one day be travelling to this part of the world, I would have assumed that this meant that the future version of myself would be enlisting in the British Army. The United Arab Emirates has had a very different recent history to much of the Middle East though.

It was only in 1971 that this independent country was formed. The discovery of huge reserves of oil has effectively allowed it to rebuild everything from the ground up, with seemingly unlimited financial backing. Much of what we would see over the next few days did not even exist a few decades ago. Futuristic buildings and skyscrapers appear to have emerged from the desert.

Our hotel was located on the man-made Yas Island, which was designed to house various entertainment projects, including the Formula One circuit that has hosted a grand prix every year since 2009.

The Radisson Blu hotel that we were staying in looked impressive and seemed luxurious to us but I imagine that it is quite modest compared to some of its competitors in the area. Incidentally, the hotel must have been fairly decent, considering that we bumped into the future UFC Lightweight Champion, Rafael dos Anjos, who was staying there ahead of his fight at the weekend.

As Abu Dhabi is three hours ahead of British Summer Time and we had arrived at the hotel over ten hours after leaving home, the day was more or less a write-off. I did not mind this too much, as we could go to sleep shortly after checking in and set our body clocks to the local time.

I caught up with the night's football scores before turning out the lights. Dad tried his best to hide his delight at the news that Manchester

United had been knocked out of the Champions League by Bayern Munich but I could tell that he was thrilled. I put this disappointment behind me by using my negative outlook to remind myself that the team would not have been good enough to win the competition in any case.

*   *   *

With a good night's sleep behind us and some cereal in our bellies, it was time to explore Abu Dhabi. We were somewhat wary of what to expect. This was the first Middle Eastern country that we had been to and we were aware that there would be different behavioural expectations.

Taking photographs of women was prohibited, as was hugging or shaking the hand of someone of the opposite sex. I am tempted to say that I would struggle to avoid receiving such close attention from my female following but the truth is that, besides my mum, I did not exactly have many women clamouring for my affection. As this was a predominantly Muslim country, we would not be able to act flirtatiously or drink alcohol in public. I guess that this meant that I would somehow have to refrain from planting a big kiss on Dad's lips.

The wariness that we felt was rather misplaced, at least in terms of what we would personally encounter. The United Arab Emirates is a conservative country but so is the United States of America, which we had visited five months earlier.

The main difference is that the conservatism of the U.S.A. is rooted in Christianity, whereas the religion of Islam is what has shaped the laws and customs of this Middle Eastern country. Both are considered to be less liberal than my home country of the United Kingdom, which in turn may be seen as less liberal than those in Scandinavia. It is all relative.

Some of the archaic laws and excessive punishments are shocking and deeply concerning but the fact that abortion and gun control are issues that are fiercely debated in every U.S. election also seems ridiculous to most British citizens. In any case, it is wise for the tourist to respect the culture of the country that they are visiting.

Interestingly, we discovered that the U.A.E. is eager to appear open to people from all backgrounds. In most tourist areas, you would not think that you are in a Muslim country. For example, alcohol is served in hotels, which often host international parties.

We asked a receptionist for advice about visiting the various tourist sites.

He said: "I know just the guy. I'll call him and he will take you to all of the important places in Abu Dhabi."

Ten minutes later, we were greeted by a taxi driver: "Hello, my name is Abubakar and I will be your guide today. I hope to give you a good experience filled with joy.

I let dad introduce us: "Hi, I am Barry. This is David."

I believe that Abubakar sensed this opportunity to lay on the charm, as he asked, "Are you brothers?"

Dad was practically gushing by the time that he clarified that we were in fact father and son.

Unperturbed, Abubakar carried on with the charm offensive: "Really? You look like brothers. You both look young."

I really hoped that he was joking, as I am thirty nine years younger than my dad. If he was being serious, this meant that I either looked depressingly old for my age or the man that was going to drive us around for the next few hours was as blind as a Texas salamander.

We began our tour and it soon became apparent that the vision of our driver seemed to be in fine working order. I had mixed feelings about this. Of course it was reassuring that we were not embarking on a drive to a certain death but it did increase the likelihood that I looked several decades older than my biological age. Perhaps all was not lost; maybe I would age in reverse like the title character from *The Curious Case of Benjamin Button.*

Abubakar informed us that Emirates Palace was our first port of call: "You have probably seen five star hotels. Well, this has seven stars. Even though the rating system only has five stars, this place has seven. Typical U.A.E."

This was the first hint of bitterness that he had shown but there would be plenty more to follow. He was right though; the hotel is marketed as having seven stars, even though such a rating does not exist.

"I will drop you off here and you can have a look around and take some nice pictures," Abubakar suggested.

We were then told that Emirates Palace should not be confused with the nearby royal palace, although it is easy to see how this can occur. We commented on how aesthetically pleasing the vast gardens were as we approached the coral pink building.

As I took some photographs of the outer structure and gardens, it did not feel like we were standing outside a hotel. Surely, only royalty could afford to stay here? This feeling only increased once we stepped inside and were faced with gold everywhere we looked. The walls, the floor and all of the furnishings are adorned with gold.

Even the ceiling of the atrium is covered with twenty two carat gold leaf. The hotel was built at a cost of over eleven billion dirhams, which is worth well over two billion British pounds. It seems that the intention was to show the world that Abu Dhabi is one of the most prosperous places on the planet. Any notion of doing this in a subtle way was clearly discarded in favour of the ostentatious.

After exiting the building, we were reunited with Abubakar, who asked: "So what did you think? Lots of gold, right? Did you have the cappuccino with gold flakes?"

We laughed off his final question, incorrectly assuming that it was a joke. Incredibly, they do actually serve coffee sprinkled with twenty four carat gold flakes. The usual posh fare of caviar and champagne was also on offer but this must not have been deemed extravagant enough to satisfy the tastes of the high-flyers of Abu Dhabi.

An even more ludicrous feature was installed a month after our visit; a vending machine that dispenses twenty four carat gold bars. Presumably, this is there just in case you are caught short and need an emergency top up of gold. Despite this, it is regarded as one of the most affordable luxury hotels in the world. The cheapest rooms are sometimes available for less than three hundred pounds a night.

Obviously this is still very expensive and it is not an option that I would even entertain, but at least it does show that you do not need to be part of Forbes' *The World's Billionaires* list to be able to afford to stay here for a night. Just to clarify, neither myself nor my father have been named on the list at the time of writing.

"That palace is crazy. Those rich Arabs spend money like it is nothing!" Abubakar exclaimed. He could no longer hold in his resentment of the inequality of wealth.

"I came here from India to work and provide for my family. I am humble. Some of these Arabs spend so much money on stupid things."

He pointed at some of the flash cars that were whizzing by and passed further comment: "Those Sheiks will buy a car, get bored, then buy another one three months later."

A more pressing concern for me than the needless acquisition of flashy sports cars was the manner in which they were being driven. I had read that the rate of fatal road accidents in the U.A.E. was surprisingly high. Despite having a world class infrastructure, the death rate was more in line with poorer and less developed countries.

To put into context how dangerous the roads were at the time of our trip, there were over fifteen road traffic deaths for every hundred thousand people in Abu Dhabi in 2010. To put this into context, the current rate in the United Kingdom is just over three deaths per one hundred thousand. Road safety has reportedly improved in recent years but, as with anywhere else, the fight to reduce accidents and save lives is an ongoing battle.

The U.A.E. Heritage Village is located a short distance from Emirates

Palace but it shares none of its extravagance . We were informed that this was a replica of a traditional Emirati village and that it was designed to show tourists what life was like before the discovery of oil. The mock village looked authentic enough; there was a water well in the centre and various tents set out as you would imagine. However, the number of stalls selling local souvenirs was a reminder that this was a tourist attraction.

Nevertheless, it served its purpose of highlighting the polarity between the traditional villages and the modern world of skyscrapers and technological advancement. What was also apparent was how foolish I had been to have left my sunglasses at the hotel. I was constantly squinting, which would have been obvious to passers-by and to anyone who had the misfortune to be shown the photographs that I featured in. We then made our way to the real highlight of our tour; the Sheik Zayed Grand Mosque. Abubakar seemed genuinely impressed by this grand structure: "It only opened a few years ago but it has already become the symbol of Abu Dhabi. It is one of the biggest mosques in the world and it is very beautiful. Inside, you will see the biggest carpet and chandelier in the world. Of course."

As we approached the building, it became clear that this was indeed a stunning example of Islamic architecture. The immaculate white marble and the beautifully constructed domes and minarets provide a striking image that continues to impress visitors from around the world.

Before entering the mosque, one is required to make any adjustments to their attire so that it falls within the strict dress code. After all, it is primarily a place of worship. Women must wear loose clothing that covers their arms, ankles and head. The mosque can provide a type of robe that is known as an Abaya or a headscarf known as a Shaya, free of charge.

This obviously did not apply to Dad and me but we still had to be mindful of some of the other aspects of the dress code. Fortunately we were both wearing a pair of jeans and a T-shirt, which were deemed acceptable clothing.

All visitors are required to remove their footwear and find a home for them somewhere within the seemingly infinite amount of shoe racking before entering the mosque. The same thought crossed both of our minds; are we going to be able to find our shoes when it is time to leave?

"We'll just take whatever is left," Dad joked. At least , I hoped that he was joking.

The mosque can hold over forty thousand worshippers during Eid. Thankfully, there were considerably less people there on the day of our visit. I am unable to even imagine the chaos of locating a pair of shoes amongst forty thousand others.

With our shoes removed, we walked through the grand doorway of the main hall, where we were greeted by the sight of one of the most splendid looking interiors of any building that we had ever seen. We marvelled at the marble columns, admired the intricately decorated walls and ceiling, and examined the chandelier and carpet that Abubakar had described to us. The equally impressive smaller chandeliers contained colourful Swarovski crystals.

The mosque was named after the first leader of the United Arab Emirates; the late Sheikh Zayed Bin Sultan Al Nahyan. If the intention was to honour him with beauty and grandeur, then this wonderful building more than succeeds in doing so.

My favourite part of the mosque was the outdoor area. The huge courtyard was covered by mosaics. On each side of this, there were rows of spectacular white marble columns and archways that seemed to go on forever; all adorned with hints of a variety of colours, as well as gold. Every square inch of this building was pristine.

Upon leaving the mosque, we realised that we were now faced with the challenge of trying to relocate our footwear. I considered what the worst case scenario would be. Perhaps, we would be unable to find our shoes. Or Abubakar. Or our wallets. In this imagined horror, we would be left without a driver to take us back to the hotel and without any money to arrange alternative transportation. We would have to walk back to our accommodation. Barefoot. In the searing heat.

My propensity for inventing the very worst situations to find myself in always makes me think of an episode of *Red Dwarf*. The central characters of the show use a virtual reality machine in which they can make any of their desires come true, simply by willing it to happen. However, Rimmer is unable to control his negativity, so he manages to turn every situation into a disaster of his own making.

I was recently surprised to find out that my blood group is A Positive. I am certainly not a positive person, so my first instinct was that this must have been a mistake. B Negative would seem to be a more fitting blood group for someone with my pessimistic outlook.

Despite my best attempts to channel Rimmer's negative energy, we had soon retrieved our shoes and we were once again in the trusted care of Abubakar.

"So, you liked the mosque? It's incredible isn't it?" he asked enthusiastically.

We agreed with him and proclaimed that it was one of the best examples of architecture that we had ever seen.

"Were people respectful?" Abubakar asked.

We nodded and told him that our fellow tourists were on their best behaviour,

"Good, because I don't like it when people are not respectful in a religious building," he replied.

He made a good point. It should always be remembered that religious buildings like the Sheikh Zayed Grand Mosque are places of worship and that we should appreciate the fact that they allow tourists to visit. It is not something that is exclusive to Islam either. The same level of respect is expected of visitors to religious buildings of any faith. Whether you are in St. Peter's Basilica in Vatican City or a mosque in Abu Dhabi, you should behave in a respectful manner and be mindful of customs that may seem unusual to yourself.

The mosque is open to the public to allow people to gain a better understanding of the Islamic faith, as well as showcasing the architectural accomplishments. The plan seems to be going well, as the number of annual visitors has risen to around three and a half million and it is consistently voted as one of the world's best landmarks. Unfortunately, there are occasions when tourists act inappropriately. This is usually due to a degree of ignorance rather than any malicious intent.

The most famous incident was when Rihanna was asked to leave during her visit in 2013. The singer was reportedly taking provocative photographs inside the building. This was probably an honest mistake, in which she was more mindful of impressing her social media following than respecting this place of worship. There was little chance of my father and me being thrown out for taking sexually charged photographs. Not there nor anywhere else.

After lavishing the mosque with praise, Abubakar returned to his criticism of some aspects of life in Abu Dhabi: "Do you see those workers over there? They are helping to build an expensive building for rich people to live in. The workers have come over from other countries to work here and they are treated very bad. They are poor and have no workers' rights. Long hours with little pay and they have to do whatever is asked off them. I am ok. Not great, but at least I get by without many problems."

He had touched upon a controversial subject that has drawn international criticism. Foreign nationals can work in the U.A.E. tax free but they have very few workers' rights, if any. There have been many stories of people coming over from poor countries and having their passports seized by their employers. Consequently, they are unable to complain about poor treatment or pay. This is not true of all workers, of course. For many, the U.A.E. provides an opportunity to make lots of money without paying taxes and to enjoy life in a developed country.

Abubakar seemed to fit somewhere between these two groups; perhaps slightly closer to the former.

It had surprised me just how many expats were living there. Astonishingly, only around one eighth of the population of the U.A.E. is formed by the native ethnic group, the Emiratis.

After a busy day of sightseeing, we were ready to head back to our hotel. Abubakar had been a brilliant guide, patiently waiting for us whilst we took our time to explore each of the places that we had visited.

During the drive back, he offered his services for the following day: "Would you like to go to Dubai? I can take you there sometime in the next few days if you like?"

Dad and I had a quick chat before deciding that we would give Dubai a miss, as we were going to attend the weigh-ins the next day and we wanted some relaxation before the UFC show on Saturday. Turning down the opportunity to travel to such a spectacular destination would be an unthinkable decision for me nowadays. However, given that we were so tired and hot, we did not fancy another busy day rushing around before the show. Instead, we asked him if he could take us to the weigh-ins and also to the airport on our day of departure.

He expressed his satisfaction at securing more business, before offering his views on Dubai. "I think Abu Dhabi is better than Dubai anyway. Dubai is all about image. Everything is for show. Abu Dhabi recently bailed out Dubai. It was spending so much money creating this luxurious place to attract tourists that it built up a large debt. The Abu Dhabi government recently gave over thirty six billion dirhams to Dubai. What is that in your money?"

Dad, who has been a self-employed accountant for most of his life, was quick to estimate that it was worth over seven billion British pounds.

Abubakar continued his rant: "Abu Dhabi has more money and power. It is less flashy but more powerful. It is the capital and the real heart of the U.A.E."

With Dubai and Abu Dhabi receiving so much coverage, it is easy to forget, or not realise, that there are five other Emirates. Fujairah, Ras Al Khaimah, Sharjah, Ajman and Umm Al Quwain hardly get a mention outside of the U.A.E. and are rarely visited by overseas tourists.

*   *   *

The following day we were due to attend the weigh-ins for the weekend's MMA show. Strangely, this was scheduled to take place in the middle of a huge shopping centre called Marina Mall. Considering the fact that I hated these kind of places, my willingness to spend a few hours there shows how deep my MMA obsession ran.

Back at home, the mere thought of visiting the Trafford Centre would make me feel ill. Crowds of people packed into an enclosed area full of stores belonging to the same old global brands? No thanks. Being as we were in Abu Dhabi, it was no surprise that this mall was gigantic and extravagant.

We attended the briefest meet and greet possible with the UFC Welterweight Champion, Georges St-Pierre, in which we were barely able to say more than five words before the heavy-handed security team moved us on.

After watching the formalities of the weigh-ins and observing our new friends in the security team struggle to control the number of people in attendance, we decided to have some dinner in the mall's food hall. Middle Eastern cuisine or burger and chips? Being the clueless tourists that we were, of course we opted for the latter.

Abubakar safely returned us to our hotel, where we watched television in our room until we were tired enough to fall asleep. The international news coverage included the upcoming U.K. General Election and the recently signed nuclear arms treaty between the United States and Russia.

The latter was an agreement for both countries to significantly reduce and limit the number of deployed strategic nuclear warheads. The treaty, commonly referred to as New START, felt like the latest step in the right direction for the world.

Unfortunately, the more conservative administration that has succeeded Barack Obama's government has taken a different view. In early 2019, the United States formally withdrew from the 1987 Intermediate-Range Nuclear Forces Treaty. Russia, which seems to have become increasingly aggressive and bold, soon followed suit.

Our first couple of days in the Middle East had been a pleasant experience. We had seen lots of places of interest and had gained some insight into the history and culture of this young country. After such a busy itinerary, it was no surprise that we were soon fast asleep.

*   *   *

We woke up feeling refreshed and with the knowledge that we had a more relaxing day ahead of us. Our first task was to collect our UFC tickets from the box office. The cloudy sky and the fact that the box office was only a ten minute walk away, convinced me that I would not need to wear any sunscreen. Ignoring the advice that Baz Luhrmann gave us all in 1999 would prove to be a foolish decision.

We passed the Yas Marina Formula One circuit on the way to the box office and caught a glimpse of Ferrari World in the distance. This futuristic looking theme park, branded with a huge logo of the automobile manufacturer, was due to open a few months after our visit.

Choosing a location in proximity to the Formula One circuit has proven to be a wise move, as interest from racing enthusiasts has helped establish the popularity of the park. One of the biggest attractions is Formula Rossa, which holds the title of the world's fastest rollercoaster. It is hardly a surprise that such an accolade is held by a theme park within the U.A.E.

We soon reached the box office, which was located within the premises of the venue that was hosting the show. In keeping with how things tend to be done in Abu Dhabi, the entire arena had been built for this one show. Once it had served its sole purpose, it would be dismantled. As the show was being held outdoors, it was not as crazy as it sounds but it was still the type of bold move that one has become accustomed to in this part of the world.

Make a proposal to host an event first then worry about the smaller details such as actually having an arena to stage it in. When you have such vast resources of money available, I guess building a single-use arena is not such a big deal. Certainly not as big a deal as the fact that the sun had escaped the cloud cover and that I could feel the intense rays burning my skin.

I had always hated the thought of collecting tickets from a box office but the event required customers to do this. I braced myself for the prospect of the staff being unable to locate my booking and informing me that there were not any spare tickets left. Travelling to the Middle East just to watch the show on a television screen would be a very expensive waste of time.

At least Abubakar would be able to take us to an establishment that was airing the action. Thankfully, we were quickly handed our tickets and we were able to head back to the hotel before I got sunburnt. Or at least, I hoped that was the case.

Upon arrival back at the hotel, it was apparent that I had been unable to avoid being fried like a steak on a George Foreman grill. My exposed skin had already started to turn red, leaving a 'builder's tan,' which perfectly resembled the shape of the T-shirt that I had been wearing. I briefly pondered what the most suitable course of action would be, before sensibly deciding that lying on a sunbed for a few hours would be the best option.

I was already sunburnt, so I foolishly believed that the best thing to do would be to try and even out my tan by putting sunscreen only on the parts of my body that had already been coloured red. I had not been exposed to this degree of heat since going on family holidays to the Balearic Islands and Florida as a child, so perhaps my ridiculous logic can be excused to some extent.

Sunbathing was a strange and unfamiliar process for me. I was struggling to understand the appeal of lying down with very little clothing on and doing nothing whilst baking in the sun. I removed all of my clothing apart from my swim shorts, positioned my towel on the sunbed and lay back on it.

I looked over to my right and saw that dad had done the same. We seemed to be doing this correctly. Now we just had to lie here for the next couple of hours, or however long seems socially acceptable, and do nothing.

After ten minutes or so of replaying yesterday's events in my mind, boredom was starting to set in. I put my iPod on and started to think ahead to the show that was set to take place later that night. I began calculating what time we would have to leave the hotel and when we would get back.

I still felt restless. Then I had an epiphany. The key to a successful sunbathing session is to switch off your mind. Or rather, to switch it to battery saving mode. All I had to do was stop thinking about things so much.

Half an hour later and I was still pleading with my mind to temporarily slow down and relax: "OK, you have stopped thinking about sport, what we did yesterday, the plan for tonight, and even managed to shut out thoughts of the other people around the pool staring at my half naked body. Now please stop thinking about not thinking."

Eventually, it co-operated and I was able to relax. I think that this was probably down to my brain overheating and triggering an emergency shutdown. Now this was more pleasant. Hot weather, some of my favourite music in my ear and a break from the stresses and worries of everyday life.

After an hour and a half of dozing, I became aware of a couple of things that had occurred. Dad had enjoyed a refreshing dip in the pool and my body now resembled a pack of Billy Bear Ham. My plan to achieve a well balanced tan had backfired spectacularly. Instead, I had various patches of sunburnt skin, each showing a different degree of red or pink.

Feeling relaxed but tender, I suggested having a bite to eat in the hotel restaurant before heading over to the arena for the show. It was an Italian themed eatery, so Middle Eastern cuisine would once again have to wait. At least we had the knowledge that we would get to sample some traditional local food during the desert safari excursion that we had booked for our final day in Abu Dhabi.

With our tummies full of delicious but overpriced pasta, we set off towards the arena that we had collected our tickets from earlier in the day. We soon located our seats and took in the view of this temporary sporting venue. It was strange to think that in a few hours time it would have served its sole purpose and that it would be deconstructed shortly afterwards.

The climate had gotten the better of me for most of the day but I was now relieved that it was warm and that there was still some daylight. I certainly would not have fancied spending five or six hours sat in an outdoor arena at night in the Manchester rain.

I heard an American sounding voice suggest that the group of men several rows in front of us were Sheiks. I am not sure what led him to believe that this was the case, as they simply appeared to be locals that were wearing traditional attire, consisting of an ankle length robe called a Kandura and a headscarf known as a Ghutra.

Perhaps, the man made this assumption due to the fact that the majority of news coverage regarding the U.A.E. focuses on the extravagant wealth of Sheiks and other prominent figures. I am pretty sure that there are many Emiratis that are not billionaires. In any case, they seemed to be enjoying the show.

Following the conclusion of *UFC 112: Invincible,* in which Anderson Silva successfully defended his middleweight title against Demian Maia, and Frankie Edgar edged out B.J. Penn for the lightweight belt, we snared a picture with Antônio Rogério 'Minotouro' Nogueira then indulged in a late night supper of fish and chips.

Sitting on a street curb in the Middle East whilst we ate fish and chips and gazed up at the stars in the night sky was a bizarre yet pleasant moment. Life can turn out so differently to what you once expected. Prior to 2009, I had never thought about travelling to foreign lands, yet here I was in the United Arab Emirates, feeling perfectly relaxed and content.

*   *   *

The final full day of our trip was upon us. We had a desert safari booked for four o'clock in the afternoon, which meant that we had all morning to relax by the pool and inflict some more damage upon my skin. I had mastered the art of sunbathing though, so the time went quickly due to my sporadic napping.

It was soon time for our excursion to Rub' al Khali, otherwise known as 'The Empty Quarter.' This section of the Arabian Desert is the world's largest uninterrupted sand mass, although the Sahara Desert has a much larger overall size.

As we boarded our minibus, I had a feeling of adventure and excitement. This would undoubtedly be the part of our trip that would take us to a landscape that was considerably different to anything that we had ever seen.

We were joined on the minibus by a Belgian family. After exchanging pleasantries, we soon broke off into our separate conversations in our native tongues. I was thankful that I could not understand what they were saying, as I imagined that they were discussing how my bright red skin looked even more ridiculous against my luminous yellow F.C. Barcelona vest.

It took less than two hours to reach the part of the desert that we were scheduled to visit. As we exited the vehicle, there was sand as far as we could see in every direction. Our desert adventure had begun.

The first activity that was presented to us was a jeep ride over the sand dunes, which proved to be rougher and bumpier than expected. The driver had deflated the tyres, as this is necessary in order to avoid them sinking deep into the sand. He would accelerate as our jeep travelled up each dune before leaping up into the air and crashing back down into the sand; all whilst he laughed uncontrollably.

The unsettling sensation was similar to that of a rollercoaster, with fear and excitement experienced in equal amounts. This was an example of how human beings are constantly finding new and strange ways in which to entertain themselves within the natural world that has existed for as long as can be documented. It felt a bit of a shame to disturb this peaceful open land with our petrol-guzzling vehicles but seeing as it was part of the itinerary, we may as well embrace it.

The driver then informed us that we were free to either partake in some sandboarding down the dunes or go for a ride on a quad bike. As we had already experienced enough exhilaration for the day, we declined both invitations. Instead, Dad and I took it in turns to run up and down sand dunes as the other took photographs.

This was a more basic type of activity but it was fun nonetheless. Aside from the sand, I think that this brought back childhood memories for Dad. Running up hills and enjoying the great outdoors provided the happiest of moments during his youth but it was becoming less prevalent with each generation.

I was fortunate enough that the majority of my childhood memories revolve around playing football in the back garden and that computers and phones had not yet taken over our lives. I played so much football with my dad and brother that the grass in our back garden completely disappeared, leaving behind a dust bowl.

Thankfully, smartphones would not become a fixture in our lives until I was an adult. I worry about the childhood that is experienced by the youth of today and I find it quite disturbing to see children as young as two or three obsessed with phones and tablets. Perhaps Dad had a point about phones and the internet after all.

We were also offered the opportunity to have a camel ride but we turned this down. I had mixed feelings about this practice. On one hand, it demonstrated how these animals have been key to the survival of the desert dwellers known as the Bedouin. They make transport across such vast and difficult terrain possible, whilst also providing meat and milk to consume in order to sustain life, and hair that can be used for textiles.

However, there is no escaping the sympathy that can be felt for the camels that are enslaved by this life. The camel rides on offer were a form of entertainment rather than something that was essential for human survival, so the feelings of sadness and guilt felt even stronger.

Dad and I were brought over to a mock desert camp, along with all the other tourists on similar excursions. The idea was to showcase what Bedouin life consisted of. We were informed that there would be a buffet of local food, entertainment provided by a traditional dancer and some stalls offering gifts and services that were associated with the desert.

Of course, this was a diluted version of Bedouin life that was geared towards tourist enjoyment but it was still interesting to be in the Arabian Desert with props that allowed you to at least imagine what it could be like.

Dad and I had a wonder around the stalls but there was not too much that interested us. We did not wish to smoke any shisha, purchase any handcrafted jewellery or decorate our hands with henna. Whilst the majority of the other visitors were drawn to the aforementioned stalls, we headed over to a gentleman who was showcasing a collection of traditional garments in his tent.

As we were admiring the clothing, I heard the stall owner's voice gently call out over my shoulder: "Hello sir, you have an interesting tattoo."

This was the opening line of an exchange that I would become accustomed to over the years. He had spotted the top part of my recently acquired ink, which read, 'We are all one.' I replied by explaining that the section of the tattoo covered by my vest included a map of the world and the Universal Declaration of Human Rights.

He was now fascinated by this: "Sir, would you be kind enough to allow me to take a photo of your tattoo?"

This felt weird but his next remark convinced me to grant his request: "If you allow me to take a photograph of your tattoo, you can try on one of my garments and have your photo taken."

When Westerners wear traditional Emirati clothing in public, it is generally deemed to be offensive unless it is in a setting such as this. Therefore, I was eager to make the most of this opportunity.

So here I was, topless and stood in a stranger's tent in the Arabian Desert as darkness descended. Our surroundings imitated a traditional Bedouin camp but the illusion was smashed as he started snapping away on his smartphone. With my dad quietly observing the unfolding events, it certainly made for a surreal moment.

After my first half-naked photoshoot was complete, I picked out a Kandura and Ghutra to try on, then posed for some more photographs, this time taken by Dad.

Wearing this clothing and being surrounded by this landscape, I felt like I was an actor on a film set. In keeping with the feeling of being a celebrity of sorts, perhaps I should be worried that somewhere in the Middle East there are a series of photographs of my naked torso doing the rounds. Hopefully, my unclothed body has not been exposed to every corner of the world via the internet. But if you do happen to see such an image whilst browsing the web, at least you now know the story behind it.

As we headed back to our cushions in the open air dining area, I realised that I would have been better off if I still had the Kandura and Ghutra on. Despite the temperature being so high all day, it was starting to feel cold now that the sun had gone into hiding for the night. At this point, my luminous vest felt like an even dafter choice of attire. There were a couple of hours to survive the cold open desert whilst I was insufficiently protected from the elements.

Fortunately, our friendly hosts had prepared a banquet to warm our souls. The serving of Arabic coffee and dates is a traditional way of welcoming guests in this part of the world. There is a great amount of importance placed on this act of hospitality and it is ingrained within the culture and heritage of the Middle East.

We were given the small handleless cups that Arabic coffee is usually served in. I was not accustomed to drinking coffee at this point in my life, so I had only tasted very weak and milky versions of the drink. Served black, the strong and bitter taste was a shock to my system. It was not necessarily unpleasant, it was just completely different to what I had previously sampled.

The look on Dad's face suggested that he was not keen, which he verbally confirmed by stating: "I think mine was off! It was horrible and bitter!"

We had each been given another cup of coffee, this time with the addition of camel's milk. "Maybe you will prefer this one," I optimistically suggested.

Dad had posed for a picture with a camel earlier on in the evening. I chose not to, as I had read about how it is common for them to spit at humans or whatever else they feel threatened by. This spit is actually more like vomit, as they are bringing up the contents of their stomach and projecting it, along with saliva, at their chosen target. Judging by the expression on Dad's face after he had taken a sip from the second cup, I became worried that we had been served coffee containing camel vomit instead of milk.

Nevertheless, I followed suit and drank my second cup of Arabic coffee. I was pleased to discover that it was indeed camel's milk that had been added to my beverage. Unlike cow's milk, this has a somewhat salty taste. Again, I did not find this to be unpleasant, but combined with the bitter coffee, it is understandable that many tourists are shocked by the difference between this and the caffeinated drinks that they consume in their native countries.

Dad was not convinced: "I certainly won't be having any more of that coffee!"

In complete contrast, the dates were extremely sweet, which Dad found more palatable. Dates are the national fruit of the United Arab Emirates and they are an integral part of the culture and heritage. The fruit that comes from date palm trees has helped sustain life in the desert for centuries.

The trees are able to survive in these harsh conditions and they provide a source of food that can either be eaten immediately or preserved and stored for future consumption. The trunk of the tree can be used to prop up structures and the leaves are often woven to create baskets. Therefore, it is hardly a surprise that this tree, and the fruit that it bears, is so revered. Remarkably, there are over forty million date palm trees in this relatively small country.

After our customary welcome drink and snack, it was time for our banquet. There was a charcoal barbecue dug into the sand, which was being used to prepare a variety of food. Traditional meats consumed by the Bedouin included camel, goat and some of the birds found around the desert.

Our hosts had catered the meal choices for Westerners, as chicken and beef were the options on offer. Vegetables such as tomatoes and cucumbers were in rich supply, as were the standard accompaniments of rice and flatbreads.

We also tried some Harees, which is a dish consisting of meat and wheat that has been cooked until a consistency similar to porridge is achieved. Dad and I thoroughly enjoyed our meals and we were pleased to have sampled some traditional dishes, even if they had been modified for Western tourists like ourselves.

I then discovered something that was even more exotic and rare; a can of strawberry Fanta. Unfortunately, this was not as nice as I had anticipated, leading me to regret not opting for the traditional after dinner drink of a mint infused red tea that is supposed to help with digestion.

Entertainment came in the form of what was effectively a belly dancing exhibition. The sole dancer must have deep reserves of energy, as she performed with great enthusiasm for a considerable length of time. We were all sat on our cushions around the edge of the carpeted stage as she showcased her agility and stamina.

Then came the inevitable moment that I had feared. She signalled to the audience that one or more of us should join her on stage and dance. My heart rate instantly doubled and my palms started to feel sweaty.

I then resorted to a technique that I had employed during every French lesson of my five years at secondary school; when the teacher is looking for a student to converse with, do not make eye contact under any circumstances. Even if you notice a fire in your peripheral vision, do not look in the direction of the teacher, as this could be a trap to lure you into making eye contact and being asked to perform in front of your peers.

Even more frightening than the thought of being chosen was the prospect of watching Dad dance with this gyrating lady. Fortunately, another father volunteered to be the sacrificial lamb for the rest of us to laugh at. He even seemed to enjoy himself, which is more than can be said for his wife and kids who looked on in horror. Much to their relief, a few more guests joined in a short while later, taking some of the attention away from him.

We returned to our hotel at around midnight and reflected on what had been a fantastic adventure in the desert.

"I am really glad that we booked that excursion. It definitely feels like we have been to the Middle East now. What did you think?" I asked Dad.

"Yeah, that was brilliant. We can tell people we have been to the Arabian Desert. We even saw Sheikh Chapman," he replied.

I chuckled to myself as I imagined that everyone who saw the picture of me in the Kandura and Ghutra would make a similar remark. Sure enough, the first person to comment on Facebook asked the inevitable question: "Is this the Sheikh that is going to buy Manchester United?"

\*   \*   \*

After our final night's sleep in Abu Dhabi, it was time to head back to the airport for our flight back to Manchester.

Abubakar picked us up on time and extended another warm greeting: "Hello Sirs. Have you enjoyed your time in Abu Dhabi?"

We stated that our trip to the Middle East had been splendid and that it had exceeded our expectations.

He used the short taxi ride to make one last sales pitch: "Next time that you or your friends are back in Abu Dhabi, you can contact me so that I can transport you around again."

We exchanged email addresses, even though I had no intention of contacting him. A year or so later, however, I received an email from Abubakar, stating that he was now out of work and back in his home country. Bizarrely, he was asking if there were any job opportunities that we knew of. I assume that he sent this message to all of his contacts but I did not reply, as there was nothing useful that I could tell him. I just hope that wherever he is in the world, he has found employment and security.

Abubakar is an example of how many people travel to the United Arab Emirates in search of a better life. Hopefully, they find this but many end up like our friendly tour guide. Once you are unemployed, you are asked to leave the country. This once again highlights the disparity between the rich and the poor that is evident throughout the land. This is true of most places in the world though.

Our flight home was much smoother than our outbound journey had been. The eight hours soon passed and we were back in Manchester before we knew it. As it turns out, we were fortunate to be able to fly home, as just a couple of days later, the majority of European airspace was closed for a few days. This was due to significant eruptions from an Icelandic volcano.

The resulting ash cloud that emerged from Eyjafjallajökull caused chaos across Europe, with people having to make alternative arrangements to travel across land or remain stranded. The bigger problem, of course, was trying to correctly spell or pronounce the name of the volcano.

# CHAPTER 6: A CITY FORMERLY DIVIDED AND EUROPE'S LARGEST GAS HOLDER
## BERLIN, POTSDAM, OBERHAUSEN AND COLOGNE, GERMANY
## NOVEMBER 2010

It has taken six chapters to reach the point from which I can write about a trip with someone other than my father. On this occasion, it was a return to Germany to see the lady that I was dating at the time. Rachel and I had only seen each other a handful of times back in the United Kingdom before she began studying in Potsdam as part of her German and French language degree.

I had managed to schedule a visit to see her during the same week that *UFC 122: Marquardt vs. Okami* was taking place in Oberhausen. As this meant that we would have to travel to the other side of the country, we decided to visit a few different places during my time in Germany.

The outbound journey was the first time that I had ever flown anywhere on my own. Naturally, this was somewhat daunting but I felt comforted by the fact that Rachel would be waiting for me at the airport in Berlin. However, there were two airports in the capital city, so I began to worry that I had somehow sent her to the wrong one.

On arrival at Tegel Airport, I was relieved to see Rachel. The prospect of making my own way to another airport somewhere else in this foreign land was not worth thinking about.

The airport was scheduled to close in 2012 following the opening of Berlin Brandenburg Airport. This was a project that was first proposed shortly after the reunification of Germany in 1990 and it was intended to show the world that Berlin was once again a major international city. The plan was to replace both Tegel and Schonefeld airports with one superior modern equivalent.

At the time of writing, the new airport has still not been completed and the older ones are still in operation. The project has become a source of deep embarrassment, with over half a million faults being detected during construction.

I find it hilarious that parts of the unused airport have been operating, despite the fact that there has not been any aircraft flying in and out of the site. The hotel that is part of the airport complex has never been open to guests but they employ staff to clean it and periodically turn on the taps so that the pipes are kept in working order. The luggage carousels are given a daily test run and the electronic notification boards are regularly used so that they do not seize up.

Laughably, the boards have been used so frequently that they have been replaced since their initial installation. They have become so worn and in need of repair despite them not showing any information that relates to flights that have actually operated from the airport. Hopefully, Berlin Brandenburg Airport opens in the early 2020s before it becomes even more of a farce.

It took less than an hour on the train for us to reach Potsdam, which I thought sounded like someone cursing after they had remembered that they still had to wash the dishes. This is where we would spend the first night of our trip before returning to Berlin to explore the tourist attractions. Darkness had already descended, so we picked up some supplies from a local grocery store before heading back to Rachel's university accommodation.

I helped to cook chicken on a stove for the first time in my life and I was amazed to see the poultry turn from pink to white. I had previously only ever used an oven or a microwave to heat meals, which demonstrates how I was still somewhat lacking in life experience at that point in time; which is a polite way of saying that I was a lazy fool.

\*　　\*　　\*

The next morning, we stopped by the university, as Rachel had to submit some coursework and have a meeting with one of her tutors. Whist we were there, she showed me around the grand domed buildings and picturesque grounds that make up part of the campus. It certainly seemed like a nice location for carrying out one's studies. Mind you, I may not have thought that way if I was the one that was rushing around trying to submit my coursework before a deadline.

With Rachel's work safely handed in, we took the train back to Berlin. I had booked a hotel room in the capital city for the next couple of nights, so the pressure was on me to have chosen a reasonable standard of accommodation.

Thankfully, upon arrival at the Ibis hotel in the west of the city, it was apparent that my selection had easily surpassed the minimum requirements of cleanliness, location and value for money. At least I had negotiated the first couple of hurdles of the trip without encountering any disasters.

After dropping our suitcases off in the room, we headed straight out to explore the sights of Berlin. Having studied the Second World War and the Cold War extensively during my time at college and university, I was intrigued to be in a city that was the scene of so much of this history.

"Where shall we start?" Rachel asked.

The most obvious landmark immediately sprang to mind, prompting me to reply: "Let's go to the Berlin Wall."

As Rachel had visited most of the places of interest during her time in Germany, she took on the role of tour leader: "I know where there is a preserved section. We will have to take the U-Bahn."

Following a smooth journey to Potsdamer Platz on the underground rail network, we had a quick look around the square that was named after the city that we had stayed in the night before. There did not appear to be anything that would interest us, as most of the modern buildings seemed to be lacking in character. The large office blocks, restaurants and shopping centres simply did not appeal to us.

Without knowing it, we had declined the opportunity to take a ride on the fastest elevator in Europe. Perhaps this was a mistake, as this would have taken us to the viewing platform near the top of Kollhoff Tower, which apparently offers spectacular views over the area where the Berlin Wall once stood.

Just before we left the square, an interesting looking structure caught my eye; a multi-faceted green block sat on what resembled stilts of the same colour. There was a clock face on each side, so I assumed that it was merely an usual looking clock tower. However, on closer inspection, we noticed that there were traffic lights on each corner. I sneakily listened to a group of American tourists that were stood next to us.

One of them said: "The oldest traffic light in Europe. 1924. How cool is that?"

Irritating accent aside, I was excited by the information that I had just heard. Potsdamer Platz was certainly an appropriate location for this pioneering technology, since it was once the busiest intersection in the continent. This is the kind of quirky history that I love, so I took a minute to marvel at the traffic tower before moving on.

A short walk led us to Niederkirchnerstrasse, where there is a preserved section of the Berlin Wall, Most of the wall was removed by one form or another, following the East German government's announcement in November 1989 that all of its citizens were now free to visit West Berlin, and West Germany in general. Most citizens were eager to tear down the wall as soon as possible and erase any trace of the structure that had brought such misery and hardship to their lives.

However, the re-unified nation eventually decided that various sections should be preserved in order to highlight the grim consequences of war and division. I certainly felt the significance of the wall as we inspected it from close quarters. As much as I had read about it during my university studies, being in the shadow of this imposing structure gave me an understanding of its nature that could not be experienced through reading about it in a book.

The wall was roped off, in order to stop people from chipping off pieces of it to take away as souvenirs.

I turned to Rachel and offered my thoughts on this: "I can't help but feel amused by the irony of people being kept away from the Berlin Wall by another structure that is designed to segregate."

The section that was standing in front of us was around two hundred metres long but the total length of the wall around West Berlin was a staggering one hundred and fifty five kilometres. We took the opportunity to learn more about the Berlin Wall at the Topography of Terror. There were numerous displays providing information about life within a city that was divided, both physically and ideologically, from 1961 until 1989.

During the years preceding the erection of the wall, at least three and a half million people defected to the West via Berlin, taking advantage of the easiest place to cross within divided Germany. Worryingly for the East, many of the defectors were young academic men of a working age, which created what is often referred to as a 'brain drain.' The construction of the wall was an attempt to stop this stream of defectors.

The East German government, known as the German Democratic Republic, officially referred to the Berlin Wall as the 'Antifaschistischer Schutzwall,' which translates as the 'Anti-Fascist Protection Rampart.' Every part of the previous sentence seems ridiculous. 'Anti-Fascist' is hardly a phrase that many would associate with the Berlin Wall. The propaganda machine was certainly in full swing.

Even the name of the East German government uses a common form of misdirection. Whenever a government or country refers to itself as a 'Democratic Republic' or a 'People's Republic,' my first thought is that those places must be anything but democratic.

Our visit to this remaining section of the wall caused us to consider just how recent it was that the wall was in use

Rachel reminded me that: "It has been less than twenty years since the fall of the Berlin Wall."

It really hit home that this terrible symbol of division was still in operation during the early years of my life. It is difficult to imagine being separated from one side of your own city, including family members, by a three and a half metre high concrete structure that was present for nearly thirty years.

The information provided at the Topography of Terror did not mention that British Prime Minister Margaret Thatcher strongly opposed the removal of the Berlin Wall and the reunification of Germany. Her deep-rooted mistrust of the country was not a view shared by the majority of world leaders, who welcomed the end to this dark chapter in European history.

It did not take us long to reach the most well known border crossing point in the city. This was referred to as 'Checkpoint Charlie' by the Allies, due to the corresponding letter in the phonetic alphabet. To illustrate this point, crossing A was known as Alpha and B was Bravo. The East German authorities called it 'Grenzübergangsstelle,' which translates as the imaginatively titled 'Border Crossing Point.'

What we saw in front of us contrasted with the preserved wall that we had just visited. There was a recently erected guard house and a couple of actors that were dressed in military uniforms. It may not have been the original checkpoint but it helped to illustrate the geographical location and it at least provided an image, however accurate it was, of what part of the checkpoint may have once looked like.

I noticed a plaque that provided some historical information about the checkpoint. It detailed the confrontation between American and Soviet tanks that had occurred here shortly after the wall's construction in 1961. Reading this conjured up a rather frightening image of opposing armoured vehicles pointing their considerable weaponry towards each other for almost a week on the very street that we were now standing on.

At this point, I realised that I was woefully underprepared for the weather. We were in Germany in November, yet most of the clothes that I had brought with me were T-shirts. Winter was setting in but for some unknown reason, I had brought the contents of my summer wardrobe. I had one relatively thin coat and one even thinner zip-up jumper to get me through the week. I was wearing both of these items but I was still very cold.

It was dawning on me that a considerable portion of the days to come would be spent shivering, whilst cursing my lack of foresight. It would become a whole lot worse if it rained, as none of my clothing was waterproof.

We travelled back in the direction that we had come from and made our way to the Memorial to the Murdered Jews of Europe. As you may have gathered, this is a memorial to the Jewish victims of the Holocaust. The slightly long-winded title of the memorial may seem unnecessary but it succeeds in making it clear that this is a place to remember and mourn the loss of the six million Jews that were killed between 1941 and 1945.

This is an important distinction, since the term Holocaust has sometimes been used to refer to the overall number of seventeen million people that were persecuted and murdered by the Nazis; including those killed because of their sexuality, mental illness, physical disability, political beliefs, religious affiliation or ethnicity.

This issue has been the subject of a certain amount of debate, given that some feel that the term should be reserved for the Jewish, who suffered losses that amount to genocide. Indeed, around two thirds of Europe's Jewish population were systemically killed during this reign of terror.

I had no idea what the memorial would look like, as I had not even been aware of its existence. Upon arrival, I was surprised by the unusual visual appearance of the memorial. There was what appeared to be a maze made up of concrete slabs. In fact there were 2,711 of them in total. I tried to delve into my memory banks in order to figure out the significance of this number but it turns out that it does not relate to anything in particular.

We walked around the grounds, navigating our way between the slabs and reflecting further on the horrors that were endured less than seventy years ago. The millions of civilians murdered by the Nazis are part of an even grimmer statistic. The resulting global warfare is estimated to have claimed the lives of between seventy and eighty five million people, which was about three per cent of the entire world's population.

Quite a few people were taking quirky pictures using the slabs to partially hide from sight whilst leaning out for the camera. I did not feel entirely comfortable with this, although I doubt that the people that had their lives taken away from them would begrudge others enjoying themselves and generally being happy.

The preservation of Berlin's remnants of war is a great example of how Germany has faced up to its problems of the past rather than sweeping them under the carpet. There is a real determination to keep this dark chapter of the country's history at the forefront of the population's consciousness, so that the mistakes of the past are never repeated. This seems more important than ever with the increase in far-right nationalism around the world in recent years.

In some ways, I feel that my home country could learn from this. Some of the more sinister elements of British history, such as its role in the slave trade or the colonisation of millions across the British Empire, are barely acknowledged and sometimes even glorified.

Brandenburger Tor was next on our itinerary. Situated just a few hundred metres from the memorial, the Brandenburg Gate, as it is known in English, is one of the most recognisable monuments in all of Germany. We joined the throngs of tourists standing in the shadow of this eighteenth century landmark, trying to find an angle to capture it all in one photograph.

There were six sets of paired columns, with a sculpture of a chariot being drawn by four horses resting on top of the gate. The location has historical significance, as it was a marker for the route to the town of Brandenburg an der Havel and later became one of the dividing points between East and West.

It was time to utilise some of the knowledge acquired during my time studying for my history degree in order to impress Rachel: "Do you know that the Brandenburg Gate was originally known as the Peace Gate?"

She countered with some information of her own: "Yes. The original German name was Friedenstor, which more or less translates as what you said. It is also the only remaining city gate."

It appeared that I would have to raise my game.

The Reichstag was nearby, so this was the natural choice for our last stop of the day. The building was being photographed by a sea of tourists, who were keen to capture its famous glass dome in all of its glory. Built in 1894, it was used by the German Empire to hold the Imperial Diet. For the sake of ridiculousness, I was disappointed to learn that the Diet was a government assembly rather than a pre-war Slimming World group. The building, however, is best known for a destructive and controversial event that happened nearly forty years after its construction.

The fire of 1933 caused significant damage but the consequences of this stretched far beyond the building itself. Blame for this act of arson was quickly attributed to a Dutch communist named Marinus van der Lubbe. The Nazi Party, with the recently elected Chancellor Adolf Hitler, painted a picture of a wider communist threat against the nation and they used this as opportunity to clamp down on opposition voices.

The Reichstag Fire Decree allowed for the detention of anyone deemed to be a threat to the state. The lack of detail and guidance included in the legislation meant that the Nazis could imprison and silence their opponents. The Enabling Act was passed just a few weeks later, which meant that the Cabinet, and Hitler in particular, could enact laws without having to gain approval from the Reichstag. The aforementioned acts allowed the Nazis to establish a one party totalitarian state.

When people talk about the importance of parliaments keeping presidents and prime ministers in check in order to prevent an individual or a party from having unbridled power, one only needs to look at this dark chapter in mankind's history to understand why. Likewise, press freedom and allowing opposition parties to be able to hold governments to account is acknowledged as a cornerstone of having an open and safe democracy.

This seems particularly important in recent years, as we seem to be in danger of repeating some of the mistakes of the past. Physical violence and intimidation directed at journalists and politicians is on the rise, with certain world leaders regularly encouraging this behaviour from their supporters.

When leaders try to bypass parliament in order to enact laws, the dangers of such actions is evident for all to see. That is why we must never forget the darkest moments in our history. We learn from these events and vow to never let them occur again. Or at least, that is how it should work.

Parliamentary sessions were no longer held in the Reichstag Building following the fire and it remained that way until 1999. As we examined the building, I pondered whether anyone could ever be sure of who started the fire.

"Do you think that the Dutch communist set fire to the building? And if so, did he act alone?" I asked Rachel.

She paused before responding: "I don't think that we will ever know. Either way, the end result was the same."

She was right. Some people believe that the Nazis started the fire themselves but this has not be proven. The only thing that we can be sure of is that they used the fire as an excuse to take away civil liberties and lay the groundwork for establishing a dictatorship.

'Reichstag Fire' has become a term that is used to refer to an attempt to damage political rivals by blaming them for something bad that has happened; therefore, encouraging the general public to cast suspicion on their opponents. This is often aimed at seeking approval for a heavy-handed response. This also seems relevant today, with so-called populist leaders trying to play on their citizens' fears.

I found our first day in Berlin to be fascinating and that visiting many of the sites that I had read about during the years that I had spent studying history was particularly interesting. The remainder of the sightseeing would have to wait until the next day though, as it was time to head back and find a place to have dinner.

Following another smooth ride on the U-Bahn, we were back at our hotel. We took our time getting ready for dinner and made the most of the opportunity to temporarily escape the cold weather. We did not venture out too far before we found a reasonable looking restaurant, which had décor suggesting that the proprietors were trying to recreate a medieval theme.

It was time to finally try some of the traditional German cuisine that I had avoided on my last visit to the country. I picked out what was a safe choice but was still a classic German dish. Schnitzel consists of a meat, in this case pork, that has been pounded into a thinner state before being coated with breadcrumbs and fried. Rachel chose something similar.

It was time to place our order and unleash my secret weapon. I had been unable to communicate effectively during my last visit to Germany but this time I had a girlfriend who spoke the language.

My idea was to step aside and let Rachel do all of the talking anytime that we were mixing with the locals. Of course, this was a ridiculous plan that fell apart whenever anybody addressed me directly. If anything, it made things worse, which is what happened on this occasion.

The waitress took Rachel's order and was met with a fluent response in German. To the extent that she must have assumed that we were a German couple; and therefore, asked for my order in her native tongue. Paralysed by fear, I was unable to respond.

The waitress laughed and said to Rachel: "Your German is very good but I knew that he could not speak the language when I saw his eyes go really big the moment that I started talking to him!"

I guess that there is no easy way of bypassing the language barrier. The food was very tasty and it was nice to be able to sit and relax after a busy day of sightseeing. At the time of our visit, I was unaware of the correct way to use a fork, at least according to the European method. In case you are wondering, which I doubt that any of you are, the fork is supposed to be held with the tines facing downwards.

Food is either to be speared or manoeuvered onto the back of the fork with the use of a knife. Like most Brits that I have encountered, I had been employing the more simplistic American method of holding the fork with the tines facing upwards and scooping food onto it in the manner of a spoon.

If the restaurant staff found further amusement at my expense, at least

I was blissfully unaware of this. As I did not fancy embarrassing myself any further, I let Rachel ask for the bill. I settled our tab, which was the least that I could do after bringing such shame and embarrassment to the table.

As we left the restaurant, I spotted a colourful sculpture of a bear with its arms held aloft. I took a picture and pointed out the strange looking creation to Rachel.

She did not seem surprised by this, which was confirmed by her response: "That is one of the Buddy Bears."

I must have had a blank expression on my face, as I had no idea what she was talking about.

Rachel then filled me in with some background information: "You will see them all over Berlin. The bear has long been associated with the city and appears on the coat of arms."

I found this quirky collection to be most charming. It turns out that Buddy Bears have been placed in over a hundred locations throughout the city, each with a unique design. Some years later, my home city of Manchester would do something similar with the worker bee, which has long symbolised its industrial history.

*   *   *

The following morning, we made our way to Alexanderplatz via the U-Bahn. We knew that there were a number of nearby attractions that we wanted to visit, so this famous city square seemed the logical place to start. We ambled along until we came across the Berliner Rathaus, which is often referred to as the Red Town Hall due to the appearance of its masonry.

We did not spend too much time looking at this, so we moved on to Neptune's Fountain. This immediately seemed more interesting, as there were four figures that represented the Rhine, Oder, Elbe and Vistula rivers. The fountain was big and impressive but it was dwarfed by what we saw when we turned around and looked behind us.

The Television Tower loomed large over Alexanderplatz. My first thought was that it looked like the type of tower that was built for the sake of being tall. This may have been at least partially true, as the three hundred and sixty eight metre high tower was constructed in 1969 with the intention of dwarfing the radio tower in West Berlin.

We left the square and headed towards Berliner Dom, which is the parish church that is commonly referred to as a cathedral. As we crossed the River Spree, I noticed that there were a number of tour companies that were selling boat trips.

I imagine that it would be nice to admire the landmarks that lined the river bank as you glide along the water during the summer months but the thought of doing this in November was most unappealing. There was something else by the river that I found to be somewhat unpleasant. Vendors were selling replica gas masks to tourists, which I thought, given the events of the past, was in poor taste.

I was instantly impressed by the sight of Berliner Dom. It is one of the most recognisable landmarks in the city and I had previously seen many images of the building online. It was even more pleasing to see the giant green domes and ornamental architecture in person, which is not always the case with tourist attractions. The current building was opened in 1905 but the history of the church goes back to the fifteenth century.

There was significant damage incurred during the Second War but the restoration process began during the subsequent period of GDR rule. Initially, it appeared that the East German government would demolish the building entirely but they eventually reached an agreement with the church authorities which secured funding for the restoration. Work was completed following the reunification of the nation, once again giving the city a church to be proud of.

I had noticed a plethora of street vendors selling something called Currywurst. Rachel informed me that it was simply sausage in curry sauce.

"Would you like to try it?" she asked.

I wanted to sample the dish but I was not yet brave enough to have any street food.

"Yes, that would be good. Can we go to a restaurant for it though?" I asked.

Sat within the comforts of a warm restaurant, I enjoyed the food, which should not have come as such a surprise, considering that I liked all of the main ingredients. In any case, it was easy to see why this was a popular snack in a city in which people are always rushing about from one place to another.

The Olympiastadion was next on our itinerary. There were a couple of facts that I had known about the stadium beforehand. Firstly, it was the home of the capital city's football club, Hertha Berlin. The other thing that I had associated with the stadium held a far greater historical significance.

Built for the 1936 Olympics, Hitler was eager for the global audience to witness the power and success of the nation that the Nazis were rebuilding. The aforementioned Olympic Games were being used by the Nazis as a propaganda exercise, with competitors told to give Hitler the Nazi salute. One athlete in particular gained notoriety for seemingly embarrassing the Fuhrer's plans. Jesse Owens, who was an African-American, won four gold medals, which flew in the face of the Nazis' theory that the Aryan race were superior in every aspect, including physical capability.

I was looking forward to visiting the stadium that, with its rich history, was so much more than just a sporting arena. The train journey was once again straightforward and rather pleasant. During the walk from the station to the stadium, I concluded that this would be an ideal location for a film about football hooligans.

We were surrounded by concrete as we made our way through a series of menacing tunnels. The only thing that broke up the grim sight of grey in every direction was the graffiti bearing the football club's name. Despite the spray painted words not mentioning anything of a sinister nature, it conjured up an image in my mind of the Galatasaray fans' infamous "Welcome to hell" sign that greeted the visiting Manchester United team coach in 1993.

As we reached the large open space in which the stadium was located, I was left wondering whether the route that we had just taken had been used in a German equivalent of *The Football Factory* or *Green Street*. Regardless, I imagine that there have been real life violent clashes between rival fans here. After all, that seems to be a big part of football culture throughout the world.

We paid for a self-guided tour, which in practice meant that we wandered around aimlessly for approximately forty minutes. Nevertheless, we were thoroughly impressed by this colossal venue that can hold nearly seventy five thousand spectators. As it had recently been renovated for the 2006 football World Cup, the facilities were more modern than one might expect from a stadium that was built in the years preceding the Second World War.

I made the most of the panoramic stitching feature on my camera phone, as this was the only way of capturing the entire stadium within a single photograph.

The track that surrounded the football pitch encouraged one to imagine the historic exploits of Jesse Owens but it also provided an insight into why football fans often disapprove of such stadium layouts. Looking down from the stands, it was evident that the fans would be sat a significant distance away from the action on the pitch below, which would more than likely have a negative impact on the atmosphere within the stadium.

After leaving the main sporting arena, we had a quick look around the aquatics venue known as the Swchimmstadion. This is where diving, swimming and water polo events were held but we did not spend too much time there due to the plummeting temperature. We probably gave more attention to the Olympic themed Buddy Bear statues that we encountered on our departure.

By this point, I had taken photos of a number of these bears that were scattered throughout the city. I have somewhat of an obsessive personality, at least in terms of building collections, so I was on dangerous ground. Part of me would have liked to have spent the rest of the day dashing around Berlin in order to complete the full set of photos but the sane part of me stopped myself from even suggesting this ridiculous idea.

We decided to take the bus back to the Hauptbahnhof before transferring to the U-Bahn for the remainder of the journey back to central Berlin. After a fifteen minute ride, we exited the bus, confident that we were within proximity of the station. However, our confidence was misplaced. We walked to the end of the road and hoped to see a landmark that would have indicated that we were heading in the right direction but we had no such luck. We carried on a little further but could not see any road names that were of any use to us.

Rachel suggested that we should ask a passer-by for directions but she should have known better than to propose such a ridiculous idea to someone like me. This was not because I was the stereotypical man that refuses to ask for help due to his male pride. Rather, it was due to the fact that, at that stage in my life, I would have done anything in my power to avoid socially interacting with other human beings unless it was absolutely necessary.

We carried on walking for nearly half an hour, feeling completely lost. Then all of a sudden, we saw a train station in the distance. It was not even the station that we were planning to use but we did not care one bit. The sick feeling in my stomach was gone and we could now return to the city centre.

It dawned on us that we needed to find somewhere to have dinner but we did not even know where we wanted to travel to. As it was getting darker by the minute, we decided to stick to an area that we were already familiar with. We were soon back at Alexanderplatz, where we quickly located a restaurant that we had remembered from earlier in the day.

We enjoyed a hearty meal consisting of a pot roast called Sauerbraten. This contained beef but other meats can be used; we were relieved that we were given options other than horse meat, which is one of the traditional variations of the dish.

After dinner, we returned to Alexanderplatz and had another look around, noting how various landmarks looked different under the cover of darkness. The TV tower was lit up against the pitch black sky, which gave it a different feel to how it had looked during the daytime. Unable to think of anything else to do and not wanting to return to our hotel yet, we sat down on one of the benches within the square and watched the world go by.

A seemingly infinite number of stars were lighting up the night, which provided a beautiful sight for our weary eyes. However, there is only so long that you can look up at the sky without losing interest or gaining a stiff neck. People watching was the more sustainable option. There were plenty of rowdy locals enjoying themselves, which at least provided us with a topic of conversation.

As a few empty beer cans were tossed into the air by one group, I turned to Rachel and expressed my genuine shock that people from outside of Great Britain were binge drinking. I had thought that this was an exclusive activity of the British and that it was part of our national identity. I was even more surprised after Rachel informed me that people in Germany can purchase beer and wine from the age of sixteen.

Regardless, I had seen a number of news stories that had labelled Britain as the binge drinking capital of Europe. This was no surprise to me, as I was accustomed to seeing towns and cities turned into a warzone during weekends. I would try and avoid small towns like Sale and Altrincham at night time; Manchester city centre was completely out of the question.

I always found it strange that people would spend all week looking forward to the weekend, then proceed to drink so much alcohol that they would have little recollection of the previous night and would spend the entirety of the next day feeling ill. In Britain, the goal seems to be to get as drunk as possible and act obnoxiously. Forget the feeling of merriment; smash straight through this and aim for total loss of cognitive function.

It was becoming clear that people from other countries shared this bizarre pastime. I have recently seen a headline saying that the Portuguese have overtaken the British as the biggest binge drinkers in Europe. Not content with defeating us on the football field, they have now taken our most precious title.

Having spent the last thirty minutes watching a series of drunkards stumble past us and establishing that I am more of a square than Alexanderplatz, we decided to head back to our hotel and retire for the night.

\*　　\*　　\*

The following morning, we caught the train to Oberhausen, in the west of the country. The journey took around four hours but the service was significantly more pleasant than what I had experienced back in England. Our train consisted of double-decker carriages and ample seating, which resulted in a spacious and comfortable ride across Germany.

After checking into the Tryp hotel that I had booked for the next four nights, we went for a short walk to gain our bearings. CentrO, the main shopping centre of the city, was situated across the road from the hotel. The König-Pilsener Arena, where the UFC show was to be held on Saturday night, was not much further away.

A ten minute walk led us to the most notable tourist attraction of the city. If Paris has the Eiffel Tower and Barcelona has Sagrada Familia, what does Oberhausen have? The answer is Europe's largest disc-type former gas holder. The Gasometer was built in the 1920s to store excess gas that could be used for industrial purposes at a later date.

With the decline of the steel and iron industries, and the increased affordability of natural gas, the Gasometer was no longer required. It was decommissioned in 1988 before it was eventually purchased by the city council four years later. It has since become a tourist attraction and the symbol of the city, serving as a reminder of its industrial heritage.

As expected, it was not the prettiest structure that we had ever visited. In truth, it looked like it was part of an industrial plant that was still in operation. As we were only in Oberhausen to watch the UFC show that I was dragging Rachel along to, I felt a certain amount of pressure to praise the virtues of the Gasometer. However, I was struggling to find the words to enthuse about the huge dull cylinder that was in front of us.

"It's big. It looks interesting," was the best comment that I could think of at the time.

I am not sure if Rachel was sold on the aesthetic value of the Gasometer but the banner attached to it seemed to offer a reprieve. It was advertising an exhibition that was being held inside: 'Out of This World - Wonders of the Solar System.'

Rachel sounded positive as she said: "That looks really interesting. I'm looking forward to seeing that."

This was most likely due to her politeness rather than a genuine sense of intrigue but I felt better about our visit in any case.

We were both legitimately impressed by what we saw as soon as we entered the Gasometer. The exhibition made use of the large area that was available by including huge three dimensional objects that told the story of the solar system. The largest of these objects, suspended from the top of the building and resting in the centre of the exhibition space, depicted the sun.

We were stood in near darkness, so the glowing 'sun' was most striking. We made our way around the exhibition, gradually ascending the ten floors and admiring the views of the different 'planets.' The displays were informative and educational but my focus was on the visual element of the exhibition, which I was not able to do justice with the quality of the photographs that I took.

The visual delights were not confined to inside the Gasometer, as there is an observation deck on the tenth floor that is accessible to the public. We made the most of the opportunity to take in the panoramic view of the Ruhr area, including the river that the Gasometer is situated next to. Despite the cold temperature and cutting wind, we enjoyed this experience. Our visit to the Gasometer had been far more pleasant than its initial appearance suggested that it would be.

All of the travelling had made us tired, so we grabbed a quick bite to eat at a fast food restaurant before getting some rest. As we had decided to take a day trip to Cologne the next day, an early night seemed a sensible decision.

*   *   *

Cologne was only an hour or so away on the train, so our journey was much quicker than what we had experienced the previous day. We headed straight for the two main landmarks of the city; the Hohenzollern Bridge and Kölner Dom.

I had visited the city with my father the previous year, so I had been singing the praises of the bridge and the cathedral when we had discussed possible cities to travel to during our time in Germany. It seemed like I had done a good job in this regard, as Rachel was rather excited to explore this wonderful city for the first time.

We went for a gentle stroll along the Rhine River in order to gain a better view of the Hohenzollern Bridge. The arches of this monumental iron bridge were just as impressive as I had remembered. It was even more pleasing on the eye to see the imposing Kölner Dom towering over the bridge. Walking over an historic bridge is one of life's great pleasures; or at least it is if you are a dork like I am.

We walked past the 'lovers' locks' that I had seen on my previous visit and browsed through them, trying to find the oldest one. Rachel spotted one from 1994, so she emerged victorious.

It suddenly felt awkward. Would she ask whether I wanted to purchase our own lock, scribble our names on it and attach it to the bridge? How would I respond to this? After a tense few seconds, it appeared that the moment had passed. I quietly took some more pictures of the locks before we moved on.

We were now standing in front of my old nemesis; the Kölner Dom. I had been unable to capture the entirety of the building in a single photograph during my previous visit and I knew that it was unlikely that I would fare any better on this occasion because I was still using the same basic digital camera. Nevertheless, I was determined to give it my all.

We backed away to the very edge of the square that stood in the shadow of the cathedral. No luck. I retreated a few steps down a side street leading away from the square. Still no luck. In my desperation, I crouched down as close to the floor as my creaking body would allow. My photos were still missing the spires. Once again, I was no match for the colossal cathedral. For the second time in as many years, I vowed to return with a better camera and exact my revenge at some point in the future.

The Cathedral must have heard my fighting talk and called upon the big man upstairs to show me who the boss is, since it immediately began to rain. This was the moment that I had feared since my first day in Germany. My coat was not waterproof; it was not even shower resistant. I had foolishly hoped that my baseball cap would provide some shelter for my face but it did nothing of the kind.

We hastily made our way towards some shelter, which was in the form of a row of shops. We briefly visited each one to escape the downpour outside, without wishing to outstay our welcome. The rain eventually eased off, allowing us to stroll down to Schildergasse, which is the main shopping street of the city.

I found a T-shirt to purchase in an H&M store but I made the mistake of not trying it on. My body was at its most muscular point of its existence, yet for some reason I opted for an extra small size. This would be a moment that I would come to regret, as I went to a pub with my friend the following month and felt extremely uncomfortable all night.

My T-shirt, which advertised the fictional fight between Rocky Balboa and Clubber Lang that featured in *Rocky III*, was so tight that I could barely breathe. Everyone in the pub must have been able to see my nipples pressed up against the fabric, which was almost certainly enough to put them off ordering any food from the bar. Upon returning home, I somehow managed to peel off the T-shirt before consigning it to the back of my wardrobe, never to be worn again.

Rachel had been teaching me how to say the odd phrase in German but I had not been able to summon the courage to use any of my newfound linguistic skills up to this point. After paying for the T-shirt, I sensed that this was my moment to shine. "Tschüß," an informal way of saying goodbye, was the phrase that I selected for my first attempt.

My pronunciation sounded like the English word 'juice,' but it was clear enough for the shop assistant to understand and reciprocate. I had mastered the German language. Rachel was spending months over here, honing her skills but I only needed this one brief exchange to demonstrate my capabilities. The worker then said something else that seemed inaudible to me, causing me to freeze.

"She just said that you forgot your receipt," Rachel explained.

Perhaps I was not a linguistic guru after all.

We passed one of the many ice cream cafes in the city centre and decided to indulge ourselves. Shortly after receiving our order of pistachio and banana ice cream, we saw what appeared to be a bowl of spaghetti being presented to the couple that were sat at the table next to us. Given that the cafe only served desserts, I was flummoxed. We kept glancing over until we figured out that the dish was in fact a dessert that had been made to look like a savoury pasta dish.

It turns out that this is a popular method within the city. Vanilla ice cream is pressed to look like spaghetti, strawberry syrup plays the part of a tomato based sauce, and white chocolate shavings resemble parmesan. Food envy had struck; our ice cream suddenly looked boring and inferior. Their dessert would not have tasted any better than ours but I was jealous of the novelty aspect.

With a nice but rather plain dessert in our stomachs, it was time to leave Cologne and return to Oberhausen. The train journey was another smooth and pleasant experience. As we travelled around the country, I noted how the cites of Germany are well connected by the efficient rail network.

Double-decker carriages provide enough seating for most journeys and the trains seem to run like clockwork. Indeed, eyebrows are raised by the news of a late arrival or departure. I would not appreciate how much superior the German rail service was compared to the British equivalent until I began taking the train to work several years later.

The daily misery that I endure during my commute through Greater Manchester often makes me think of the efficiency of rail networks in Germany and across much of continental Europe. I am relieved when there are four carriages instead of two; despite there being enough passengers to fill six units.

I consider it a victory when my train arrives only ten minutes late. Even the trains themselves are inadequate. Rather than the state of the art vehicles in Europe, I have to make do with the abysmal 'pacer' trains that were converted from old buses decades ago.

*    *    *

*UFC 122: Marquardt vs. Okami* was held the following evening, so we had a relaxing Saturday wandering about the area nearby to our hotel. With the temperature dropping as the day progressed, we entered the enclosed CentrO shopping centre, where we killed some time by browsing the shops before consuming some more fast food, much to Rachel's dismay.

A group of obnoxious Americans were discussing their recent trip to Berlin: "We partied hard there! Berlin is badass!"

Rachel and I looked at each other and smirked. Then I realised that they were almost certainly attending the same UFC show that we were going to that evening. This was further confirmation that I did not want to be associated with the stereotypical mixed martial arts fanbase.

The show lasted around six hours. In hindsight, this was probably an awful evening for Rachel but she did not complain at any stage. After leaving the König-Pilsener Arena, we headed back to the hotel.

Before we reached our destination, I heard a voice over my shoulder, "Hi David, it is Christoph."

It took me a while to realise that Christoph was a fellow member of the UFC Fight Club, which includes an online forum for fans. We had the briefest discussion about Yushin Okami's victory over Nate Marquardt in the night's main event before he said that he was heading to a bar.

Thankfully, Rachel's presence provided me with the perfect excuse to decline his invitation to join him. As nice as Christoph seemed, I was ever so pleased that I had successfully managed to avoid socialising with people that I hardly knew.

# CHAPTER 7: MISTAKES MADE IN THE DUTCH CAPITAL
## AMSTERDAM, THE NETHERLANDS
## NOVEMBER 2010

The journey from Oberhausen had taken just under three hours but this had not diminished my excitement about exploring the Dutch capital. The architectural beauty of Amsterdam Centraal has resulted in the train station that we had just arrived at being regarded as a tourist attraction in its own right. In fact, it is the Netherlands' most visited Rijksmonument, which is the name given to national heritage sites.

Perhaps this is a little unfair on the others on the list, as the station was always likely to achieve this feat, considering the fact that it is one of the main transport hubs in the country. I had a quick look at the interior of the station as we made our exit but I did not think that it looked particularly remarkable.

Once we exited the building, however, I could finally appreciate its splendour. The ornately decorated red brick facade has been providing visitors a charming first impression of Amsterdam ever since the station opened in 1889. It looked more like a palace or parliamentary building than a train station.

Similarly to the Eiffel Tower, plans to erect the station were initially met with hostility from sections of the local population, with many people believing that this huge structure would be an eyesore that was not in keeping with the beauty of the city. The station, again like the Eiffel Tower, managed to win over the critics in the following years.

Before leaving the surrounding area, I was eager to locate a grouping of letters that has become very popular with tourists. It almost feels like an obligatory task for any visitor to the city to take a photograph stood in front of, or on, the 'IAMsterdam' sign. As a friend had told me that the letters were just outside the train station during his recent visit, I did not bother to research this. We walked around the perimeter of the building but we were unable to see any trace of the sign.

I was left wondering whether I had done something to fall out of favour with my friend, to the extent that he had provided me with incorrect information just to spite me. As it turns out, there had been a sign outside of the station at some point but this was a temporary one that was being briefly displayed at various places around the city before being moved on to the next location.

The widely photographed sign was situated by the Rijksmuseum on Museumplein at the time of our visit. However, I did not discover this until after returning home from my trip. Perhaps this was my punishment for electing not to visit any of the famous museums of Amsterdam due to time constraints.

Incidentally, the 'IAmsterdam' sign has recently been removed from Museumplein due to the large unsightly crowds that it attracted. Many people felt that it was encouraging individualistic selfie-obsessed behaviour that went against the principle of the sign, which was supposed to be about inclusiveness. I do hope that a considerable percentage of these people, unlike myself, went on to visit at least one of the museums located on the square.

It was midday, which meant that we had around eight hours to explore the Dutch capital. Our first port of call was at a type of establishment that Amsterdam is renowned for; a cafe. It was not a 'special' cafe selling 'herbal alternatives' but a regular coffee shop. This suited us perfectly, since caffeine was our drug of choice. Despite the city being famed for its liberal attitude towards cannabis, the more traditional European cafe culture is still thriving here.

As we stocked up on caffeine ahead of the sightseeing that lay ahead, I asked Rachel what she wanted to see in Amsterdam.

Thankfully, her reply confirmed that she had not come here merely to sample the seedier side of the city: "I would like to see Anne Frank's house, if that's ok?"

I nodded enthusiastically as I replied: "That is great. I would really like to see that too."

I was worried that I had appeared too happy to visit the house. After all, it is a site that shines a light on the horrors that humans inflict on each other.

After leaving the cafe, we immediately made a mistake that is typical of a tourist in Amsterdam. We started walking down a red path, oblivious to the fact that this was a cycle lane and that we were in danger of being mowed down by one of the many locals travelling on two wheels. Cyclists must be irritated by the familiar sight of their path being blocked by ponderous visitors who have their heads buried in a map as they amble along.

Fortunately, we were only greeted by the gentle ringing of a bell rather than vicious verbal abuse or a head-on collision.

It was time for me to use my famed powers of deduction, as I declared that: "We must be stood in a cycle lane."

We promptly made our way to the pedestrian pavement with our tails between our legs. I felt embarrassed, given that I had read about the abundance of bicycles in the city beforehand. Indeed, Amsterdam is the most bicycle-friendly capital city in the world, with this method of transportation accounting for more than half of the journeys taken in the city centre.

Whilst most cities are almost brought to a standstill by a slow trickle of seemingly endless cars, Amsterdam has recently faced the issue of bicycle traffic congestion. I am quite confident that Londoners and Mancunians would envy such a problem.

Despite my embarrassment, it was refreshing to see so many bikes being used in an urban environment. I looked around and appreciated how the roads were more suitable for bicycles than those back in the United Kingdom. Designated cycle lanes are a rare sight in England and the ones that I do see are clearly either an afterthought or have been specifically designed to endanger the lives of those brave enough to use them.

There is one particular junction in Wigan in which the cycle lane and the regular traffic lane diagonally cross each other. Surely only a sadist could have conjured up this road plan. Therefore, I would never dream of taking to the roads of Great Britain on a bicycle. As much as I like the idea of this form of transportation, I prefer being alive.

Aside from the abundance of bicycles, there were a number of other things that are strongly associated with the Dutch capital that lived up to expectations, both in terms of numbers and beauty. The canals and bridges of Amsterdam are a visual treat for visitors and locals alike. The combined length of the canals within the city exceeds one hundred kilometres and there are over fifteen hundred bridges providing safe passage over them.

It is, therefore, unsurprising that the first photograph that I had taken since leaving the train station featured a canal, a bridge and a bicycle. What is even less surprising, is that Amsterdam has, like many other cities around the world, been labelled 'The Venice of the [insert compass direction].' In this case, it was the north.

Whilst it is, of course, very different to the man-made Italian city, the comparison at least holds some merit. Just as in Venice, it is possible to wander along the canals of Amsterdam and admire their beauty without feeling the need to plan a route or even caring where it takes you. At least that provided me with an excuse for when I inevitably lost my way when trying to lead us to the next city landmark.

The canals were functional as well as beautiful. They were part of successful seventeenth century city planning, with concentric canals lined with residential properties and a series of interconnected smaller canals providing routes for merchant ships to navigate and trade.

Traditional Dutch townhouses flank the numerous canals. They are a wonderful sight but they were built for practical rather than aesthetic purposes. Following the introduction of the aforementioned canals, trade within the city was booming, which in turn brought an influx of people to the area. Subsequently, there was an increased requirement for residential and commercial properties by the canals. Due to an overwhelming demand for properties and a lack of space to accommodate them, the government allocated narrow plots of land so that they could pack in as many units as possible.

Restricted by such narrow dimensions, the property owners then came up with a clever solution by building tall townhouses. They have become synonymous with the city and they are popular with tourists. If you go shopping for a souvenir fridge magnet in Amsterdam, you will find that a large proportion of them feature these buildings.

There was at least one thing missing from the scene in front of us, as many photographs of the Netherlands feature an abundance of tulips. This colourful flower has become synonymous with the country, attracting tourists from all across the world. The vibrant fields of tulips are often photographed alongside windmills, thus creating the quintessential Dutch image. Unfortunately, we were in an urban environment during November, so there was little chance of encountering either of these items.

As I was taking pictures of our beautiful surroundings, I noticed that Rachel had not yet taken a single photograph.

I asked her whether she had forgotten her camera but her response stated otherwise: "I prefer to take it all in with my eyes. The memories will be more vivid this way."

Her reply surprised me and also made me ponder whether my snap-happy approach was resulting in a failure to truly appreciate my surroundings. In the end, I concluded that I should endeavour to combine the two methodologies. I love looking back at my photographs, as they instantly fill my soul with joy whilst also documenting my overarching journey through both the world and life itself. I have also made an increasingly conscious effort to 'live in the moment,' rather than just capturing the photographic evidence.

I would have quite happily spent the day wondering aimlessly around the city whilst admiring the canals, bridges and townhouses. However, Rachel and I both wanted to visit the Anne Frank House. This was obviously going to be a sombre moment within the trip but one that we felt would be the most worthwhile. Map in hand, I was entrusted to lead the way.

*    *    *

Not only did I manage to locate the building with relative ease but I also avoided any collisions with the countless number of cyclists that we encountered. We even got to visit the iconic Westerkerk without deviating from our route along the Prinsengracht. This seventeenth century church is the largest in the Netherlands and remains one of the most picturesque buildings in the city.

In truth, it was by chance that the church was located along our path to the Anne Frank House but I was pleased that we saw it and I was grateful that it gave the impression that I was an accomplished tour guide.

Upon arrival, we joined the queue to enter the Anne Frank House. There is always a strange atmosphere at places like this, given that everyone is eager to see the site in question but they are fully aware of the misery and horror that the place represents. The house has been partly converted into a museum, whilst also preserving much of the original structure and detail in order to show visitors the conditions that the Frank family had to endure in order to hide from the Nazis during the Second World War.

Perhaps it gives away my lack of experience in visiting museums but I was left a little confused by a security guard indicating that I should wear my backpack on my front. He must have seen the cogs in my brain slowly turning, as he reiterated that I should either wear my bag on my front or take it off. After my brain caught up, it finally made sense. With so many visitors in such a confined space, it was inevitable that any backpacks worn in the conventional way would probably knock into something at every turn.

Throughout the house, there were quotations from Anne Frank's diary, in addition to photographs and other documents. This helped build a picture of the circumstances that led to the family having to hide in the secret annex that we were heading towards and it gave some degree of insight into what life was like in there.

Some of the quotes from her diary were unexpectedly uplifting. "How wonderful it is that nobody need wait a single moment before starting to improve the world," was a surprisingly optimistic sentiment for a young girl in her situation to express. This really struck a chord with me; it was the most idealistic period in my life up to that point and I felt that such words could not fail to inspire oneself to become a better person.

Along with the various artefacts on display, some of the other excerpts from her diary were a stark reminder of the grim reality that she and her family faced: "I long to ride a bike, dance, whistle, look at the world, feel young and know that I'm free and yet, I can't let it show."

It was becoming clearer why her diary was so well regarded throughout the world and why it was so important to keep her story alive in the global consciousness. Horrific events such as the Holocaust must not be allowed to happen again and we should all endeavour to appreciate the freedom and happiness that we have been blessed with.

With the recent increase in white nationalism and terrorism, this message feels more relevant today than it has at any other time during my relatively short existence.

The sense of sadness was building as we worked our way through the house, passing through the workplace of Anne's father, Otto. He transferred control of the business, which sold pectin and spices used to make jam, to non-Jews so that it could continue to operate. In 1942, Otto and his family went into hiding in a secret annex that was concealed behind a bookcase.

The information that we had read during our journey through the house had informed us that they were later joined by the van Pels family and Fritz Pfeffer. Otto's colleagues, Johannes Kleiman, Miep Gies, Victor Kugler and Bep Voskuijl helped the family by bringing them food and keeping their secret. I had been unaware that so many people were hidden in the annex for such a long time or that so many people risked their own safety by helping them.

As we made our way through the entrance that was no longer concealed, Rachel and I were not entirely sure what to expect in the annex. It was obviously in an entirely different condition to what it would have been like for those hiding from the Nazis. The air must have felt stale with so many people stuck inside and it must have been dark as they hid from sight. It was much cleaner now that it was open to visitors than it would have been for the Frank family.

It was bigger than I had expected in terms of overall size, yet the rooms were fairly small. Space was at a premium as we climbed up the ladder staircases that linked the various floors. Indeed, the layout of the annex was completely different to what I had imagined. I had a picture in my head of one room but it was actually a small house hidden behind the main part of the building.

I tried to think of what it must have been like for them but it was impossible to grasp the emotion that they would have experienced. I walked towards the attic window that they looked out of on occasion but I did not have the fear of somehow being spotted and knowing what the consequences would be. Although I could see that the rooms were small considering the amount of people that lived there, I did not have to stay there for over two years, locked away from the outside world. Constant fear yet constant boredom.

Although it was a sobering experience, I was left feeling that this was the most valuable and effective form of exploring historical events; to stand where they stood, to feel the closeness of the walls that they were trapped within and to see the limited view of the outside world that they could. Although it is not possible to feel what they did, visiting places such as this can be a very powerful way of demonstrating the terrible events of the past.

Reading about such events can build a picture of what happened but to walk through the sites in question adds an emotional element. Places such as the Anne Frank House perform an invaluable role in keeping the lessons of history in our minds. We must not forget the horrors of the past and we must not let them happen again.

As with most museums, we had to pass through the gift shop in order to exit the building. I did not have a problem with this, as I understood the importance of keeping the message alive. I purchased a copy of Anne Frank's *The Diary of a Young Girl* to read on the journey home and reflected on how lucky we were to be able to freely explore this beautiful city.

We decided that we should visit the home of Rembrandt, who moved here to kick start his career as a professional portraitist. I looked at the map that had been crumpled up inside my pocket and attempted to locate the seventeenth century artist's former residence.

\* \* \*

We took one or two wrong turns as we made our way through the city centre but we eventually stumbled upon a neon sign that read 'Rembrandt Corner.' We were confident that this was a strong indication that we were in the right place. As it turns out, Rembrandt Corner was the name of a bar and restaurant next to the Rembrandt House Museum.

The neon sign was shining brightly against the dark sky, so it was not particularly surprising to discover that the house museum was now closed for the day. We were not too disheartened, as we were simply satisfied to have finally found it and been able to examine the exterior of the building. At least it gave me the opportunity to take another photo, even if it was of poor quality due to the lack of light.

We recommenced our walk through the centre of Amsterdam and eventually ended up in Dam Square. A seventy two foot stone column immediately caught our eye. Situated in the centre of the square, the National Monument was officially unveiled in 1956, with the intention of commemorating the lives of those killed during the Second World War.

In keeping with the nature of most war memorials, it did not appear to be particularly elegant on first inspection. It was certainly big but it looked like many other similar shaped monuments. The aesthetic quality improved as we approached for a closer inspection. The level of detail of the design and, more importantly, the message of remembrance is better conveyed from close quarters.

The square was fairly busy but if our trip had taken place a few weeks later, there would have been lots of stalls across the square for the Christmas markets and it would have been absolutely heaving with people. Whilst I was relieved that it was not so manic, I also felt that it would have been nice to see the area decorated for the festive period.

I expressed this sentiment to Rachel but I was left confused by her response: "How would you react if we were here next month and you saw people dressed as Black Pete?"

I paused for a few seconds but I was still unable to figure out what on earth she was talking about.

"What do you mean?" I tentatively enquired.

Rachel proceeded to inform me that: "Traditionally in the Netherlands, people wear black face paint and dress up as a character called Black Pete during the Christmas festivities."

She was right; Black Pete, or Zwarte Piet, is a helper of Saint Nicholas, or Sinterklaas as he is known by the Dutch. Whoever plays the role of Zwarte Piet will usually wear black face paint and hand out presents during Sinterklaas events held around the country.

This has been the source of protest in recent times, with it becoming part of a wider debate about the practice of 'blackface' and racism. There are many who staunchly defend the tradition, stating that the black face paint signifies soot picked up from chimneys that the character has journeyed down.

However, the number of people objecting to this character being paraded around has increased over recent years. The person playing Zwarte Piet will usually have their lips painted bright red, will wear a curly black wig and large earrings, and be dressed extravagantly.

Critics say that this clearly represents the appearance of African slaves who were brought over to the Netherlands during the colonial era. I was surprised that this was a tradition belonging to a fairly liberal country such as the Netherlands and I was somewhat relieved that we would not have to encounter such activities that I knew that I would be uncomfortable with.

It was now that awkward time of the day in which it was too late to visit most tourist attractions but a little too early for an evening meal. Just as we were discussing how we needed to find something to do for the next forty minutes or so, we realised that we were walking towards De Wallen, the main red light district of the city.

"Would you like to see what it's like there?" I sheepishly asked Rachel.

"Erm, not really," she replied, with a nervous laugh.

For most tourists, this would be the ideal place to visit when looking to kill a bit of time. In fact, a lot of people would name this in their top five things to see in the city. However, here we were with time to kill, yet we declined the opportunity to even have a quick look around. Maybe we were both too sweet and innocent, or we were just too embarrassed to walk through this seedy area in each other's company.

I looked around and started to think to myself that we were clearly in the minority. Perhaps people would find it really strange that we had travelled to Amsterdam but we had not visited the red light district, nor sampled any cannabis that we were legally entitled to. We had not even touched a drop of alcohol. I know that there are some who would say: "If you did not do any of those things, why did you go to Amsterdam?"

This was reflected by the souvenir shops that we were now browsing. There were hundreds of T-shirts with marijuana leaf designs or crude references to prostitution. I am sure that there must be some residents of Amsterdam who feel a little embarrassed by the image of the city that is being capitalised on by those involved in tourism and merchandising. Nevertheless, I managed to find a suitable gift for my mother, in the form of a miniature townhouse ornament.

We had successfully occupied ourselves with trivial activities for long enough that is was now an acceptable time to have dinner. I was becoming more accustomed to travelling around Europe, so I was happy to sample some continental cuisine. In an Italian restaurant. It was the wrong country but at least it was the correct continent.

As it turned out, I then made a catastrophic error that will never be repeated; I chose a carbonara dish. I already knew that I did not like this type of meal, especially when it is made in the inauthentic, extra creamy way, so this was a rather foolish decision. My twisted logic was that it would be prudent to pick the dish that I was most confident of pronouncing correctly when placing my order with the waitress, regardless of whether I would enjoy it or not.

I looked on with envy as Rachel enjoyed her tomato based pasta. Unwilling to lose face, I pretended that I was enjoying my meal.

I turned the conversation to a generic topic about the Netherlands: "Did you know that Dutch men are, on average, the tallest people on Earth?"

She responded by saying: "Yes, I had read about that before," which was a little disappointing, given that I had my facts about the height of people in the Netherlands ready to be uncorked.

"Do you think that I could pass off as a Dutchman?" I joked.

I received a token gesture of a laugh borne out of politeness rather than appreciation. In case you are wondering, the average height of a Dutchman is six foot, whilst the average British man is five feet, ten inches tall.

Five feet, five inches is the average height of a British woman; which is also my height. Hence, my woeful joke. Perhaps I should have made a humorous comment about being more likely to be, from a statistical point of view, a woman than a man. Alas, it was yet another missed opportunity to be funny.

I was becoming concerned that there was some confusion about my gender, so I conformed to the stereotypical role of the British male by paying for both of our meals. Despite being in the Netherlands, I declined the opportunity to 'go Dutch,' which is a phrase that is commonly used to describe situations in which each person pays for their share of the bill.

Perhaps this phrase came about due to this practice being commonplace throughout much of Europe, including the Netherlands. However, it seems probable that this can be traced back to the seventeenth century, which saw a rivalry between the British and Dutch Empires that were fighting over trade routes and foreign lands. To 'go Dutch' may have been a derisory term, implying that the Dutch were stingy.

Indeed, there are several commonly used phrases that have negative connotations in relation to the Netherlands. 'Dutch courage' implies cowardice, as any notion of bravery is only acquired after consuming a large volume of alcohol. The term 'Double Dutch' refers to someone talking nonsense, although this may have been directed at the Germans, who shared a similar language and a border with the Netherlands.

With the evening meal consumed, and at least one of us having enjoyed it, we left the restaurant and began walking back to the train station. We had just over half an hour to spare before our train was scheduled to depart. As we passed a café, I noticed a sign that stated that they were selling a slice of cake with a cup of coffee for five Euros. Against all my instincts, I suggested going in and making the most of this offer.

"Are you sure? Do we have enough time?" asked an increasingly worried looking Rachel.

Normally, I would have already been at the station at this point, in order to rule out any risk of being late. However, I had spent the last week waiting around in cold train stations across Germany, so I fancied a warm drink and a dessert instead. Besides, the station was only a couple of hundred yards away.

"Yeah, we will be fine. It will only take us a few minutes to have a coffee," I confidently proclaimed.

Service was quick and we were soon enjoying our carrot cake and cappuccinos.

I felt nice and content as I said to Rachel: "You see, we have got plenty of time left."

Upon finishing our beverages, I checked the time on my watch; our train was due to depart in just over ten minutes' time.

"We will pay now and walk to the station. We should have plenty of time to spare," I declared.

What I had not accounted for was the possibility that the staff would all go missing at the same time. They had taken our order and served our food and drink promptly but they were nowhere to be seen now that I wanted to ask for the bill. I wandered around aimlessly for a few minutes, hoping that a member of staff would become available to take my money. A bold and assertive person would have just left ten Euros on our table and exited the cafe. Unfortunately, I possessed neither of these characteristics.

Eventually, a waitress emerged from the kitchen and I asked for the bill. Again, a more decisive person would have just handed ten Euros over without going through the formalities of asking for the bill. It was if I was conspiring with the staff in order to sabotage my own night. With the bill finally in my possession, I settled up. I even gave them a couple of extra Euros for holding up their end of this imaginary agreement to ruin our night. We left the café six minutes before our train was due.

"It is only a couple of hundred yards away, so we will be fine," I stated.

At this point, I was attempting to reassure myself rather than Rachel. As we reached the junction before the station, the lights changed and a wave of cars now blocked our path.

"We can still make it," I said, with a much less confident tone.

After what felt like an eternity, we were finally able to cross the road and enter the station. We quickly located our platform and hurried towards it. We could still make it if we were quick. Unfortunately, I decided to walk at a brisk pace rather than sprint. I had never ran to catch a train before, as I always prioritised my desire to avoid looking foolish in front of others.

In most scenarios back in Manchester, I would, as ridiculous as it sounds, hope to arrive at a station and see the tram or bus already leaving, so that I would not be faced with the dilemma of whether to try and make it in time. The fact that I would sooner risk missing my international train than look slightly silly in front of people that I would never see again in my life tells you how self-conscious I was at that point in my life.

Just as we reached our platform, we heard the whistle of the rail guard. The train was stationary, so I convinced myself that maybe we could still make it. I pressed the button to open the doors but they were no longer operational.

I would like to say that this was a rare occasion in which pressing a button was futile but that would be inaccurate. Nearly half of the pedestrian crossing buttons in Manchester do not need to be pressed during busy periods of the day. The percentage is even higher in other cities across the world, with New York citizens often bringing up this subject.

The reason why pressing these buttons often has no effect is due to the system that is used to control the traffic lights. At busy junctions, the sequence is either controlled by a timer system or another method that is too complicated for me to attempt to explain. For many simple road crossings, the button can work almost instantly. Unfortunately, there are many crossings that appear to be operated by some form of timer system but still require the pedestrian to press the button.

Therefore, I still press the button on every occasion, despite knowing that there is a good chance that it will be a waste of my time. These redundant switches are often referred to as 'placebo buttons,' as it has been suggested that they exist simply to placate us by giving us the illusion that we are in control. I can understand this principle, as I believe that most people feel better when they have at least tried to remedy a situation, regardless of whether this has actually had any effect or not.

The 'close door' function in lifts is often given as another example of a 'placebo button' within the United States. The discovery that these buttons are indeed operational within the United Kingdom was a huge relief. The prospect of being unable to close the lift doors and ensure that nobody else would turn up and enter was unthinkable. During my time living in a flat in Baguley, I would usually weigh up the decision of whether to take the stairs or the lift based on the probability of bumping into a neighbour.

If I saw someone getting in the lift, I would take the stairs and travel so slowly that it ensured that I would not bump into them once they exited on the relevant floor. If I used the lift, the 'close door' function was absolutely essential.

The guard at Amsterdam Centraal whistled again and gestured for us to retreat from the platform edge. It was most out of character but my poor time management had caused us to miss our train back to Germany. Rachel had a pained look on her face but she was far too polite to vocalise any of her anger or frustration.

I apologised for the inexplicable decisions that I had made and sheepishly suggested that: "We will have to go to the ticket office and book seats for the next train."

The stern looking woman that was sat behind the window of the ticket office asked: "What service do you require?"

I explained that we had just missed our train back to Oberhausen and that we would like to purchase tickets for the next train.

"There are no more trains to Oberhausen tonight," was her matter-of-fact response.

I tried to calm myself down by formulating a logical plan. We just needed to take a train to any location in Germany and from there we could transfer to a regional train to take us back to Oberhausen. I relayed this plan to the ticket office worker but this was met with another blunt response of: "That was the last train to Germany for the day."

I had a sick feeling in the pit of my stomach and it was not due to the carbonara that I had eaten earlier. I managed to compose myself before enquiring when the earliest train back to Germany was scheduled for on the following day. At this point, my fate rested entirely on her response.

My flight home to Manchester was scheduled to depart Berlin the following evening at around five o'clock. In order to make this, we would have to take the train to Oberhausen, return to our hotel to collect our luggage and check out, then catch another train at eleven in the morning that would take us from one side of Germany to the other. I felt like a boxer, or a mixed martial artist, who had his hopes of victory in the hands of the judges.

The lady began her response: "The first train that goes to Oberhausen tomorrow departs at...."

The tension was palpable. As she began talking, I quickly calculated that I needed her to finish her sentence with a time that was no later than seven thirty. I looked up at her with pleading eyes, in the hope that this would somehow make a difference.

Fortunately, she finished her reply with "....seven in the morning."

I was hit by a wave of relief and euphoria, as if I had just been announced as the new world champion of train travel. I paid around seventy Euros on my debit card and gleefully accepted our train tickets.

I walked away from the ticket office with a smile on my face, which was soon wiped away by Rachel's next question: "So where are we going to stay tonight?"

I hesitated before stating that: "We will have to find a hotel near the station, so that it will be easy to get back here in the morning. There will be lots of hotels in a big city like Amsterdam. We will have a look around and choose a good one."

We walked a couple of hundred yards before heading into the first appealing hotel that we saw.

"Sorry, there are no rooms left for tonight," was what we were duly informed by the receptionist.

This one setback was all it took for panic to set in and for my standards to nosedive. I was now willing to stay in any hotel, regardless of how grubby it was. If grubby was what I was after, then the next hotel a few doors along, certainly fitted the bill. The huge neon sign that simply stated 'Hotel' instantly conjured up a seedy image. The neglected, crumbling building did not leave any better impression. We cautiously made our way to the front desk.

"Do you happen to have any rooms available for tonight?" I tentatively enquired.

I was not sure what answer I was hoping for at this point but I was soon told by the man on duty that: "You are in luck. We have a room available. Would you like to take it?"

Feeling quite tired and fearing that this could be the only available room in Amsterdam, I nodded my head.

"That will be sixty Euros. I will require your passports."

This seemed normal enough, so I agreed without hesitation. I handed over the passports and waited for him to photocopy and return them, as is the norm in many hotels in Europe.

He must have noticed the look of confusion on my face, so he explained that: "We will hold on to your passports for the night and you will collect them in the morning. You see, we receive a lot of stag parties who leave the hotel in a mess and refuse to pay the damages."

I felt extremely uneasy at leaving our most important documents with a complete stranger in a scruffy looking hotel that seemingly had no name attached to it. Especially as I had an international flight to catch the next day.

Unable to muster the energy to retrieve our passports and find alternative accommodation, we agreed to this request. We trudged up to our room on the second floor and we saw that, although it was basic, it was just about clean enough to stay in for the night.

"We can honestly say that we missed our train due to taking a drug from a café in Amsterdam. We will laugh about this one day," I suggested.

I do not think that Rachel shared this sentiment at the time but I do hope that she can now look back on our misadventure with a certain degree of fondness.

\*　　\*　　\*

My mother probably did not find it too funny that the opening line of the text message that I sent her in the morning read: "Hi Mum, we have overslept and missed our train....only joking!"

After a surprisingly decent night's sleep, we made our way down to reception, praying that our passports were still there and not in the possession of a criminal gang that specialised in human trafficking. Thankfully, they were returned upon checkout and we arrived at the train station with plenty of time to spare.

I started to read Anne Frank's *The Diary of a Young Girl* on the train back to Germany whilst Rachel was napping. This visit to the house in which she had hid was the most poignant moment of the trip but as we crossed the border back into Germany, we were reminded of the other side of Amsterdam.

Border Patrol made their way on to the train, accompanied by sniffer dogs. All the passengers were inspected, since the authorities are always on the lookout for drugs being smuggled across the border.

Despite not possessing any drugs other than some paracetamol tablets and my asthma inhalers, I sat nervously whilst checks were carried out. I started to imagine scenarios in which someone had dumped some drugs in my pocket or that one of the officers would plant something sinister on my person.

After a tense few minutes, I let out a huge sigh of relief when the authorities left without apprehending me. I was also pleased that I had successfully undertaken another method of transportation between countries.

Upon our return to Oberhausen, we collected our luggage and headed back down to reception to check out. It dawned on me that I had spent an extra one hundred and thirty Euros with our unexpected overnight stay in Amsterdam. I tried to add up the amount that I had spent on my debit card in Germany and the Netherlands during the last week and came to the conclusion that I would not have enough money left in my account to pay for the hotel stay in Oberhausen.

I warned the man behind the reception desk that: "There won't be enough in my account to pay for our room. I may have to pay the rest with Rachel's card."

He replied that he would try to take the full amount from the card and that we could split the payment if it was unsuccessful.

"The payment has gone through OK," he informed me.

It was only when I got back to Manchester that I discovered that my account had an emergency overdraft, which helped pay for the hotel. I was charged an extra fifteen pounds per day for a week until I checked my bank balance and rectified the situation. Prior to this, I had never even heard of an overdraft, which is an indication of my lack of life experience at that point, and also how I am fortunate to have always been in a sound financial position.

In any case, my trip across Germany and the Netherlands had been a success, despite the mishaps along the way.

# CHAPTER 8: A CONFRONTATION WITH A KOALA AND A KANGAROO
## SYDNEY, AUSTRALIA
### FEBRUARY 2011

It was only when we were preparing to board our flight from Manchester Airport, that I truly thought about how long it would take to reach Sydney. We would have to get on another plane at London Heathrow, before changing aircraft once again in Singapore. When you factor in time spent waiting at the various airports, it would be more or less twenty four hours before we reached our destination in Australia.

This was the longest journey that I had ever undertaken, so like many intrepid explorers before me had done, I decided that I would need an expert to accompany me on the trip. My mother. This would be the first time that we had been abroad together since 1999 but I was pretty sure that we would not be partying like it was still that year.

The decision to make the trip to the other side of the Earth was the result of all the stars aligning. My Uncle Wai Lun, my mother's brother, was working in Sydney for six months, during which time, *UFC 127: Penn vs. Fitch* was scheduled to take place in the city. The company he worked for had provided him with a spacious apartment that was big enough to accommodate a couple of guests, so we only needed to pay for our flights.

Ever the opportunist, I made the most of this scenario. In addition to being happy to visit my uncle and to watch another live sporting event, I was also pleased that Mum would be able to see a new part of the world whilst visiting her sibling.

By the time that we arrived in Singapore, I was starting to feel the effects of all the travelling. It was understandable, as it had already been the furthest that I had travelled as an adult. It was a little demoralising to think that we had another eight hour flight to come. It was beginning to make sense why my friends had said that our trip would be too short to make it worthwhile. We would only be in Sydney for nine nights yet the combined time of the outbound and return journeys was more or less the equivalent of two full days.

Australia is so big that it is often referred to as the 'island continent.' It would be the largest island in the world if it were not for the fact that it is considered too big to meet the definition of such a body of land. This states that an island must be smaller than a continent. The entire duration of our trip would be spent in one city within this huge country, adding to the feeling that we were not making the most of our long journey.

Nowadays, I would feel extremely frustrated to land in a country that I have not yet visited and being unable to leave the airport. This was not really a concern during our time in Singapore's Changi Airport, since we were feeling tired and my enjoyment of frequent travel had not yet developed into a full-blown obsession.

*　　*　　*

After wandering around the airport for nearly two hours and then trying to get some sleep on the flight to Sydney, we finally set foot on Australian soil.

"That was not so bad. Everything went smoothly," I proclaimed; perhaps tempting fate.

We made our way to the luggage carousel to collect our suitcases. This is always a tense moment, as each passenger hopes that their cargo does not become part of the estimated one to five percent average that is lost or damaged. Unfortunately, Mum was one of the unlucky few on this occasion.

She was quick to tell me that I "should not have said that about everything going smoothly."

Whilst it was extremely unlikely that my previous assertion had anything to do with her suitcase going missing, I apologised nonetheless. After filling out a form and handing it over at the lost luggage counter, we were informed that once her case had been retrieved, it would be sent on to Uncle Wai Lun's address.

We greeted my uncle and made our way out of the airport, before taking a taxi to the city centre. The heat and humidity immediately hit us, prompting Mum to declare that it was a disaster that her case had been lost. Even though it would likely be returned the next day, I could understand her reaction. We were dressed for winter, as it had been very cold back in Manchester, but we were now facing the intense heat of an Australian summer.

Uncle Wai Lun offered some hope by stating that he believed that his wife had left behind some suitable clothes following her visit the previous month. Thankfully, Mum was able to find some clothing that fitted her and that was light enough to be able to wear without making her pass out in the heat. As Mum tried on some more of my Auntie Josephine's clothes, I had a look around the apartment, which was located on the fifty second floor of the building. It was very nice inside but the best thing about it was the stunning view of Darling Harbour below.

This was all paid for by the multi-national financial company that my uncle worked for. As he had worked hard for many years and had been sent to a number of countries, he had certainly earned such perks. This was not enough to inspire me to carve a similar career path though. After a somewhat sheltered childhood and adolescence, I was more interested in exploring the world rather than earning money whilst sat in an office.

\*   \*   \*

The following morning, Uncle Wai Lun suggested that we could have breakfast by Sydney Opera House and Harbour Bridge. Looking up at the grey cloudy skies prompted me to make an extremely foolish decision. Thinking that the clouds would remain throughout the day, I opted to wear just a vest with my jeans and, inexplicably, I did not put any sunscreen on.

To do this in a country with the highest rate of skin cancer in the world, in which it is estimated that two out of three Australians will be diagnosed with a form of this disease by the time they are seventy, was more than a touch silly.

My sunglasses and plain white vest probably gave me the look of a wannabe gangster. Hopefully, the Marks and Spencer label that was sticking out from the bottom of my vest was a clear indication that I was an idiot but not a criminal.

It was the kind of vest that brought back memories of being in school, where some unfortunate soul would have to go through their Physical Education lesson wearing just their underwear because they had forgotten their kit. I imagine that this would not be allowed to happen today but back in the 1990s, if you forgot your kit then you would have to face the humiliation of exercising with only your undergarments to cover your modesty.

We were soon sat on a restaurant terrace, enjoying our breakfast whilst admiring the view of the Harbour Bridge. It was very pleasant to be able to do this during the month of February, which is one of the dullest times of the year back in England. We took some pictures of the steel arch bridge and discussed its aesthetic appeal.

"It is a very impressive structure. What do you think?" I asked Mum. She replied that: "It is nice but it does look a bit like a coat hanger."

Mum was right, as this is the nickname often given to this famous landmark. Tourists have the opportunity to climb the distinctive arches of the bridge but we were content to simply admire it from ground level.

The bridge could have had an entirely different appearance if various other proposals had come to fruition. The three-span design that was put forward in the 1920s would have resulted in a Y-shaped structure, which would have looked nothing like the current creation. A cantilever bridge was also mooted but the final design ended up being based on New York City's interestingly named Hell Gate Bridge.

We walked the short distance around the harbour to the Opera House and gazed upwards at the sail shaped features of the roof. This was the most famous building in the city and it was interesting to see it up close. We decided to take a tour inside the Opera House, which took around forty minutes.

The intricate design could be appreciated more once we were stood within the bowels of the building and we were able to consider what it would be like to witness a live performance here. The tour guide talked impressively about the grand pipe organ and how the main concert hall and the opera theatre were located in different sized sails within the venue.

As I did not possess any knowledge of the opera scene, I was unaware that the design has actually caused both the concert hall and the opera theatre to gain a reputation for having extremely poor acoustics. Apparently, the concert hall has a ceiling that is far too high and the room is too large to carry the sound created on stage.

Meanwhile, the orchestra pit within the opera theatre is too small and cramped, resulting in a compromise in the quality of performance. I believe work is currently being done to help alleviate some of these problems.

In any case, I was oblivious to any of this, so I simply admired the unique beauty of the building. Perhaps ignorance is bliss when you are taking a look around a building that scores higher for style rather than substance. For some reason, I enjoyed looking out at the harbour from within the Opera House and imagined how many times people had been blessed with this glimpse of beauty on their way to a show that they were attending.

It had been interesting to see the Harbour Bridge and Opera House at close quarters but I was keen to take in a particular view that I had in mind before embarking on the trip. A short walk further along the harbour would take us to a point from which both of these iconic structures could be seen from. This was the image that I had seen countless times on the internet whilst planning our trip and it was something that I was keen to recreate.

My photo was not particularly great, partly due to the poor lighting caused by the sudden increase in cloud cover, but I was simply happy to have captured the view that I desired.

Even though some of my favourite photographs that I have taken over the years are of lesser-known quirkier scenes or more personal moments, I still feel the necessity to take what is essentially the same photograph that has been captured thousands, or even millions of times before. The value of such a photo may be that it instantly conjures up an image or a memory of a place that is unrivalled.

The next place that I had in mind was another popular place of interest but one that is not on the scale of the Harbour Bridge or Opera House. Situated on a peninsular further along Sydney Harbour, Mrs. Macquarie's Chair is a sandstone rock that has been cut into the shape of a bench.

Mrs. Elizabeth Macquarie was the wife of Major-General Lachlan Macquarie, who was the Governor of New South Wales from 1810 to 1821. The bench was hand made by convicts for Mrs. Macquarie to sit on whilst she enjoyed the panoramic view of the area; it is said that she would look out for British ships sailing into the harbour. This is what intrigued me, as I was fascinated by the prospect of sitting in the same spot and taking in the same view that she enjoyed two centuries ago.

The Macquaries are regarded as pioneers in regard to their attitude towards ex-convicts. They were amongst the first to push for a greater acceptance, including employment opportunities, for those that had served their prison sentence.

I took some photos of the chair and the inscription above it, before asking Mum to take my photograph whilst sat on the rock. Wearing my plain white vest and scruffy jeans, I probably looked more like one of the convicts that had helped build the chair as opposed to an acquaintance of the Macquaries.

Mum would have to get used to taking photographs of her son at various tourist locations throughout the trip. The bigger challenge for her would be to meet the particular demands that I placed upon her in order to capture the image that I desired. I was not necessarily concerned about the technical aspects of the photos but I would often become a little frustrated when, for example, the top of a building was cut off. Hopefully, I managed to avoid displaying any childish, temperamental behaviour and kept the nature of our calm and patient relationship intact.

At the start of the trip, Mum did what the majority of people do when taking a photograph of someone; she focused on the person being photographed rather than the buildings and landscape within the scene that is being captured. This would often result in the landmark in question becoming an afterthought and only partially visible in the photo.

Surely the purpose of the photograph is to record the moment that the tourist visited the attraction rather than just a close up of their face? Over the course of the next nine days, Mum would show the patience of a Saint, as she would re-take photograph after photograph without complaining.

We discovered that our best approach would be for me to take a photo of Mum, before showing her the image as an example of what I would like my photograph to resemble. She would then line up the shot without me in it before I positioned myself in the perfect spot.

"I never knew how to take a good photo before. Thank you for teaching me. You are very patient," Mum remarked.

I felt embarrassed to have received such praise after making my poor mother take hundreds of almost identical photographs. By the end of the trip, she was my perfect photographer. I am not too concerned about being in the photo these days but it is good to know that I can always be confident in Mum's ability to take a good picture at family functions. At least I can attempt to alleviate my guilt by convincing myself that my obsessive behaviour helped to improve my Mum's skills behind the camera.

Aside from the laborious task of photographing her youngest son, Mum actually enjoyed taking lots of photos of our beautiful surroundings. She had been on many holidays around the world during her lifetime but she had dedicated the last couple of decades to raising her children.

In many ways, she had missed out on some of the pleasures that life can offer, as she always put the happiness of her two sons first. With this in mind, it was heartwarming to see her full of excitement and joy as she snapped away with her camera and stared with amazement at some of the breathtaking sights that we encountered.

My uncle's friend joined us at this point and offered to drive us to a couple of places that were too far to walk to. Our first stop was by a cliff edge on a peninsula that overlooks the ocean, known as The Gap. We admired the view of the cliff edge against the blue backdrop of the Pacific Ocean and gazed across at the city skyline. No wonder why this had been such a popular tourist spot for many years. We took our usual set of photos, snapping images in all directions and taking it in turn to pose for the camera.

The only thing that looked out of place in this beautiful scene was all of the tall fencing in front of the cliff edge. Obviously, safety should always be a priority but it did seem a little excessive. It was only after I had returned home that I carried out some research and discovered that The Gap has long been a notorious suicide location like Beachy Head in England. It is estimated that the one hundred metre cliff edge is the suicide site of around fifty people a year.

This number would have been even higher if it was not for a remarkable individual named Don Ritchie. He became known as 'The Angel of The Gap,' after news outlets became aware of the heroic deeds that he had carried out for over half a century.

Ritchie was a former life insurance salesman who served in the Royal Australian Navy during the Second World War. He moved into a house overlooking the ocean in 1964 and lived there until his death in 2012. In an era in which suicide prevention was not given the resources and focus that is required, he would go out and approach people that appeared to be considering ending their life at the cliff edge. Apparently, he would gently ask them if he could help in any way and he even invited them back to his house for a cup of tea.

It is acknowledged that his kind actions saved the lives of at least one hundred and sixty four people. Don Ritchie was awarded the Medal of the Order of Australia in 2006. Reading about the compassion that he demonstrated makes me feel bad for considering the fences to be an eye sore and it inspires me to become a better person.

Next up on our itinerary was a trip to the world famous Bondi Beach, which incidentally gets its name from the Aboriginal word meaning 'water breaking over rocks.' Located around seven kilometres away from the centre of Sydney, the beachfront is about one kilometre in length. We only saw a fraction of this during our flying visit. As we were fully dressed, the others did not wish to step foot on the beach and get sand in their shoes.

I had a task to complete though. I was dating a German lady called Mandy at the time and she had suggested that, since she could not visit Bondi Beach herself, I should bring the beach back to her. I assumed that she was joking but, nevertheless, I decided to fill a small bottle with sand from the beach and bring it back with me to Manchester. Mum, of course, was tasked with ensuring that there was photographic evidence to authenticate my gift.

This short episode is probably a good example of tourism at its worst. We drove up to the site, in this case the beach, briefly got out to take some pictures and admire the view, before crudely removing some artefact, which on this occasion was a bottle full of sand. The present day version of myself would look disapprovingly at such actions, despite the good intentions. In any case, Mandy appreciated the gift, especially as I had photographic evidence that the sand was indeed from Bondi Beach rather than Blackpool.

With our sightseeing for the day complete, we headed back to Uncle Wai Lun's apartment in the city centre. Mum was feeling anxious about the fate of her suitcase. If all had gone to plan, it would be waiting for us back at the apartment block but there was no guarantee that this would be the case.

If it had not arrived, Mum would have to continue wearing her sister-in-law's clothes until the luggage was returned. If it was ever located. The tension was released when we were informed that the suitcase had indeed been returned and that it was being stored in the building's luggage room.

I was relieved that Mum had her luggage back in her possession but I was now facing a new concern. My arms, my neck and my shoulders had been exposed to the deceptively strong sun all day, so when I had a look at my slightly pink skin in the bathroom mirror, it was clear that I had been sunburnt. The worst part about this was that it had not yet turned red but I knew that there was nothing that I could do to stop this from happening over the next day or two. The damage had been done, I just had to wait to find out how ridiculous I would look.

*   *   *

Our next day of sightseeing revolved around a trip to see the most imposing area of natural beauty in New South Wales; the Blue Mountains. Uncle Wai Lun had arranged a tour for the three of us, which involved an early start and a full day of tourist activities. I fell asleep almost immediately after getting on the coach and only awoke when we arrived at our first port of call less than an hour later.

Featherdale Wildlife Park offered our only chance to see hundreds of species that Australia is renowned for, so it was a welcome part of the itinerary. Although we were not seeing them in their natural habitat, it was still nice to see them in their native country.

The first animals that we encountered were some kangaroos that were wandering around the pathways.

"Would you like your picture with one, David?" Uncle Wai Lun asked me.

"Yeah, that would be nice, thanks," I replied, before realising that I would have to get closer to the marsupial than I was comfortable with.

I had seen documentaries that had highlighted the powerful blows that they can dish out when they feel threatened. Their bulging biceps are an indication of the strong punches that they can throw but it is their kicks that are amongst the most powerful of strikes delivered by any living creature.

The kangaroo that I was having my picture with was bigger than a Joey but it was not one of the huge ones that I had seen on television and it was not roaming around in the wild, so I was not likely to face any physicality. However, this did not stop me from being so wary of it that I stayed as far away as possible whilst remaining in the same camera shot.

"Go on David, you can get closer," Uncle Wai Lun suggested.

I channelled my inner Steve Irwin and overcame the insurmountable challenge of edging a few centimetres closer. My picture was taken and my bravery was confirmed to everyone in attendance. As we were walking away, I saw a young boy walk straight up to the kangaroo without a moment's hesitation before he had his photo taken. My moment in the sun had cruelly been taken away from me by this fearless explorer.

We then made our way over to another marsupial that is synonymous with Australia. Koalas, often incorrectly referred to as koala bears, are famed for sleeping for around twenty hours a day. I jokingly asked Mum if she had ever suspected that I was a koala during my teenage years, in which I would often stay in bed until lunchtime.

"So does that make me a koala?" was her puzzled response.

Fearing that the joke had been lost on her, I changed the subject: "Would you like your photo taken with the koala?"

She declined and suggested that I should have my picture taken instead. Here we go again. Whilst most people were commenting on how adorable the spoon shaped black nose and fluffy white ears were, my eyes were trained on the claws that were gripping the tree trunk and the teeth that were munching through an abundance of leaves.

After reading about some of the occasions in which koalas had viciously struck out at humans and dogs, I was unable to remove an unlikely image from my mind. Would everyone still regard the koala as cute when it was slashing my face with its claws and biting my nose off?

I tried to look as cheerful and relaxed as possible as my photo was taken in front of the modest crowd. I can only imagine what my heart rate would have been like if I had known that chlamydia was ravaging its way through the koala population, as it has in the last few years, and could be passed on to humans through exposure to infected urine. The prospect of encountering both koala urine and chlamydia does not bear thinking about; no pun intended.

Now that I was a safe distance away from these killing machines, I could once again appreciate their cuteness. Despite being wary of them, I could not help but feel dismay at how humans have once again endangered another species. Following many years of being hunted by Homo sapiens, koalas now face the threat caused by loss of habitat.

With a feeling of guilt running through me, I bought a koala teddy bear with an Australian flag affixed to its claws. Along with the kangaroo teddy that I also purchased, these items could either be handed out as gifts for friends and family or they could simply serve as mementoes of my brush with death. I chose the former.

After a short break for lunch, our tour trundled on to the main attraction, which we arrived at around an hour later. The Blue Mountains only form part of the Great Dividing Range, which is the third longest land-based range in the world. We would only see a fraction of the three and a half thousand metres that make up its length. You would certainly need longer than the few hours allocated for a day tour to see it all.

The vast expanse of the area was breathtaking, which made me consider just how enormous the whole mountain range must be. I attempted to take some panoramic pictures but it was impossible to capture the sheer scale of it all.

Our tour included a ride on the Scenic Cableway at Scenic World in Katoomba. This entailed a descent through Jamison Valley for a closer look at Katoomba Falls, Orphan Rock and the most popular feature that is known as the Three Sisters. Slightly more impressive than the wildlife wetland reserve of the same name back in Wigan, the Three Sisters refers to a rock formation that has three distinct points.

The scientific explanation is that this was caused by the land being eroded by rivers, wind and rain. Alternatively, the most widely told Aboriginal legend is that there were three sisters from the Katoomba tribe who fell in love with three men from the neighbouring Nepean tribe but were forbidden from marrying them. A tribal battle ensued with the men attempting to capture the sisters.

The legend states that the sisters were turned into rock by an elder so that they could not be taken but he was killed in the fighting. With nobody able to restore them to their human form, they would forever remain as rock. The three sections of the formation are named after the sisters; Meehni, Wimlah and Gunnedoo.

Regardless of the origins of the rock formation, it was an impressive sight that we would soon be seeing from the vantage point of the cableway. This was essentially a large yellow cable car that would transport us across the valley, descending to the bottom before travelling back up to the top.

I was unsure whether I would be able to appreciate and enjoy the closer view, knowing that over eighty of us would be suspended from a cable that was over six hundred and fifty feet above the land below. The mixed emotion of excitement and apprehension was becoming the theme of the day. We climbed into our cage and awaited our fate.

I tried to console myself that if we were to perish here, then at least we would do so within the most beautiful setting imaginable. This comforting thought was soon replaced by the vision of us all falling over six hundred feet during the most terrifying death possible.

The cage was a little shaky as we began our journey but I managed to occupy myself by taking pictures of the rugged landscape. It ended up being a thrilling experience that afforded us views that would not otherwise have been possible. And we did not die, which is always a bonus.

After stopping off at a few more vantage points, we left the Blue Mountains and began our journey back to the city. It had been a successful day. We had seen a variety of indigenous wildlife and some awe-inspiring natural beauty. We rounded off a lovely day by going for some Chinese food.

As you may have gathered, Uncle Wai Lun is a quiet man of a gentle nature. Therefore, I was surprised by his willingness to navigate through traffic on foot and dart across the road whenever the briefest of openings presented itself. Maybe he was an actor playing his part in the 'let's scare David' theme of the day.

It was obvious to Mum that I was reticent to cross the road without the safety blanket of the little green man, so she reassured me that Uncle Wai Lun knew these roads well and that he would not endanger us. Unconvinced, I followed them through the endless stream of cars, dodging death as well as Toyotas and Fords. Incidentally, the Chinese food was almost worth dying for.

* * *

Seemingly unable to escape our Chinese roots, we visited the Chinese Garden of Friendship the following morning. This was an example of the strong links that exist between Australia and China. It was pleasant and peaceful to walk around the garden and admire the waterfalls, the lake, the bamboo trees and the Dragon Wall that symbolises the bond between the two countries. I find that quiet secluded places like this provide a welcome relief from the hustle and bustle of a sprawling metropolis.

We then bumped into one of the fighters that was scheduled to compete in the co-main event at the weekend. Taking a break from his preparation to do battle with Michael Bisping, Jorge Rivera was taking a stroll around Darling Harbour. He granted my request for a photograph before finding it brilliant that I had told him that I wanted him to defeat my fellow Brit. He asked me to repeat this on camera, which he duly uploaded to his Vlog.

The video is still available online, so if any of you want to see me embarrass myself on camera, just search for 'UFC 127 Rivera Vlog' on YouTube and skip to the part that begins at around two minutes and nine seconds into the video. Needless to say, I had given him the kiss of death and he went on to lose the bout.

We then moved on to a site that demonstrates Australia's links with a different country. The name of the Queen Victoria Building probably gives away the fact that the country in question is the United Kingdom. This grand historic building was opened in 1898, when Australia was still under British rule. We arrived at its location within the central business district and I could not help but be impressed by the grandeur of the building.

The green domes that lined the roof were more akin to the appearance of a European cathedral than a shopping centre. I wondered whether it was originally designed for religious or government use but I discovered that the building was first used as a marketplace, which is not too dissimilar to its current incarnation.

After admiring the historical value of the building, we entered the shopping centre in search of something of a modern nature. The battery of my mobile phone had become increasingly feeble and the large amount of photos that I was taking was putting severe pressure on its endurance. However, that was the least of my problems. The power button on my phone was barely operational, which meant that whenever the phone was shut down, it could take up to an hour of continually pressing the power button before it was brought back to life.

This led to the ridiculous situation of anxiously keeping an eye on the charge level of the phone and hoping that it would not die before I found a power source. I would need to keep it on charge overnight, which further diminished the battery life. It reminded me of the movie *Crank*, in which the central character, played by Jason Stathom, must keep adrenaline flowing through his body in order to stay alive. My scenario was not quite as dramatic, so the jury is still out on whether Hollywood will come calling for the film rights.

The search was on for a portable power source for my phone but this would be a time consuming task, given that the Queen Victoria Building takes up an entire block and has four main shopping floors. We found an electronics store and I approached a member of staff to try to explain my predicament.

As I was not entirely sure what product I required, this led to some confusion. The man I was speaking to did not seem to have a clue as to what I was referring to, so he directed me to another similar store within the shopping centre, no doubt relieved to get rid of this strange English man asking for an item that may or may not have existed.

The staff at the next store at least seemed to have some inkling of what I required and eventually came up with a suggestion. The store sold a piece of equipment that could be charged up at home and then used to charge my phone when required. My mission had reached a successful conclusion and my phone would live to text another day.

After returning to the apartment, I had a look at my increasingly sore skin in the mirror. It was the most disappointing thing that I had seen in a mirror since examining a breakout of pimples in my teenage years. My arms and shoulders had now turned an angry looking shade of red, yet my chest and back were still pale. I was topless but it looked like I was wearing a white vest.

I tend to retain a tan for a very long time, which I normally consider to be a good thing. On this occasion, however, it meant that the reverse imprint of the vest that I had worn on the first day would remain with me for over six months. Mandy would find this most amusing. In fact, this probably made her happier than the sand from Bondi Beach did.

Any prospect of the sunburn not looking as bad as I thought was immediately squashed within seconds of showing it to my mum: "That's bad. Very bad. It looks silly."

I should have expected this, as Mum has always demonstrated a stereotypical Chinese trait; her comments are often blunt but never mean spirited. There were many occasions during my teenage years in which I had spent the entire day trying to convince myself that the spot on my face was not as bad as it seemed in my own mind. After all, it would probably look worse to me as my focus was locked in on the spot, whereas most people would either not notice it or not care.

On such occasions, I could always count on Mum to destroy any such illusions. "You have a big spot on your face," would be the last thing that I wanted to hear but it would just be a truthful comment that was intended to inform rather than humiliate me.

Just in case I needed a reminder that there are much worse things that can happen in life, the news broadcast on television was focusing on a tragic event that had occurred in New Zealand. An earthquake that had measured 6.3 in magnitude had struck close to Christchurch earlier that day, causing significant damage and loss of life. It would later be established that one hundred and eighty five people died. For some reason, this news seemed even sadder to us, given that we were enjoying a holiday in this part of the world.

*   *   *

The next day would be spent in the suburb of Parramatta in the Greater Western Sydney region. I dragged my poor mum along to a meet and greet with UFC competitors Chris Lytle and Jason Reinhardt. It was not as bad as it sounds, as I had done some research into what tourist attractions could be of interest to us. The train journey only took about half an hour, which meant that we were soon heading out to explore the area.

Those thirty minutes were spent with me stood up and Mum sat down on one of the available seats. I was reluctant to take any of the other seats, as it would potentially lead to an awkward social dilemma. If I took a seat, my instincts would tell me to offer this to anyone that would be deemed as being in more need of it than I was; which is where the problem lies. Who exactly would be a suitable person to vacate my seat for? This is the type of decision that an over-thinker like myself despises.

The obvious candidates do not offer any problems; it is not difficult to work out that a disabled or pregnant person probably requires the seat more than I do. The trouble lies with those that are not so easy to determine. I have offered my seat numerous times to people that I thought may be in need of it but they refused to take it and even looked disappointed to have been asked. How old does someone have to look before it is deemed appropriate to offer them your seat without offending them?

Any acts of chivalry, such as vacating my seat for a woman, can be met with a variety of responses. They may be pleased by the gesture, feel patronised or just find the whole exchange as awkward as I do. In order to avoid this grey area, I often stand up, even if this means leaving the seat unoccupied for the entire journey.

With a straightforward journey behind us, we exited the station in Parramatta. The sun was fierce once again, which was not exactly ideal for my already damaged skin. I was wearing sunscreen but for some reason, a phrase about a horse and a stable door springs to mind.

We made our way down to Parramatta River, which did not seem like anything more than a gentle flow of water. However, the online research that I had done prior to the trip had informed me that this was in fact the main tributary of Sydney Harbour. Without this understated river, the world-famous harbour would not exist. Armed with this information, I was able to play the role of tour guide and relay the aforementioned facts to my mother.

"You are so clever, David." Mum was clearly impressed by my regurgitated information.

This emboldened me to deliver some more facts acquired from my Google search: "The indigenous Burramatta, of the Darug people, lived by the river for at least forty thousand years, which makes sense given that water is a source of life all around the world. However, this was interrupted, unsurprisingly, by the arrival of the British."

Mum gave a rueful smile before responding: "The British again. We know all about that back in Hong Kong."

The fresh water of the river leads to salt water closer to the harbour, making it an ideal place for eels to breed. This provided a source of food that helped sustain Aboriginal life. Indeed, Burramatta loosely translates to 'the place where eels lie down.' In an apparent tribute to the history of the indigenous people, the Parramatta Eels is the name of the local rugby league team.

We left the river bank and walked across to Parramatta Park. This was a tranquil green space in which one can temporarily escape their urban surroundings. However, it is also home to a number of historically significant sites. We had a look at Old Government House, which is the oldest remaining public building in Australia.

I decided to impress Mum with some more local history: "The park was the site of Australia's first successful farm and it had a steam tramway running through it until 1993."

Mum replied by saying: "I am glad that I have you to tell me what I'm looking at. I would not have a clue."

I silently expressed the same sentiment about Google.

The George Street Gatehouse was what I was most interested in. The Tudor-style structure was built in 1885 and it has become one of Parramatta's most well known landmarks, often referred to as 'The Tudor Gates.' We took some pictures of the red brick gate before moving on. As was often the case, the park was an important Aboriginal site before European settlers arrived and created their own history there. Today, the park is keen to acknowledge both Aboriginal and Colonial history.

I queued up in a mixed martial arts apparel store to attend the meet and greet. Mum was on camera duty once more and performed her task admirably. The photos were pretty much the same as every other; the fighters would clench their fist for the camera and I would stand next to them, unsure whether to smile or attempt, and fail, to look mean.

The only difference that stood out on this occasion was that one of the fighters, Chris Lytle, had managed to burn his face to the same degree that I had damaged my arms and shoulders. In addition to the photographs and autographs that I obtained, I was also provided with the feeling that, in comparison to Lytle, I should be less embarrassed about my sunburn. Thanks Chris.

Elizabeth Farm was our final port of call before getting the train back to the city centre. Here we saw the oldest remaining colonial house in Australia, which was the home of wool pioneer John Macarthur and his family. We also had a quick look at another of Macarthur's properties, Hambledon Cottage, but this was borne out of a sense of obligation rather than genuine interest.

We had travelled all of this way and we would never likely return here, so we thought we might as well check out these former colonial homes. They did not appear to be any different than any other old cottages that one may encounter but there was historical value, whether this was considered good or bad, attached to the buildings.

Back at Uncle Wai Lun's apartment, we were pleased with ourselves that we had managed to conquer the public transport system of Sydney and that we had successfully navigated our way around an area that was not covered by our guidebook. We were king and queen of the travel world. Actually, I will rephrase that; we were prince and queen.

*   *   *

Speaking of queens, we headed back to Sydney Harbour the following morning to see a majestic lady or two. Uncle Wai Lun had informed us that the world-famous Cunard Ships, *Queen Mary 2* and *Queen Elizabeth,* had arrived at Sydney Harbour the previous day. Whilst we had missed the opportunity to see these two iconic ships dock simultaneously, there was a chance that we could see at least one of them sail away from the city.

As we approached the harbour, the large crowd that had gathered and the deafening sound of a horn indicated that the ship had begun its departure. Sure enough, we could see *Queen Elizabeth* was slowly inching away from where it had docked the previous day. This huge vessel was the latest Cunard cruise ship, although it was difficult to distinguish it from the other members of the uniformed fleet.

Both of the ships that had docked in Sydney were circumnavigating the globe, which added to the sense of occasion as we watched *Queen*

*Elizabeth* sail under Harbour Bridge and begin its journey to the next port of call. Although I had never felt any desire to undertake an ocean voyage, I could not help but feel slightly jealous that the passengers would get to see a glut of countries across several continents.

We went for a gentle stroll around the harbour and encountered an outdoor wedding that was taking place. They certainly chose a beautiful setting. Our attention turned to Sydney Tower on the other side of the bay. Despite it standing out from the rest of the cityscape, it looked quite unremarkable in many ways. Its appearance was what you would expect from the city's tallest structure. It fell in line with the usual design of a tall, narrow body with a turret near the top. This was where the observation deck and some restaurants were housed.

Towers such as this one seem designed simply to be the tallest. In this case, it is the second tallest observation tower in the Southern Hemisphere. To be fair, it was not unpleasant looking. It just did not appear to be much different from its contemporaries.

Uncle Wai Lun asked if we would like to visit Sydney Tower and Hyde Park.

Before I had time to answer, Mum interjected: "I thought Hyde Park is in London."

This was a fairly reasonable assertion but it turns out that the same name was given to the oldest public park in Australia. The area, which was once an Aboriginal contest ground, was given its name by Governor Macquarie, in honour of its famous counterpart in London. After the confusion was cleared up, we decided to visit both attractions, which were located within a short distance from each other.

The double-decker lift journey to the observation deck near the top of the tower only took around forty five seconds. Although it is not close to being the fastest in the world, it is remarkable to think that within the space of a minute we had ascended over eight hundred feet and that we were now faced with a panoramic view of the city below. We took a series of photos from different vantage points but the view over Hyde Park provided the best image.

I asked Mum if she would like to visit the Skywalk, which is an open-air glass floored viewing platform surrounding the deck.

"No. That's too scary for me," was her blunt reply.

I was relieved, as I also had no desire to leave our safe enclosure until we left the tower. We would not have been given the opportunity to make such a decision if we had visited a few years later. The Skywalk was temporarily closed in 2018 after someone removed their harness and jumped to their death. A second suicide a few months later once again prompted the closure of the Skywalk; this time indefinitely.

After leaving the tower, we walked across to Hyde Park. It was only a fraction of the size of its namesake in London but it was still a pleasant and tranquil place to temporarily escape city life. My curiosity had been piqued by a large arched structure when looking down at the park from the tower's observation deck. On closer inspection, it became apparent that this was the ANZAC Memorial, which was built to commemorate the sixty thousand Australian lives lost during the First World War.

The Australian and New Zealand Army Corps bravely fought alongside The Allies between 1914 and 1918. Although the war primarily took place in Europe, the memorial was a reminder of how this terrible conflict claimed the lives of people from all around the world. After all, the war featured opposing imperial powers, who called upon their colonial states to join the war effort. The Pool of Reflection provides a place to gather such thoughts and pay one's respects to those that sacrificed their lives in the name of war.

One of the most elegant sections of the park that we walked through was the Avenue of Hill's Weeping Fig, which runs the full length of the park, leading to the Archibald Fountain. This central pathway was lined with the aforementioned fig trees, which created a picturesque setting for a gentle stroll and provided some welcome shade from the intense sun. The shape and layout of the trees gave the walkway an appearance of a horticultural tunnel, which certainly made for a nice photograph.

*   *   *

A couple of days later, we took the ferry from Sydney Harbour to Manly. The journey only took thirty minutes and it allowed us to view some of the iconic sights from a different angle. We sailed past the Opera House and Macquarie's Chair on our way to the tourist friendly suburb that forms part of the Northern Beaches. "Manly is a funny name. Is it because everyone is manly and masculine?" Mum joked.

As it turns out, she was not too far from the truth. Captain Arthur Phillip is credited with the creation of the area's current name. The "confidence and manly behaviour" of the Aboriginal clan that he and his men encountered on arrival in the late eighteenth century inspired him to select the name of Manly Cove.

Manly Beach is the main reason that tourists flock here, so we thought that we may as well join them. It did not take long after leaving Manly Wharf to reach the promenade, or Corso as it is often referred to, which was lined with cafes, restaurants and bars. Many visitors were having some food and drink whilst admiring the view of the beautiful golden sand but we were content to amble along without a care in the world.

We took our shoes off and briefly walked along the beach before abandoning this idea and returning to the promenade. We did not have anything in mind to see; therefore, we carried on plodding along until we reached something of interest. In this case, it was an ice cream stand. There are not many things that are as enticing as an ice cream when the weather is sunny and one is on holiday.

After enjoying our pistachio ice cream, we decided to head back to the city centre. It may have seemed a little odd to catch a ferry here just to have an ice cream and go for a walk but we felt content with our day. We had seen some beautiful views of the iconic attractions at Sydney Harbour during our ferry ride and we had found our brief visit to Manly to be most pleasant. Ferries depart regularly so we were soon sailing back in to the harbour.

I was starting to feel a dreaded case of the sniffles coming on, so we found a pharmacy to buy some decongestant tablets. I asked the pharmacist for some Sudafed but I was rather taken aback by her response. She stated that in order to purchase them, I would have to provide my identification details, which would be logged into a database.

This seemed rather extreme for some cold and flu medicine but it turns out that these measures were introduced to combat the increasingly common practice of using the pseudoephedrine in these products to make other drugs, such as methamphetamine and ecstasy. It is a good job that I did not know about the register beforehand, as I probably would have opted to suffer in silence rather than go through this rather awkward exchange.

*   *   *

*UFC 127: Penn vs. Fitch*, was held the following day at what was then known as Acer Arena. For what it is worth, Qudos Bank have since acquired the naming rights. As the arena is situated within Sydney Olympic Park, Mum and Uncle Wai Lun decided to accompany me on my journey there, even though they were not attending the show.

Uncle Wai Lun was particularly keen to have a look around the site which hosted the Summer Olympics just over a decade beforehand. The train journey did not take long, as Sydney Olympic Park is located only fourteen kilometres away from the heart of the city.

We walked along the main thoroughfare and noted how big the different Olympic arenas were. The ANZ Stadium, most commonly used to host rugby league matches, can hold over eighty thousand spectators, whilst the aquatic, athletic, tennis and hockey centres each have a capacity of at least ten thousand. The Olympic Park is a good example of how the various arenas can be put to good use long after the Olympics have left town. There have been many instances of Olympic or World Cup arenas in other countries being left largely unused and becoming little more than an eyesore.

We took some photographs before I left the others and headed to the Acer Arena for the show. The venue could hold over twenty thousand people and was regularly used for concerts and sporting events. I had arranged to meet a couple of fellow UFC Fight Club members, Andy and Sergio, that I had been chatting to on the online forum. We briefly said hello, and little more than that, before making our way inside.

We were sat apart for the show but we met up again after the event had finished. We were a collection of socially awkward individuals who were brought together by our obsession with the sport. Inevitably, this meant that there were long periods of silence that were only broken when one of us mentioned something that had happened during the show, such as the controversial draw between B.J. Penn and Jon Fitch in the main event.

We made our way back in to the city and wandered around aimlessly for an hour or two. I was calculating how long I would have to wait before it no longer seemed rude for me to leave the others. I imagine that they were both doing the same. We did a bit of window shopping to kill some time but the enjoyment levels remained pretty low.

I am unable to recall much from that afternoon other than a woman with a strong American accent pointing at my retro football shirt and sounding excited as she yelled, "Manchester United! Yeah!"

I imagine that she would probably sound markedly less excited if she saw a United shirt these days. After an awkward goodbye, in which we insincerely said that we may meet up next time that any of us travels to the other side of the planet, I returned to the apartment.

\*     \*     \*

Our last full day in Sydney was spent casually walking around Darling Harbour and eating more Chinese food in the food court of the nearby shopping centre. Mum worried about her luggage being lost again during the journey home but unless there was a special way of packing a suitcase that ensured its safe return, we would just have to hope for the best.

With our cases now packed, we stood on our balcony and watched a fireworks display over the harbour on our final night. I have no idea what the display was in aid of but we thought that we may as well take in the view from our impressive vantage point. I am not usually a fan of fireworks but I was able to take some decent photographs before spending much of the night gazing up at the stars, reflecting on the wonder of life.

I felt blessed to have been able to travel this far without incurring huge costs and I appreciated how fortunate I was to have been able to see so many beautiful sights during my time in Sydney. It was a bit of a shame that I had not been able to explore more of the wonders of Australia, such as the Great Barrier Reef or Uluru, otherwise known as Ayers Rock. However, I was grateful for what I had been able to experience during the nine days that I was in Sydney.

I hoped that Uncle Wai Lun and Mum did not think that I was too selfish and obsessed for arranging the trip to coincidence with the UFC event. Although this was certainly part of my decision to travel there, I think that we had all enjoyed each other's company and it was nice being able to explore this beautiful city together. We created some wonderful memories and I felt that this gave Mum a belief that it was once again possible for her to travel and embark on adventures around the world.

If I had the power to ensure that one journey during my lifetime would be unaffected by any flight delays, the mammoth trip home from Sydney would certainly have been a strong contender. Much to our dismay, this was the scenario that we faced upon touching down in Frankfurt following the first two flights of the journey. A six hour delay after flying from Australia to Europe was a pretty gruelling affair and it meant that our total travel time exceeded twenty four hours.

One has to keep things in perspective in this type of situation because there are much worse things that can happen in life. To illustrate this point, we later found out that the delay was caused by a terrorist attack at the airport, in which a gunman killed two United States Airmen and injured two others. Oblivious to this incident, we were happy to finally arrive home following a successful trip to the 'land down under.'

# CHAPTER 9: NOT THE TALLEST TOWER AND NOT THE LONGEST STREET
## TORONTO AND NIAGARA FALLS, CANADA
### APRIL 2011

Just a couple of months after our trip to Australia, Mum and I were back on our travels. We were once again visiting one of her siblings, this time her sister Becky. The selfish part of me had timed this to coincide with *UFC 129: St-Pierre vs. Shields*. I had been to Toronto on a few occasions when I was younger but this was the first time as an adult.

I could not remember much from my previous visits apart from Mum being terrified whilst she was stood on the glass floor of the CN Tower, looking straight down at the streets below from a height of over three hundred and forty metres. Just to clarify, bringing her back here was not intended to act as a form of psychological torture.

It was afternoon when we arrived in Toronto but it would have been evening time back home in Manchester. We felt surprisingly fresh despite the long journey and the time difference, so we were happy to dine in a Chinese restaurant with a group of Auntie Becky's friends. My understanding of the Cantonese language was on par with what you would expect from the average Chinese three year old. I could say a few phrases that Mum and I would exchange in the family home when I was growing up but I was incapable of holding down any sort of conversation.

Everyone at the table knew this, so my tongue-in-cheek proclamation that: "Ar hay bat fan bat jung got yan" drew hysterical laughter. This phrase translates to: "I am one hundred percent Chinese."

If I could not converse with our fellow diners in their native language, I may as well get a cheap laugh using the limited Cantonese that I had at my disposal.

Auntie Becky's partner, John, found this particularly amusing and he was still chuckling to himself as he dropped the three of us off at Becky's apartment. He was probably laughing at me rather than with me but I did not mind. Before going to sleep, we expressed our gratitude that we were fortunate to be able to stay with a relative. Mum had the spare bed whilst I was given a waterbed. I would have to learn to stay as still as possible over the next few nights so that the others would not be woken every time that I turned over.

*　　*　　*

As we felt quite tired when we woke up the next day, we decided to take it easy. A lazy morning was most notable for examining Auntie Becky's kitchen. North American refrigerators are known for being much larger than their European counterparts; therefore, I expected to see an enormous kitchen appliance. The reality failed to live up to my unrealistic expectations. At least the contents of the fridge seemed to encapsulate North American kitchen life.

Cardboard cartons of milk and probiotic yoghurt were a sign that we were indeed on the other side of the Atlantic Ocean. The kitchen had a few other items that I was familiar with from television shows; the sight of a few big bags of Cheetos and various brands of potato chips, as they are called in North America, was strangely pleasing.

The apartment complex had its own gym on the ground floor, so I decided to make use of the facilities whilst we were not venturing outside that day. Rather impressively, each treadmill and exercise bike had a built-in television screen. As I burned off the calories that I had consumed earlier by demolishing a family size bag of Cheetos, I watched the Canadian news coverage of the upcoming royal wedding between Prince William and Kate Middleton that was scheduled to take place back in the United Kingdom at the end of the week.

I do not usually pay much attention to royal affairs but I was left feeling short changed as the presenters reminded me that Friday was to be a national holiday back home. Despite being on an adventure in another continent, I felt like I had somehow not received full value from this public holiday.

In the afternoon, John volunteered to take us to the Royal Ontario Museum. This was not somewhere that was at the top of my list of places to visit but I was grateful for the time and effort that he was willing to sacrifice. My levels of excitement increased upon arrival, as the appearance of the museum was extremely unusual. The original building was opened to the public in 1914 and various sections have been added over the years without causing many raised eyebrows.

However, four years prior to our visit, the museum's aesthetics were drastically altered by the addition of the Crystal. This glass and aluminium structure was pointing outwards in all sorts of directions, in complete contrast to the more traditional brick building. It looked like someone had thrown a gigantic glass vase at the old building and that some of the fragments had remained attached to the brickwork.

John was clearly not a fan of the architecture: "The glass section was created a few years ago. I don't know why they did this as it looks terrible. It has been voted as one of the world's ugliest buildings."

I was not sure if I found this to be interesting or just hideous. I think a more valid criticism of the Crystal relates to its lack of functionality. There must be a lot of unusable space due to the bizarre angles that exist throughout this modern section. Either way, I can certainly understand why John hated it so much.

What was not in dispute was the quality of the artefacts and exhibitions within the museum. We enjoyed seeing the dinosaur skeletons, art and fossils. John and Becky were generally more interested in museums than Mum and I were but we still appreciated the impressive collection on show. It was no surprise to discover that this was the most visited museum in Canada. After leaving the dinosaurs behind, we spent the evening in another Chinese restaurant before taking up the opportunity to have an early night.

\*   \*   \*

We felt more energetic the following morning; therefore, Mum and I decided to visit the main attractions of the city. It would be our first experience of Canadian public transport, so Auntie Becky, who had to go to work that day, gave us an overview of the transit system. Conveniently, we could purchase tokens that were valid for travel on buses, trams and on the subway. She even gave us some tokens that could be used until we bought some more at one of the subway stations.

We deposited some tokens as we boarded a bus on the main street by Auntie Becky's apartment and then did the same as we went through the turnstiles of the subway station.

I could not contain my excitement: "This is brilliant. The transition from one form of public transport to another is seamless. I love it."

It was apparent that although I had the biological age of a twenty six year old, I had the mindset of a pensioner. Mum made me feel a bit better about this by also expressing her approval of the transport system, albeit in a more understated way: "That was easy. Very good."

There were a few seats available but I was reluctant to take one, as I had been scarred by a recent misunderstanding back in England. A few months earlier, I had boarded a Metrolink Tram travelling to Manchester city centre. I had caught a glimpse of a woman from behind, who had moved over to the right hand side of the tram. I assumed that this meant that she had sat down in one of the chairs. Without thinking anything of it, I took a vacant seat on the left hand side of the vehicle. Everything seemed normal so far.

She swiftly turned around to face me, at which point I was horrified to see that she was pregnant and had been parking her pram, which contained her other young child, in the allocated space that had been obscured from my vision by the guard rail. I rose from the chair, apologised and attempted to explain to her what had happened but I could tell that she did not believe me. The look on her face painted a picture of absolute disgust and incredulity.

Despite my best efforts, there was nothing that I could do to change her opinion that I was the scum of the earth. I knew that I had not intentionally done anything wrong and that I considered myself to be a fairly polite person but I just had to accept it. In her eyes, I would forever be the poor excuse of a human being that seized the opportunity to steal the seat of a pregnant woman whilst she attended to the pram that was carrying her young child.

As I stood by the doors of the tram, I did not particularly enjoy the awkward atmosphere during our journey towards Manchester.

Worse was to come when she exited the vehicle and delivered a sarcastic comment: "The seat is free now. You can have it."

Still reeling from the latest awful episode in my life, I did not sit down and I instead left the seat unoccupied for the duration of the journey. Since that moment, I have rarely sat down on a tram or a train.

The CN Tower was the main attraction that we planned to visit that day. The last time that we had ascended the tower, it was the tallest free standing structure in the world but this had been surpassed by Dubai's Burj Khalifa in 2007.

Although the prospect of travelling to the top of the tower may not have seemed quite as exciting as it did fourteen years ago, it was still the landmark of the city and it dominated its skyline. We took one of the six high-speed elevators up through the largely redundant main body of the tower until we reached the observation deck.

Just in time for our visit, gloomy clouds had gathered in all directions, so the view was rather dull. We wandered around the perimeter of the observation deck, which provided us with a closer view of the increasingly grim looking weather rather than the city below.

We could still appreciate how high up we were but the image that we had in our heads of looking out across the top of the other buildings in the city did not materialise. The view that we had in front of us was not necessarily the worst that I had ever seen, it was just that it would probably have been best appreciated by a meteorologist rather than a tourist.

I did not dare mention the glass floor sections to Mum, so we made our way back down to street level via the elevator. We had a quick walk around the nearby harbour but found the cold temperature and chilling wind to be most unpleasant.

Bizarrely, we made the brave decision to book a boat ride around the harbour and the surrounding islands. It may not have been ideal weather for it but we did not know whether we would return to this area at any point in the trip. In any case, the alternative of travelling on foot would not have protected us from the elements either.

Although the boat had a canopy, this did little to shield us from the bitterly cold weather. We were now faced with what felt like a stronger wind that was being generated by the movement of the boat. The decision to book the trip was seeming less inspired by the minute; I began to consider whether we had effectively paid a fee to catch pneumonia.

The tour included a journey that passed by the Toronto Islands, which was a chain of fifteen islands that contained parkland and a number of attractions, such as Centreville Amusement Park. Considering the weather, we were glad that our trip did not include a land tour of the islands. The gloomy weather actually gave the islands a mysterious look, which may have helped disguise the impact of human interference on this land.

Our guide informed us that the area was once home to various groups of indigenous people, who used to bring the sick members of their population to the islands due to its healing qualities. Predictably, things changed drastically with the arrival of European colonists.

The British acquired land from the indigenous people through the Toronto Purchase of 1787. Various items were exchanged for land. Although it is not clear what the value of these items were, the amount of money paid for a revision to the agreement in 1805 may be a good indicator; it was as little as ten shillings.

The Mississaugas of the New Credit First Nation, who are the descendants of the indigenous people, contested the inclusion of the islands in the agreement before finally reaching a settlement in 2010. At least there have been attempts in recent years to educate tourists about both the indigenous and modern Canadian history of the islands.

The boat's return to the harbour coincided with an improvement in the weather, at least in the visual aspect, which allowed us to take some deceptively pleasant looking photographs. In fairness, the view of the CN Tower and the adjacent Rogers Centre was delightful. The symbol of the city was side by side with one of the most impressive sports and entertainment stadiums in North America, which also happened to be the location of the show that I was attending on Saturday.

We decided to take refuge from the cold and try some warm Canadian comfort food. I had seen many references to poutine on television shows and films but I had not been aware of what it consisted of. Originating from Quebec, it was ridiculed as a cheap trashy food for decades before it became a popular meal throughout the country.

Mum and I both ordered an ample sized portion and discovered that it was as basic as the menu description had indicated. It simply comprised of French fries, cheese curds and gravy. It resembled something that one could order from a late night takeaway shop at two in the morning after a boozy night out was reaching its conclusion; at least that is what I had imagined in the fictional reality in which I actually had a social life.

Nevertheless, I really enjoyed my bowl of poutine. It may be a simple dish but it is tasty comfort food and I found it hard to believe that anybody could dislike it. However , I only had to look to my left to find someone who was not so impressed.

Mum gave her verdict: "Too salty. It was OK but very salty."

This did not surprise me in the slightest, considering that it was Mum's standard opinion on any food that she tastes. Even if she had just eaten something that had absolutely no salt in it whatsoever, Mum would still say the same thing. Her other common complaint about food is that it is too dry. At least she could not say that about the meal in front of us, which was swimming in gravy. It is not that Mum is particularly demanding about food; she just has a few things that she really does not like.

*   *   *

We then returned to the subway and headed for downtown Toronto. When I had researched the best things to see in Toronto, Yonge Street was mentioned several times. This was mostly due to the decades-old misconception that it was the longest street in the world. The entire route of Highway 11 had, incorrectly, been regarded as being part of Yonge Street. This false claim was widely believed until the turn of the century, with the *Guinness Book of Records* still listing it as the world's longest street until 1999.

This added to my flustration because at the time of our previous visit to the city in 1997, the CN Tower was the tallest in the world and Yonge Street was widely regarded as the longest in the world. I was oblivious to these records at the time but now that I had researched them, both had been taken away.

I tried to phrase my description of the length of Yonge Street in a way that would provoke Mum's interest without feeding her with any false information. "We are heading towards what used to be regarded as the longest street in the world."

She seemed suitably impressed: "Very interesting. So how long is it?"

I had no idea, so I attempted, and failed, to make a humorous comment: "We are going to walk the entire length of the street. It will take us three days. Is that OK?"

Mum looked confused as she replied: "Why do you want to do that? I could never do that."

I should have known better than to try and be funny. Yonge-Dundas Square seemed the logical starting point, as it was one of the most prominent public spaces in the city. We were met by a sea of tourists and workers, who were rushing around the square. I am not really a fan of such hectic, crowded places but I was still keen to observe the chaos in front of us. There were clusters of people watching various street performers dotted around the square.

We briefly watched part of one man's act, which mostly involved standing completely still. I made a quip about him "displaying all of the qualities required to play for Manchester United."

As usual, my joke went down like a lead balloon with Mum, who replied: "What makes you say that? Wouldn't he need to move more and run about if he was a football player?"

We left the square and picked a direction to walk down Yonge Street. It did not really matter which option we chose, as it all looked pretty similar. There were office buildings, retail units and restaurants lined along the street, which I found it to be rather bland. We walked down the street for a while then turned around and did the same in the other direction. What great fun we had.

At least I had been able to keep up to date with the football results whilst we wandered around. Manchester United had defeated Shalke of Germany in the first leg of their Champions League semi-final. I told Mum the good news, which resulted in her giving a rather confusing response: "Does that mean that they have won the FA Cup?"

I thought that it was fantastic that we lived in a world in which one can keep up to date with current affairs, live sport or communications from their friends via the internet from anywhere in the world. What I did not realise at this point was how data roaming charges worked.

I had been browsing the internet sporadically from the moment that we had arrived in Canada, blissfully unaware of the huge phone bill that I was racking up. Unfortunately, it was not yet common practice for phone companies to cap the charges that one could accumulate in regard to data roaming. Around ten days after returning to the United Kingdom, I had the pleasure of discovering that my monthly phone bill was an eye-watering seven hundred and fifty pounds.

After having a walk along a street that is not the longest in the world and naively adding to my ever increasing phone bill, we made our way back to Auntie Becky's apartment. Aside from the weather, we had enjoyed our day exploring some of the city's most well-known tourist sites.

*   *   *

The following day, we left the city to visit one of Canada's most famous attractions. In fact, it is a site that is shared with the United States. Situated on the border of the two countries, Niagara Falls can be accessed from either the Canadian or American side of the border. My memories of our previous trip in 1997 were as misty as the falls themselves, so I was looking forward to witnessing one of the natural wonders of the world as if it were for the first time.

Auntie Becky drove to the falls, which took around an hour and a half. As we exited the car, we could hear the crashing sound of the immense movement of water. This was not a surprise, as a total of three waterfalls comprise what is collectively known as Niagara Falls.

The largest of the three, the Horseshoe Falls is situated almost completely on the Canadian side, whilst the Bridal Veil Falls and the American Falls are, not surprisingly, entirely on the American side. Apparently, up to six million cubic feet of water travels over the crest of the falls each minute. I am not sure how to put that into context but it certainly sounds like a lot of water.

We made our way towards the mist and noise and could soon see the two waterfalls that were on the American side. We went through all of the different photography combinations of the three of us, which always involved one person taking a photo of the other two. Little did we know but the individual that is credited with inventing the modern day selfie stick a few years earlier was a man from Toronto called Wayne Fromm.

We could have done with a chance encounter with him and his

contraption at that moment but it would be another few years before the selfie stick became one of the most sought after gadgets throughout the world.

Interestingly, the origin of the selfie stick can be traced all the way back to the 1920s after a photo recently emerged of a man holding a stick whilst posing for a picture. Perhaps the first attempt to make a commercial product was by Hiroshi Ueda of Japan in the 1980s. As well as the extending stick, his invention was based on a camera that had a convex mirror on its front so the user could gain a general idea of what they were taking. However, it was not until the invention of smartphones with front facing cameras that the selfie stick really took off.

Perhaps unaware of the potential for the selfie stick, Ueda's product was listed in the 1995 book, *101 Unuseless Inventions: The Art of Chindōgu.* The Japanese term 'chindōgu' is attributed to the process of inventing something that seemingly solves a particular problem but is, in practical terms, useless. A couple of decades after being branded as useless, the selfie stick has been recognised as one of the most widely used inventions of recent times and has become one of the world's most popular gadgets.

I certainly appreciate the selfie stick, since it helps me to avoid a couple of unwanted scenarios. I do not have to engage in conversation with a stranger when I want a photograph taken of the whole group and I also no longer have to worry about a stranger's thumb obscuring the camera lens or my head being chopped off the top of the image.

We decided to get a closer look at the falls by taking a boat trip on The Maid of the Mist; which is one of the major operators, along with Hornblower Niagara Cruises. Incidentally, 'Hornblower' was also the name that my brother, John, gave me when I was blowing my nose, which he had given the name of 'Norman,' during our childhood years. I had nasal problems when I was younger, which resulted in having my adenoids removed. My loud nose-blowing irritated John but not as much as my heavy breathing and snoring.

We had shared both a bedroom and a bunk bed until I was thirteen years old, so bedtime was always a tense affair.

"Stop snoring!" and "Shut up! You're breathing heavily!" were regular comments that were dished out from the top bunk. I could finally relax when it became clear that John was asleep due to the change in his breathing pattern, which was more than a touch ironic. Despite this, my brother and I have always had a good relationship. It was more of a case of quarrelling siblings rather than anything more sinister.

We were all given blue cagoules before boarding the boat. This led us to take another series of photos, this time whilst looking rather silly in our new waterproof clothing. The main thing that I could see on the boat was a mass of blue cagoules. It was difficult to distinguish anyone from the rest of the hundreds of other passengers. The sea of cagoules was only occasionally broken up by the mist and spray that was being produced by the waterfalls.

The boat journey itself was more exhilarating than I had anticipated. This involved sailing close enough to each of the waterfalls so that we were battered by the spray of the water. Suddenly, the cagoules did not seem anywhere near as ridiculous or embarrassing. We all seemed to appreciate this opportunity to see a natural wonder of the world at such close quarters and nobody reported feeling nauseous.

There was an optional extension to the trip, which involved walking up to and then behind one of the waterfalls but we were content with our water-based journey. As our ride came to an end, I reflected on how the incredible force of nature certainly makes one appreciate how insignificant we all are in the context of the planet as a whole.

Following the boat trip, we stopped by one of the gift shops. I am unable to recall whether it was compulsory to travel through the shop in order to exit the falls but this is usually the case with souvenir stores at tourist attractions.

I used this opportunity to purchase a gift for Mandy, who I was still seeing at the time. I had brought her back some sand from Bondi Beach when I travelled to Australia, so what could I possibly return with from my Canadian voyage? A gimmicky souvenir provided the answer to this quandary. The gift shop was selling bottles of water that had 'survived a plunge over Niagara Falls.' Although I had not retrieved the water myself, I hoped that the sentiment would be appreciated.

The water may have survived the plunge over the falls but the track record of human beings attempting this was mixed at best. The first documented attempt was made in 1829 but the famous example that I had read about involved a sixty three year old school teacher going over the falls in a barrel in 1901. Against all odds, she emerged from this publicity stunt with only minor injuries.

This only encouraged others to attempt similar feats, who often met a gruesome death in the process. I asked Mum if she would consider such an attempt.

She simply replied: "No. Why? Do you want to kill your mother?"

I reassured Mum that I did not want to throw her over Niagara Falls in a barrel before we moved on to our next destination. Niagara-on-the-lake is a town that is located a short distance from the Canadian side of the falls. It lies within the Niagara region, which is not to be confused with the region of the same name on the American side. To complicate matters further, both countries have a town called Niagara Falls.

Almost immediately after arriving in Niagara-on-the-lake, we passed one of the major landmarks of the town. The Memorial Clock Tower was unveiled in 1922 with the intention of honouring residents of the town who had lost their lives during the First World War.

The town was virtually destroyed following the American invasion of 1812 but it was subsequently rebuilt by the British. The restored colonial style buildings are now regarded as a major tourist attraction. It was a picturesque small town so it was not hard to see why it is one of the most popular places that Canadians choose to reside after retirement.

I initially suspected that Auntie Becky, who had become somewhat of a wine connoisseur in recent years, was only interested in the wineries of the town, as the area has a reputation for producing exceptional wine due to its fertile soil and mild climate. Then I remembered that she was driving, rather than drinking, so she must not have taken us there for that reason.

Wine was on the menu later that evening though. Back in Toronto and reunited with John, we dined together in a French restaurant in what seemed a quiet suburban area. The food, beef bourguignon in my case, was very nice but I imagine that the prices were not as agreeable. This did not seem to be a concern for John, who was well accustomed to sampling the finer things in life. John and Auntie Becky ordered a bottle of expensive red wine, which was promptly brought to the table.

The sommelier, whom I learned was a waiter exclusively designated for the serving of wine, poured a small amount into John's glass and encouraged him to try it before letting him know whether the drink was of an acceptable standard. John brought the glass up to his nose and closed his eyes as he lost himself in the aroma of the wine. He then swilled the contents of the glass around his mouth before giving the sommelier the all clear to dispense some more alcohol.

John seemed to be in his element and it appeared that this process was part of his enjoyment of the wine. I, on the other hand, would have found this whole exchange extremely awkward and I would have been willing to pay money in order to ensure that I did not have to partake in any such social interaction.

John would continue to enhance his dining experience through further conversations with the restaurant staff. After we had all finished our meals, he asked to speak to the chef, which I gathered was a common occurrence when John was dining out. This request was duly granted and he warmly embraced the man that had emerged from the kitchen. I had no desire to join in with such activities and I certainly did not want to know what the cost of the meal was. Even though John had already insisted on paying, I felt somewhat uncomfortable with him footing the bill.

On one occasion at The French in Manchester, he ended up paying around seven hundred pounds for a tasting menu for five of us and an accompanying wine flight. It was also on this night that he gave my brother and me a lesson on the complexities of red wine. I think that my brother was impressed by the grandeur and sophistication of it all, as a few days later he had abandoned the beer that he had once favoured and had been transformed into a red wine aficionado.

*   *   *

The following day, we returned to the CN Tower. This time we had Auntie Becky for company and we were also blessed with glorious weather. It appeared that we would finally be afforded the opportunity to truly admire the city from above. We rode the elevator to the observation deck once again, where we were met with the view that we had hoped for. With clear blue skies and unobstructed sunshine, visibility was infinitely better than it had been during our previous visit a couple of days earlier.

We walked around the perimeter of the observation deck, taking pictures of the city below and also taking it in turns to pose for pictures. As impressive as this bird's eye view was, most of the city looked rather bland to me. There were many skyscrapers in downtown Toronto but none of them appeared to have any character or interesting features.

The area that provided the best view was Mum's old nemesis; the glass floor. After some gentle encouragement from Auntie Becky, Mum stepped onto the glass. Much to our surprise, she managed to remain calm. I am not sure that I would go as far as to say that she enjoyed it, as she spent most of the time stood completely still and staring down at her feet, but she had conquered her fear.

Part of the glass floor was positioned so that it overlooked the adjacent Rogers Centre far below. The famed retractable roof was open, which resulted in a perfect view of the baseball pitch within the stadium. The Rogers Centre was huge, which highlighted just how high up we were. Auntie Becky convinced me to lie down on the glass so that she could take a picture of me suspended above the stadium. I had hoped that this photograph would look stylish but my chubby cheeks and scruffy beard ruined this close-up image.

With fears conquered and photographs taken, we made our way back down to street level and moved on to the next port of call. Most major international cities have a Chinatown of some sort; Toronto has one of the largest in North America. Therefore, it seemed like an obvious place for three people of Chinese descent to visit. I had read that Canada has a substantial Chinese population, including Auntie Becky, which caused me to ponder what it must be like for those that emigrate to distant lands.

Whilst Mum and Uncle Wai Lun left Hong Kong for a more prosperous life in England, Auntie Becky had settled in Toronto, where she had enjoyed a successful career within the banking sector. I am unable to imagine how scary it would have been for them to leave their homeland at a young age and relocate to an unfamiliar country on the other side of the world. Especially since many of their relatives remained in Hong Kong, including their siblings, Dickie and Pak Lin.

Mum came to England when she was just eighteen. When I was that age, I regarded a twenty minute tram ride into Manchester city centre as a bit of an ordeal. It is clear that I have had a very easy life in comparison.

We had some nice Chinese food before walking around a shopping arcade. I was browsing through the various items that were for sale, as I had one eye on purchasing what I had incorrectly referred to as a Chinese lucky cat. In fact, the cat figurines are of Japanese origin.

The 'maneki-neko' is said to bring its owner good fortune and prosperity, which unsurprisingly appealed to Chinese people. Such is their popularity, it is hard to imagine going into a Chinese owned store anywhere in the world without being able to see one of the figurines, complete with a moving paw beckoning potential customers to enter.

We looked at a few of the cats and I asked Mum what the various inscriptions on the base of each one meant. She told me that they all referred to money, since the most common wish for Chinese people was to gain prosperity. I decided not to purchase one because money was not a driving force of my life. It is understandable that many Chinese people desired this, as they are more often than not coming from a less privileged background than what I have been blessed with.

*   *   *

There was a big UFC fan expo being held on Friday and Saturday, which kept me occupied for a couple of days. I met up with a fellow Fight Club member called Jonathan, who was accompanied by his younger brother. They were also of Chinese origin but lived locally. I think that we all found it comforting to be in each other's company rather than being a lost soul within this sea of sports fans.

The expo was being held in what was then known as The Direct Energy Centre, which was certainly more than big enough to host the festivities. There were countless stalls that were set up for meet and greets with a plethora of MMA competitors and there were stages that had been constructed for demonstrations.

For your average MMA fan, this was heaven but I had mixed feelings. I felt a certain amount of excitement about meeting the stars of the sport but I knew that there would be a lot of time queueing up in order to exchange a few awkward lines of conversation that the other person had probably gone through hundreds of times before.

After a full day of visiting as many stalls as possible and posing for photographs with the competitors, it was almost time to leave. I had one more meet and greet to complete before I left the expo. After queueing for around thirty five minutes, I realised that I would not be able to reach the front without keeping Mum and Auntie Becky waiting.

They were due to pick me up at five o'clock before we all had dinner with some of Auntie Becky's friends. Unfortunately, my selfishness and determination to see a task through to the end, resulted in my choice to remain in the queue to meet the UFC Heavyweight Champion, Cain Velasquez, at the expense of my timekeeping.

I emerged from the expo, with a photograph of the champ, around thirty minutes later than we had agreed. I, quite rightly, felt guilty for my actions and apologised profusely. Auntie Becky was angry as she had been looking forward to showing off her nephew to her friends.

My lateness would surely create a poor first impression. However, it turned out to be the perfect icebreaker. A couple of the guys within our dining group were MMA fans, so they were interested in the expo and the live show that I was due to attend on Saturday. Normally, I would remain quiet in such social settings but the sport of MMA proved to be an effective introductory topic of conversation.

*   *   *

Saturday was again spent at the expo with Jonathan and his brother. It was almost an identical day to the previous one, with the only difference being that there was a new group of MMA competitors attending the meet and greets.

During the two days of the fan expo, I had my photograph taken with some legendary mixed martial artists, such as Royce Gracie, Anderson Silva and Mauricio 'Shogun' Rua. I also met Antônio Rodrigo 'Minotauro' Nogueira, who should not be confused with his twin brother, Antônio Rogério 'Minotouro' Nogueira, whom I had encountered in Abu Dhabi. To have chosen such similar names for the twins, their parents must have taken enjoyment from watching the rest of us struggle to distinguish between the two of them.

Just as we were about to leave the expo, I made the mistake of absent mindedly rubbing my tired eyes. I had, not for the first time, forgotten that I was wearing a pair of contact lenses, so I inadvertently dislodged one lens from my pupil and moved it onto the back of my eyelid. I now had the difficult task of locating the lens and removing it. This involved lifting up my eyelid and frantically blinking until the lens separated itself.

In this situation, I have found that there is more or less a fifty per cent chance of being able to successfully place the dry contact lens back in my eye. Unfortunately, I was not able to complete my mission on this occasion. Of all the times to effectively lose the vision in one eye, this was a bad one. My seat was located at the very top of a stadium that had been configured to accommodate over fifty five thousand people. The competitors would look like toy soldiers even if both my eyes were in full working order.

With only one eye operating to an acceptable standard, they would seem more like ants. In the end, I spent the entirety of the evening looking up at the action being shown on the big screen. For the record, Georges St-Pierre successfully defended his welterweight title against Jake Shields and the featherweight champion, Jose Aldo, defeated hometown favourite, Mark Hominick. At least, that is what I think that I saw with my one good eye.

The following day, Mum and I headed back to Toronto Pearson International Airport, as we had arranged a three night break across the border before we returned home. The next adventure beckoned.

# CHAPTER 10: CITY PLANNING AND LONG WALKS
## NEW YORK, THE UNITED STATES OF AMERICA
### MAY 2011

Although we were about to spend a few days in New York, our flight from Toronto was scheduled to touch down in Newark, New Jersey. This was not because I was so incompetent that I had accidentally booked a flight to the wrong state but it was due to the fact that it was much cheaper to fly there rather than to one of the airports in New York. I would have to wait until the return journey before truly experiencing the horrors of Newark Liberty International Airport though.

Following the usual interrogation by the U. S. immigration officers, the train journey to New York City was rather uncomfortable, as it was hot and crowded. Even worse than that; it was full of Americans. I am kidding of course, as I was not bothered what nationality they were. It was just irritating to be surrounded by so many noisy people.

Thankfully, it was only about thirty minutes before we arrived at Pennsylvania Station. Although it was not as big and famous as Grand Central, we still found the station to be visually impressive. The grandeur and architectural elegance of the building provided a positive first impression of New York.

Our accommodation for the next three nights, Hotel Pennsylvania, was located opposite the station, so even a couple of hapless tourists like ourselves could find it with ease. The smartly dressed doorman was stood in front of what was effectively a giant porch in front of the hotel. He let us through the grand entrance and into the expansive lobby. It looked so clean that every inch of it seemed to be glistening.

I was cautious not to place too much value in this, given that we had been warned that the grandeur of the lobby areas in New York do not reflect the state of the rooms. This was certainly true with the hotel that we were staying in. The walls in our room were crumbling, the décor was dull and the state of the plug sockets looked rather dubious. We were not too bothered, as we had chosen the hotel because it was relatively cheap and it was in a good location.

It was time to attempt to impress Mum with some topical knowledge: "Do you know why they say 'New York, New York'?"

She looked confused as she replied, "Who says that?" Mum was not going to make this easy for me.

"You know the song by Liza Minnelli and Frank Sinatra? Or the hotel in Las Vegas?" I asked.

This seemed to make things even less clear for Mum.

"What has Las Vegas got to do with it?" she asked, with a puzzled look on her face.

"Nothing really. I just mean that there is a hotel in Las Vegas called 'New York, New York'. It has a rollercoaster that runs along the outside of the building," I explained.

Mum then asked: "What does a rollercoaster have to do with this?"

I was now eager to finish the conversation as quickly as possible: "It doesn't matter. The main point is that people often say 'New York, New York' because the city of New York is situated in the state of New York."

She did not look particularly impressed. "Oh, I knew that. We stayed with my friend in New York State many years ago."

This surreal conversation must have been some form of punishment for attempting to show off and make myself sound clever.

After unpacking our small cases, we picked up a map from reception and ventured out to explore the Big Apple. I thought that this would be sensible, considering that the book that Mandy had given me was written in her native German language. Although her intentions were good, the idea of walking around an unfamiliar city with a guidebook that was written in a language that I did not understand was rather comical.

We headed out to get some food from one of the many 'delis' that the city is famous for. Rather than choosing a dish that originated from New York, I opted for a Philly Cheesesteak. I had only been in the city an hour, yet I had already disrespected its culinary heritage by ordering a dish from Philadelphia. It was tasty though.

One of the most famous department stores in America was close by to our hotel, so we decided to have a quick look inside. Macy's flagship store has stood at its current location since the beginning of the twentieth century and is said to be one of the largest in the world. I had seen it featured in many films and television shows, usually set at Christmas time. Therefore, I viewed it as a tourist attraction rather than a place to shop.

We had no intention of buying anything but it did not take long before I was seduced by the rampant capitalism that is synonymous with the United States. I had been frustrated by the quality of photographs that I had taken on recent trips but I did not want to spend a fortune on a new camera. A persuasive salesman was able to convince me to purchase a digital camera that was of a much higher quality than the one that I currently used.

*   *   *

A couple of hundred dollars lighter, we left Macy's and made our way over to Times Square. It was getting dark now, which provided the perfect backdrop for the bright lights of the electronic advertising boards that were visible in every direction. Large groups of people had congregated on a set of red steps, which seemed to be the favoured spot for posing for photographs to post on social media. I was content to have my picture taken stood in the middle of this busy intersection.

"David, why don't you smile for photos?" Mum asked.

Her question caused me to reflect on why this was the case. I concluded that it was a hangover from my teenage years that were spent believing that there was a cool way of doing things and that any deviation from this would cause me embarrassment. My brother, John, was the main person that I had looked to for this warped guidance. If he made a throwaway comment about how to act, I would take that as gospel.

For example, he once said that the way that I was holding a bottle of Coca-Cola was "lame." I was simply holding it like ninety nine per cent of people would; upright, like it is supposed to be held. However, John said that bottles should be held halfway down, with the lid pressed against your wrist.

He probably forgot that he said this almost immediately after he had uttered the sentence but I ended up utilising this technique through to adulthood, before I realised how ridiculous it was. Similarly, the influence of my teenage brother could be felt when I was posing for a photograph. Cool people did not smile for photographs. Therefore, I rarely did so; right up until that moment in Times Square.

We decided to find an even better view of the city that was being lit up by electricity. Mandy had advised me to visit the 'Top of the Rock' rather than the Empire State Building, as the latter could be photographed from the vantage point provided by the former. Mum and I followed her advice and entered the Rockefeller Center.

I had always thought that it was just one building but I discovered that it is actually a complex consisting of nineteen buildings that are linked by a series of underground walkways. Even the concourses are lined with restaurants, shops and a post office. The complex is so big that it has its own private street, called Rockefeller Plaza.

We took the elevator to the observation deck that was located over eight hundred feet above street level. Mandy's tip proved to be fruitful, as we were blessed with splendid views of the Empire State Building that was being illuminated in a range of alternating colours. We also had a clear view of the Art-Deco Chrysler Building, which preceded the Empire State Building as the world's tallest.

It was wonderful to take in the night time view of the city that had featured on our television screens for decades. This pleasant feeling was enhanced by the knowledge that we would also get to see a different version during daylight hours at some stage of our trip.

After returning to street level, we spent a few minutes in the sunken Lower Plaza that contains the famed statue of Prometheus. It is during the Christmas period that this area really comes to life, when hordes of tourists and locals come here for the ice rink and the huge Christmas tree that has been erected here each holiday season since 1934. The ice rink and the tree have become synonymous with Christmas in New York and have been immortalised in popular culture.

Whilst admiring the plaza, it was hard not to imagine all of the scenes that had been filmed here that I had watched on television. I first saw an image of the plaza shortly before my eighth birthday, when Mum took me to the cinema to watch *Home Alone 2: Lost in New York.*

I reminded Mum of this memory and took the opportunity to make what I thought was a fairly witty comment: "We would have been the ones lost in New York if we had used that German guidebook!"

Mum replied by saying: "I think that we would have been okay. It has a map and we could figure out what each landmark is."

Judging by Mum's response, my joke was the only thing that had been lost in New York.

Before retiring to our hotel for the night, we had a quick look at another New York institution. With a capacity of around six thousand, Radio City Music Hall is one of the largest theatres in the world. It is often referred to as the 'Showplace of the Nation' and special editions of a variety of popular television shows have been filmed there. More recently, the venue has hosted a number of music concerts, which has proven to be a key source of revenue.

It was not particularly pretty but like so many of the attractions in the 'Big Apple,' the appeal is the familiarity that you feel for it despite having not visited it before. Images of all the buildings, bridges, parks and streets are so ingrained in our collective consciousness due to the films and television shows that most of us have watched over the course of our lives. A considerable percentage of the most widely used film locations can be found in New York City, with Central Park being the most popular of them all.

On our way back to the hotel, we saw another sight that was familiar from the world of film and television; people were drinking bottles of alcohol out of a brown paper bag. I had always wondered why Americans did this. Was it simply the traditional way that shops in the United States sold alcoholic beverages or is it because they are hiding something more sinister? In any case, I always thought that this made the person with the drink look like a vagrant or an alcoholic.

I did a quick online search and discovered that this custom is actually due to the rather bizarre laws regarding public drinking and how these laws are enforced. Laws vary from state to state but in most places within the United States, people are prohibited from consuming alcohol on the street. However, the nuances to these laws and a lack of appetite to pursue every such case has resulted in the frequent sight of an American citizen downing a bottle of their favourite alcoholic tipple whilst it is wrapped in a brown paper bag.

The law in the state of New York outlines that it is illegal to drink from or carry an open container of alcohol. However, a police officer is unlikely to challenge you if he or she does not have visual confirmation that you are drinking alcohol. Therefore, people conceal their bottles or cans in this manner.

Obviously, this will not stop a law enforcement official from apprehending you if you are acting drunk and disorderly in public. This was hardly a concern for me though. I could hardly imagine Mum walking along the streets of New York whilst swigging a bottle of vodka. At least, I hoped not.

We walked through Times Square again on our route back, at which time we saw some breaking news on the big screens. Al-Qaeda's leader, Osama Bin Laden, had been killed during a military operation in Pakistan. In some ways it felt fitting to find out this news whilst in the city where his terrorist group had carried out the horrific attack on the World Trade Center ten years beforehand.

The next headline was a little more troubling though, since it stated that the threat level for a terrorist attack in New York had been raised as a result of his death. I could not help but think that the timing of his killing could not have been much worse for us. In the end, I told myself that the threat level has been high across the Western world for the past decade and that at least one monster had been eradicated from this planet.

\*    \*    \*

The following day would prove to be a very taxing but enjoyable one. Mum let me create the itinerary, which our poor bodies would come to regret. I really wanted to walk across Brooklyn Bridge and then look back at Manhattan from the other side. Given that our hotel was situated opposite Penn Station, most people would have taken the subway to the station that was located by the bridge but I decided to walk there and back.

After building up our energy levels with a breakfast of cereal and fruit, we set off on our quest. It would not be a simple walk to the bridge though. I routinely checked our map for places of interest, which resulted in us deviating from our route every time that we were near one.

We began our journey by walking along Broadway. This is one of the most famous streets in New York, on which the city's theatre scene is found. Similarly to the West End in London, the majority of theatres are concentrated here. I had no real interest in theatre shows at the time but if I return to the city one day, I imagine that I will book a show at one of the numerous venues.

As we walked along the street, my fascination with Broadway was limited to something very simple.

I turned to Mum and posed a question: "Have you noticed anything different from most of the other streets that we have seen in New York?"

She paused for a moment before providing a response that was lacking in conviction: "Well, you said that there were lots of theatres here."

Finally, it was my time to shine: "Nearly all of the streets in New York City form a grid pattern, with the streets appearing to run vertically or horizontally on a map. However, Broadway is one of the only ones that cuts diagonally through the city."

I showed her our map in order to illustrate my point. This seemed to pique Mum's interest, which led to the logical questions of how and why this grid pattern originated. I gave Mum a condensed, simplified version of the Commissioner's Plan of 1811. It is regarded by many as one of the greatest examples of efficient city planning but I find it to be a little boring, even if it is practical.

Broadway escaped the 'gridiron' design as it was already an established major route through Manhattan prior to the Commissioners Plan. Originally it was a Native American trail and later it became an important road, called Brede weg, in what was then known as New Amsterdam during Dutch colonial rule.

Following the arrival of the British, the road became known as Broadway and the city was renamed New York. Two hundred years after the conception of New York's gridiron design, Mum and I were stood on the very streets that were included in the plan and we were in agreement that the layout was practical but unimaginative.

New York, with its carefully designed grid of skyscrapers and apartment blocks, can be seen as a rather uninspired city that resembles an example of a basic attempt to create a metropolis in the early incarnations of the *Sim City* franchise of computer games. From a visual point of view, I certainly prefer the organic, although sometimes confusing, maze of streets that forms the city of London. The fact that we had spent so long analysing just one street that did not conform to the grid design shows how rigid and dull it can seem at times.

It was not long before we stumbled upon a rather more unusual and intriguing sight. A forty four feet tall sculpture of a girl's head was staring at us from Madison Square Park. *Echo* was the latest creation of the renowned public artist, Jaume Plensa. It was inspired by the Greek legend of the same name, who had her voice taken away. This resulted in her being able to vocalise the thoughts of others but not her own. Apparently, the artist hoped that the sculpture would provide a place for people to reflect on their inner thoughts.

He has made sculptures in various locations throughout the world, such as Calgary and Dubai. However, his first project of this kind was unveiled in a rather unremarkable town in the north west of England called St. Helens. In fact, *Dream* is located less than ten miles away from my current home town of Wigan. Maybe I will check it out one day. Perhaps not, as this would involve visiting St. Helens.

Mum asked me about the sculpture but I had no idea what it was at the time. It appeared to be a recent addition to the city, as it was not listed on my map and I could not recall reading anything about it when I was planning our trip. Nevertheless, I took a few photographs of it. Amusingly, it looked liked the giant head, which was completely white, had been superimposed on all of the pictures.

The Flatiron Building was the next landmark that we encountered after walking a little further along Broadway. This is widely regarded as one of the original skyscrapers of New York; although its twenty two stories seem miniscule next to the colossal buildings that now occupy much of the city.

Situated on a triangular block, due to the angle that 22$^{nd}$ Street and 23$^{rd}$ Street cross Broadway, the name of the building derives from it having a similar shape to a cast-iron clothes iron. The building was a shining example of the increased character and individuality that can arise from deviations from the rigid grid pattern that we had discussed within the last half hour.

We took some photographs whilst I waited for Mum to ask me why it was called the Flatiron Building.

I had the relevant information loaded and ready to distribute but she surprised me with her next comment: "I can see why they call it Flatiron. It sort of resembles the shape of an old fashioned iron."

Through Mum's pre-emptive strike, I had been denied the opportunity to dish out some more regurgitated information. Therefore, order had been restored.

*   *   *

We were soon on the fringes of Greenwich Village. My eagerness to explore the area caused us to deviate from our direct route to Brooklyn Bridge. Washington Square Park is the heartbeat of The Village. Students from the nearby New York University often congregate around the fountain and Washington Arch, which resembles a much smaller version of the Arc de Triomphe.

There were a set of statues that indicated that the area was more interesting for the events that had taken place there over forty years beforehand. Despite my passion for human rights, I did not possess any knowledge of what the statues in front of us represented. The Gay Liberation Monument is an example of how travelling can help people learn more about history and the world around them.

In 1969, The Village was the site of a hugely significant and symbolic moment in the history of civil rights. The area had long been associated with bohemian culture and it was a haunt for those with progressive, liberal attitudes. Gay people had very few civil rights, so many were naturally drawn to Greenwich Village, where there was a greater level of acceptance.

In a country where consensual sexual relations between people of the same gender was illegal in every state apart from Illinois, the bars of The Village offered refuge. Gay people faced prejudice in the legal system and were expected to conform to the established norms of society. Many people were arrested for trivial things such as their choice of attire and were subjected to the public humiliation of being identified as indecent criminals in newspapers.

The Civil Rights Movement was reaching boiling point in the 1960s, with violent clashes with the authorities an inevitable by-product of the fight for equality. Perhaps inspired by the success of the more aggressive and organised approach employed by many of those seeking to end racial discrimination, there was a growing anger and appetite to protest against the increasing number of police raids that were targeting bars that were regularly frequented by the gay community.

After seeing an opportunity to exploit the situation for financial gain, the Mafia stepped in and acquired many of the bars. This in turn, resulted in even more raids. The police raided the Stonewall Inn during the early hours of the twenty eighth of June, 1969. This was a fairly common occurrence but it was what followed that changed the course of history.

The arrests took longer than anticipated and accusations of rough treatment riled up the crowd. Vastly outnumbered, the police were unable to keep control of what was now a violent mob. The protests continued for a number of days. Whatever the rights and wrongs of the events of those nights were, it was a turning point in the fight for gay rights. After years of hiding in the shadows, there was now a visible battle being fought for equality.

Thousands of people took part in the first Pride march in New York on the anniversary of the Stonewall riots. The following decades saw the reversal of many laws that had effectively made homosexuality illegal and had allowed discrimination in every area of life. Pride marches now take place all across the globe and there is generally a higher level of acceptance in wider society. However, there is still a long way to go in the fight for equality.

Right-wing governments around the world have divided society once again and hate crimes have been on the rise in recent years. Over half of the states in the U.S.A. do not offer any legal protection against discrimination based on a person's sexuality, meaning that someone can be fired from their workplace for this reason. The Democratic Party have unanimously backed the proposed Equality Act but efforts to implement this nationally have been met with resistance from the other side of the political aisle and from various right-wing organisations.

Since we were keen to rejoin our intended route to Brooklyn Bridge, Mum and I swiftly made our way through the streets of SoHo, which were lined with the cast-iron buildings that the neighbourhood is famed for. Similarly, we did not spend long in Little Italy. There did not appear to be much to see there, in any case.

The area was once a thriving community of Italian immigrants that resembled a self-contained subculture within New York.

"Where is Little Italy?" Mum asked, oblivious to the fact that we were now walking through it.

To be fair, there were only a handful of Italian restaurants and stores that remained. In truth, it did not feel different to anywhere else in New York.

Chinatown, on the other hand, was still a large area that retained the Chinese vibe that had been ever present since the first significant wave of immigrants arrived during the Gold Rush. There were Chinese restaurants and shops in every direction. Everywhere 'looked' Chinese.

Mum tapped me on my shoulder and proudly gave her verdict: "Of course, Chinatown is much bigger and more successful than Little Italy. Our people have established themselves in countries all around the world. China has the world's biggest population."

I would like to say that it was my turn to put a dampener on Mum's proclamations but she was right. In the vast majority of countries I have visited, I have noticed a substantial Chinese presence. Indeed, there are over fifty million Chinese people residing in foreign lands. New York has the largest ethnic Chinese population outside of Asia and its Chinatown has the highest concentration of Chinese people in the Western hemisphere.

However, Mum's statement about China being the most populous country in the world may soon become outdated, given that India is on course to take this title within the next decade.

We felt compelled to have a look at the statue of Confucius that was highlighted on our map. The fifteen foot bronze statue of the ancient Chinese philosopher stood proudly in the plaza that also bore his name. His influence on Chinese culture has remained strong over two thousand years after his death. Family loyalty and respect for one's elders are obvious examples of Confucianism that are key aspects of the traditional Chinese way of life. His wise words, such as: "What you do not wish for yourself, do not do to others," have been embraced across various cultures throughout the world.

Having worked up a considerable appetite, we were glad to be in Chinatown. The McDonald's restaurant that resembled a pagoda caused us to chuckle rather than consider it as a serious option for lunch. Instead, we opted for an ordinary looking Chinese restaurant. After a lovely meal, we felt re-energised and ready to continue our trek to Brooklyn.

After leaving Chinatown, a man approached us and started to mumble some racist comments as we approached Brooklyn Bridge. Like most racists, he was severely lacking in intelligence and decency. He mistook Mum for a Vietnamese woman and he thought that my Chinese tattoos were written in Vietnamese.

He said to me: "Why have you got that [offensive phrase that is commonly used in America to describe Vietnamese people] [expletive used to describe excrement] written on your arms? Why are you with her?"

Mum encouraged me to just walk away, which was sound advice. After all, when you argue with a fool, bystanders may not be able to tell the difference between the two of you.

Perhaps it would be more fitting to take advice from Confucius, who said: "When you meet a man of worth, think how you may attain his excellence. When you meet an unworthy one, then look within and examine yourself."

In truth, I am no different to anyone else and I most likely subconsciously harbour various racial stereotypes. Perhaps if I had lived the life that this stranger in New York had, I would be more likely to hold such abhorrent views. Maybe he fought in the Vietnam war and is still scarred by the things that he witnessed. Or maybe he was just a random idiot.

Our experiences certainly contribute to racism. I remember working alongside an elderly lady in a British Red Cross shop. She seemed to have a kind nature but one day she turned to me and said: "The Japanese are terrible people."

Although I was shocked and disappointed by her comment, further contemplation made me realise that she had lived through the Second World War and her views would undoubtedly have been influenced by the war crimes of the Imperial Japanese regime. This does not excuse her racist sentiment but it does help explain how this came to be.

Thankfully, this was the only overtly racist incident that I have personally been confronted with during my travels around the world. I suspect that this is because I have a mixed racial background that many find difficult to distinguish. Therefore, I am not a particularly obvious target for racists. Some people can tell that I am half-Chinese, whilst many others just suspect that I have a mixed background of some sort.

In fact, there have been occasions in which Chinese people's actions have demonstrated the racial assumptions that I mentioned earlier. On a couple of visits to Chinese restaurants, the staff have taken away my chopsticks and replaced them with a knife and fork before I have started eating. If they had not done so, they would have seen that I am perfectly capable of eating with chopsticks, having used them all of my life.

\* \* \*

After an unexpected incident had led to more contemplation of the wisdom of Confucius than I had anticipated, we were finally ready to cross Brooklyn Bridge. The fact that the bridge itself has become a tourist attraction in its own right is testament to both the engineering triumph and the visual impact that it has had on the city since its opening in 1883. Most of us are accustomed to seeing the sweeping aerial shots of the steel-wired suspension bridge and the city that are so often featured in film and television.

It soon became apparent that we still had a considerable distance to walk before we reached our final destination on the other side. After all, the length of the bridge is just shy of sixteen hundred feet.

There were throngs of fellow tourists posing for pictures along the bridge and taking photographs of the cityscape on either side. With the U.S.A. flags proudly displayed on the stone towers, it felt like we were walking across a true American landmark.

Brooklyn Heights Promenade and the nearby park were effectively the finish line of our outbound journey. I had read that the view from this area was spectacular, and that one is able to simultaneously admire Manhattan, Brooklyn Bridge and the Statue of Liberty. The promenade was to our right but we were unable to see a direct route to it. Eventually, we realised that we had to carry on travelling away from the bridge before following the road that spirals down to the lower level, where we were able to join the promenade.

The view was certainly worth the day's exertions. The mid-afternoon sun made the East River glisten and provided a glow above the skyscrapers of Manhattan. We took numerous photographs of Brooklyn Bridge, Manhattan and the distant image of the Statue of Liberty.

We repeated this process whilst taking it in turns to pose for the camera before I took a few panoramic shots of all three landmarks. With the photographic evidence secured, it was time to do something that often slips my mind; we took our time and simply enjoyed the amazing view before our eyes.

It was during this time that I took a moment to really think about what we were looking at. Brooklyn Bridge may have been a tourist attraction for us but its creation benefitted the lives of many New Yorkers by providing a direct route between Brooklyn and Manhattan.

I could appreciate the scale of it all now that we could see the distance that separated the most populous borough of New York with the most densely populated. Feeling relieved to have temporarily escaped the concrete jungle of Manhattan, I suggested taking a stroll along the promenade whist having an ice cream. Taking time out to just enjoy the moment was a most pleasant change of pace.

A lovely afternoon was drawing to a close, which meant that it was time to begin our mammoth trek back to our hotel. In order to sample a different viewpoint, we decided to use Manhattan Bridge for our return journey across the river.

The sun was starting to come down as we approached Manhattan, which provided a nice backdrop to the city skyline. I noticed a baseball pitch near the main road at the edge of the Manhattan side of the river and I imagined locals congregating there for a game after work. Mind you, given how long it seems to take to play a game of what is often referred to as 'America's national religion,' it would probably be sensible to meet on a Sunday morning instead.

I resisted the temptation to deviate too much from the route back to the hotel by exploring the financial district but every so often I was tempted to take a photograph of the city. By the time that we reached our hotel, it was late enough that we decided that we may as well stay out for dinner before returning to our room. Somewhere relatively near Times Square, we gave up on the idea of finding a nice restaurant and settled for a quick meal at McDonald's. That is part of the appeal of the franchise, I guess.

As soon as we walked in, we witnessed the tail end of an argument that was taking place between a customer and a member of staff. The customer, who was a dishevelled man in a wheelchair, seemed to be ranting that the worker had stolen his shoe. The shoe in question was in his hand. He then proceeded to place this on the counter, before once again shouting, "You stole my shoe!"

The member of staff that had served him tried to remain calm, as he replied: "Sir, you just placed your shoe on the counter."

A resolution did not seem to be close, as the customer once again said, "You stole my shoe!"

We were in McDonald's in one of the busiest cities in the world at night time, so we should not have been surprised to have encountered such a bizarre and chaotic scene. If there had been any doubts about it before this moment, it definitely felt like we were in America now.

I am guessing that the customer eventually accepted that the member of staff had not stolen his shoe, given that he left with his meal and his footwear. I think that the staff were relieved that the most drama that Mum and I unleashed was our polite request for a couple of sachets of tomato ketchup. By my estimations, we then scoffed our meal in less time than the previous customer had spent arguing about his shoe.

As we had just spent the majority of the past thirteen hours walking around Manhattan and Brooklyn, we had earned the right to stuff our faces with junk food.

"Am I terrible for making you walk for thirteen hours?" I asked Mum.

Her reply was one that I had heard many times during my childhood: "God gave you legs, so you should use them."

Bearing in mind the scene that we had just witnessed with the man in the wheelchair, who was obviously struggling with various issues, I was not sure if her standard line of response was somehow more poignant or less appropriate.

Almost immediately after leaving McDonald's, we walked by a homeless man. He had a sign that stated that he was a veteran of the Vietnam War and that he was in need of money.

"Got any change?" he asked.

He did not give me the opportunity to reply, as just a second later he unleashed a torrent of expletive ridden abuse in my direction.

I was rather shocked by this and I instinctively hurried along. I turned back and watched him repeat this process with the next person. And the person after them. It was if he was shielding himself from the rejection that he was anticipating.

This self-defeating behaviour was most likely the result of mental health issues, possibly Post Traumatic Stress Disorder, so it was probably something that I should have shown more empathy towards. Like everyone else around me though, the shock of this strange verbal exchange caused me to quickly move away. After walking through Times Square again, we returned to our hotel for the night.

*　　*　　*

The following morning, it was time to take on the beast that had been towering above us for the duration of our trip. I am, of course, referring to the Empire State Building. Rather than scaling the outer surface of the building in the manner of the title character of the 1933 film *King Kong*, we opted for the boring alternative of taking the lift with our fellow tourists. The queues were as long as expected but there was a fairly well organised system in place, which meant that the time seemed to go reasonably quick and was not too unpleasant.

There were various information displays to examine during our wait for the lift. We read about how the 1,453 foot skyscraper took only two years to build. This seems mightily impressive when you consider how long similar projects have taken almost a century later.

To illustrate how the building techniques and regulations differed from what one would expect to be in place today, there were a number of displays featuring the famous images of workers balancing upon steel beams, without a harness, hundreds of feet up in the air as they carried out the required tasks.

We were soon on the observation deck, on the eighty sixth floor of what was the world's tallest building at the time of its opening in 1931. The long-held desire to achieve the status of the world's tallest building was at the forefront of the design. Indeed, the 'Race into the Sky' had gripped the city of New York in the years prior to the opening of this iconic building.

In order to surpass the 40 Wall Street Building and remain taller than the yet to be built Empire State Building, the Chrysler Building had added a 185 foot steel tip to its roof. This did not deter the owners of the Empire State Building though, as five extra floors and a spire were worked into the design.

Overcome by paranoia, those in charge then decided to add a two hundred foot crown shaped structure and an even taller antenna for good measure. This obsession to be the tallest was one of the main reasons that the building plans were changed a total of fifteen times. Just three decades later, the target was much higher up, as the 'Space Race' was at the forefront of the public's imagination throughout the 1960s; culminating in Neil Armstrong becoming the first person to walk on the moon in 1969.

As soon as we stepped out onto the observation deck, it felt completely different to when we had visited the equivalent section of the Rockefeller Center. We were now faced with a brilliant blue sky and a chilling wind. It felt more like what I had expected from a skyscraper. The buzzing city below felt alive, whereas it seemed calm and still whilst we were at the Top of the Rock on our first night.

The safety bars around the edge of the observation deck did not detract from the view too much, since I had seen them on so many people's photographs over the years. They almost served as a signpost that one was at the top of the Empire State Building.

The view was magnificent, allowing one to look over much of the city. The financial district and the glistening top section of the Empire State Building's old rival, the Chrysler Building, were clearly visible on this sunny day. We were provided with a different perspective of Brooklyn Bridge, which had been the focal point of our previous day's activities.

This was the quintessential image of a sprawling metropolis; at least it was in my mind. People had come from all over the world to take in this view and now we were jostling with them, trying to find the perfect angle for our photos.

After capturing a satisfactory amount of photographs, we took the lift down to street level. We had the option of paying extra to visit the second observation deck on the 102nd floor but there did not seem to be much point in standing in a smaller area that was even more tightly packed with tourists. Besides, we would only be taking in a view that would surely look almost identical to what we had just seen. I guess we were not embracing the spirit of the 'Race into the Sky.' Or King Kong.

"What did you think of the building?" I asked.

"Just a tall building really. We have many in Hong Kong," Mum replied.

In some ways she was right, as this type of skyscraper was obviously built with the primary objective of becoming the tallest. In its defence, the Art-Deco design was more appealing than most.

Next up on our itinerary was the site of what was once the World Trade Center. The Twin Towers had succeeded the Empire State Building as the world's tallest in the early 1970s but a tragic event thirty years later would see the building that we had just visited return to its status as the tallest in New York City.

The towers were, of course, destroyed in the terrorist attack of September the eleventh, 2001. Our long walk to Ground Zero, which largely resembled the route that we had followed the previous day, was filled with a feeling of uneasiness rather than the usual excitement when making our way towards a tourist attraction.

It was an eerie feeling when we reached the site of where the towers once stood. There was effectively a huge crater where construction work was taking place. Nearly ten years after the terrible events of that day, the scene in front of us demonstrated the lasting impact made on the city. It took eight months to clear the debris and it was not until 2005 that the process of identifying human remains at the site concluded.

There were 1,629 victims that were identified but 2,753 death certificates were filed. It would be another three years after our visit that One World Trade Center, the centrepiece of the new complex, was completed.

We entered the Tribute WTC Visitor Center, where we booked a place on the next tour of the site. This non-profit operation involved survivors of 9/11, who felt it was important to ensure that people do not forget about the events that transpired or the lives that were lost. Our guide, whose name escapes me, was a rescue volunteer who had risked her life by attempting to locate people amongst the rubble.

She began the tour by laying down some ground rules. We were not allowed to record any videos of her relaying information to the group and we were told not to wander off and start taking photos. She paused before lambasting somebody who was stood by and may or may not have been listening in. It was clear that she was a proud woman who was, understandably, passionate about the tour that she was giving.

As we walked through the site, she began by providing her personal account of that day and how it has deeply affected her life: "I was not part of the fire service that showed incredible bravery by running into the burning building. God bless them all. I entered the site long after the towers had collapsed but I remember the hairs on the back of my neck standing up."

She went on to recall how the area was still unstable during their search and how the day's events would damage her both physically and mentally.

She developed respiratory problems in the months and years that followed and she was still suffering from them as she gave her talk: "I can still taste the dust. It will never leave me."

The efforts of those that risked their own safety was not in vain; it was reported that twenty people were pulled out of the rubble alive. Over four hundred members of the emergency services were killed.

Our guide then introduced a man, whose name I am once again unable to recall, that survived both 9/11 and the previous terrorist attack on the World Trade Center that took place on the twenty sixth of February, 1993.

He described how he thought that the first attack was a fire of little note until he got word of an evacuation of the towers that he worked in. It was only later on that he discovered that the damage was caused by the detonation of a truck full of explosives in the underground car park of the North Tower.

Our tour guide stepped in at this point and offered a frank assessment: "We got lucky that time. If they had planned it better, they would have parked the truck next to one of the building's support pillars, which may have caused the tower to become unstable and eventually collapse."

The male survivor then recounted the horror of the second attack: "There was no doubt in my mind about the second attack. Both 40 Wall Street and the Empire State Building had been accidentally struck by small army planes in the 1940s but I knew that this was different. Although we did not know for sure what had happened, I just felt that we had to get out of there straight away. Thankfully, I was able to make it out. Many people that worked in the same building as me were not so fortunate."

I cannot even imagine what it was like trying to escape one of the world's tallest buildings in the midst of a terrorist attack.

Our guide once again analysed the details of the murderous plan: "Those evil men were smart though. They chose flights that were scheduled to travel right across the country from nearby Boston to Los

Angeles. This meant that the planes were full of fuel when they crashed into the towers, which caused big explosions and meant that the fuel travelled down the buildings, spreading the fire."

The tour was informative, as well as highly emotional. I was unaware that, in addition to the Twin Towers, there were another five buildings that formed the World Trade Center complex. Two of the other buildings collapsed on the day of the attack, whilst the remaining three were extensively damaged and were eventually demolished.

Many nearby buildings also suffered damage and were discontinued but our guide struck a more hopeful tone as she told us about how a small church across the road emerged unscathed: "The little chapel that stood. That's what people call St. Paul's Chapel after it somehow survived that day."

Our tour concluded with a summary of why our guide felt it was important to keep giving the tours: "We lost friends and colleagues that day. We must keep their memory alive and show them that we have not been defeated. We got Bin Laden a couple of days ago. United States Navy SEALs. God bless them."

We returned to the visitor centre, where it was very sobering to look at exhibits that had been recovered from the debris and photographs of people in tears as they paid their respects in the days after the attack. The sheer number of tributes that had been documented was overwhelming.

One of the most poignant exhibits was from a seemingly unrelated event that had taken place on the other side of the planet, over half a century earlier. There was a tiny red paper crane in a glass box, along with a picture of a young Japanese girl called Sadako Sasaki. I had not heard of her story before but it was extremely sad.

She was two years old when the Americans dropped an atomic bomb on Hiroshima in 1945. It initially appeared that she had emerged unscathed but she later became one of the many people that developed leukemia as a result of the radiation. She set herself the goal of folding a thousand origami cranes, as it was believed that this would grant her wish of returning to full health.

The popularised version of the story states that she fell short of her goal before her death in 1955 and that her friends completed the target on her behalf as a tribute to her. Her brother later confirmed that she had actually exceeded her target and that he had hoped that displaying her paper cranes in museums around the world would help to keep her message alive.

There were an additional ten thousand paper cranes on display that had been sent in from families of Japanese victims of 9/11.

A quote from Sadako accompanied the exhibit: "Please treasure the life that has been given to you. It is my belief that my small paper crane will enable you to understand other people's feelings, as if they are your own."

It is estimated that up to 129,226 people were killed as a result of the atomic bombs that were detonated over Hiroshima and Nagasaki but it is hard to ascertain a true figure, due to the scores of people that died as a result of illness in the decades that followed. Sadako and her cranes have become synonymous with the devastating effects of nuclear warfare and are seen as a symbol for peace.

We headed to nearby Battery Park to locate a symbol of hope that our guide had mentioned during the tour. A large globe-shaped metal sculpture had stood in the plaza of the World Trade Center for over thirty years prior to 9/11.

Remarkably, it emerged from the colossal amount of debris with very little damage. It had been moved to the park the following year and on the first anniversary, an eternal flame was lit in memory of those that lost their lives as a result of the events of that day. The past couple of hours had been a sombre reminder of the terrible atrocities that human beings inflict on one another.

\*   \*   \*

It was time to take a ferry ride away from Manhattan. Rather than visiting the Statue of Liberty and Ellis Island, we took Mandy's advice and made use of the free service to Staten Island. The twenty minute ferry journey passed the statue, which allowed us to see the attraction without having to negotiate the long queues of tourists.

Besides, we had seen it up close on our previous trip to New York State in the 1990s. The winds were getting stronger, which resulted in us putting our hoods up like a couple of teenage tearaways, which we were most certainly not. This may have meant that we looked a little strange in our photographs but we were glad for a little protection from the elements.

The Statue of Liberty looked much smaller than I had remembered. I suspect that this was due to how far away it was rather than it having shrunk in the last couple of decades. Although we were travelling away from the mainland, I imagined how it would have felt for the wave of immigrants that caught their first glimpse of the famed monument on their way to starting a new life in America during the end of the nineteenth and the start of the twentieth century.

Ellis Island was home to the largest immigration centre in the country and it was where most of the people arriving from Europe and Asia first touched down on American soil.

Mum then vocalised her thoughts: "When I first arrived in England, people used to ask me if I made the journey by boat. The immigrants who came here actually did."

The United States is a country built on immigration, with much of today's population being able to trace their family's history in America back to the arrival of one of their ancestors at Ellis Island. Many others can look back even further to colonial time, with the Dutch, Spanish and English attempting to lay claim to American land.

For others, the slave trade brought their ancestors over to the United States. Indeed, only around one percent of the population are Native Americans. Mind you, they would probably be mistaken as foreigners by many anti-immigration campaigners, who ironically are themselves descendants of immigrants.

Mandy had advised that a lot of people who take the ferry to Staten Island will run from the exit of the vessel to the area where people embark and end up boarding the same boat back to Manhattan. Whilst this seemed a bit extreme, we did not venture out of the terminal before taking the next service that we were able to board in half an hour's time.

This seemed to amuse Mum: "We get a ferry to another island, then immediately get a ferry back to where we came from."

I guess we were just a couple of cheapskates making use of a free service.

Upon our return to Manhattan, we wandered through the financial district. Although the area did not particularly appeal to Mum and me, it was undeniable that Wall Street and the Stock Exchange are synonymous with modern America. We were at the epicentre of capitalism and greed.

I looked around and thought about how decisions will have been made in these buildings that will have had an impact around the world. The popularity of some commercial products had probably soared due to discussions that had taken place in those very buildings.

One of the key events of the global financial crisis originated from here. Lehman Brothers, one of the biggest investment banks in the United States of America, found itself in financial trouble after the mortgage sector that it was heavily involved with went into a severe decline. The firm, which held over six billion dollars of assets, issued the biggest bankruptcy filing in the history of the United States. Various other financial institutions followed, as the depth of the crisis became apparent throughout the world.

We made our way back to the hotel, where we took the opportunity to have some rest after a couple of very busy days that involved lots of walking. We may have been in the 'city that never sleeps,' but we were in desperate need of some shut-eye. After a power nap, we ventured out for some food and had another look at the Empire State Building, which was being lit up in a variety of alternating colours.

*　　*　　*

The following day was our last in the 'Big Apple.' As we were due to fly back to Toronto in the early evening, we were determined to make the most of our final few hours in the city. Central Park, which as I mentioned earlier, has provided the setting for more movie scenes than any other location, was the most obvious landmark that we had not yet seen. Therefore, the day would revolve around visiting the park and any other places of interest that were nearby.

We began our journey along the iconic Fifth Avenue, famed for its fashionable shops and swanky hotels, occasionally stopping to admire some of the landmarks that are dotted along the street. We did not have the time nor the inclination to stop off at Saks, given that we had already visited Macy's during our stay in New York. After all, we were aware of the size of Central Park, so we did not want to take up all of our time inside of another department store.

The spires of St. Patrick's Cathedral looked particularly striking against the bright blue sky. The Neo-Gothic Roman Catholic church is, unsurprisingly, a focal point of the St. Patrick's Day Parade held every year in the city. The significant proportion of Americans with Irish heritage, which is just shy of thirty five million, ensures that the annual celebrations attract large crowds of revellers. Indeed, the number of New Yorkers with Irish heritage is around seven times larger than the population of Ireland itself.

German is the only ancestry with more significant numbers in the United States. Our route then saw us walk by a building belonging to an individual of German descent. Trump Tower is the headquarters of Donald Trump's business empire. At the time of our visit he was merely a real estate tycoon and reality TV star but he would later become, in a sad indicator of the state of the world, the forty fifth President of the United States of America.

We did not stop to examine the building, instead opting to continue with our walk towards Central Park. Perhaps we somehow had a feeling that he would one day become a divisive, racist, misogynistic president. Or perhaps we just did not think that the skyscraper was particularly impressive enough to take up any of our limited time.

Just before we reached Central Park, we stumbled upon a familiar sight, albeit in an unfamiliar format. Located in front of the Plaza Hotel, there was a group of bronze statues that depicted the heads of the twelve animals that represent the Chinese zodiac symbols.

We did not know why the statues were in the middle of New York but we could not resist taking photographs next to our correlating zodiac animals. I posed in front of the rat's head, which provides a clue as to what my age is, at least in terms of twelve year intervals. As I am a gentleman, I will not reveal which animal Mum posed with.

It turns out that the statues were a temporary exhibition called *Circle of Animals: Zodiac Heads* by the Chinese artist and activist, Ai Weiwei. He had been detained by the Chinese authorities for rather vaguely worded "economic crimes," prior to the opening of the exhibition, where he would remain for eighty one days.

Despite contributing to the design of the 'The Bird's Nest' national stadium that was the centrepiece of the 2008 Olympics, he had fallen foul of the Chinese government for repeatedly speaking out against the country's alleged human rights offences. Previous incidents had seen him placed under house arrest and allegedly beaten by the police. Since our visit, the exhibition has been showcased in a number of cities across the world, including London and Paris.

We reached Central Park a little later than we had anticipated, which meant that we already had one eye on the time. Our flight was not until the evening but we did not want to find ourselves rushing back to New Jersey and worrying about missing our flight.

For this reason, we did not seek out any of the famous landmarks within the grounds, such as the Tavern on the Green or the Strawberry Fields memorial to John Lennon. Instead, we were happy to make our way through the huge park almost as quickly as Kevin McCallister did whilst fleeing the 'Sticky Bandits.' We did not need saving by the pigeon lady though.

The park was pretty much what we had expected; it is a vast area of parkland right in the heart of Manhattan. We did not walk the entire four kilometre length of the park but we travelled far enough to get a feel for the place that provides New Yorkers with sanctuary from the chaos of the city. We did not have time to visit some of the famous buildings that surround the park but we managed to have a brief look at their exterior.

We would have to console ourselves by watching scenes from various films that were set in the Guggenheim. Unfortunately, *Night at the Museum* was not filmed on location, so we could not even rely on the film industry for this.

Visiting the neighbourhoods at the top of the park, such as Harlem, was out of the question, given our time constraints. We decided to get some food on our way back to the hotel but we were unable to find a restaurant that appealed to both of us. Perhaps it was the anxiety about our upcoming journey that prompted Mum to declare that every food establishment that we encountered during our three or four kilometre route seemed too spicy, too heavy or generally not to her liking.

Just before checking out of our hotel, we stopped by Madison Square Garden, which was located across the street. Opened in 1968, it was one of the first multi-purpose arenas to be built above an active railway station. The historic venue has played host to countless basketball, ice hockey, boxing and music events.

"It is not square," was Mum's initial observation.

She was indeed correct, as 'The Garden' has an almost circular shape.

"Its name is not due to the shape of the building. It is based on a location. Madison Square," I explained.

Mum examined her surroundings before offering further assessment: "But we are not on Madison Square and I can't see it nearby."

Again, she was correct.

I tried to shed some light on the matter: "The original building was located by Madison Square Park, which is around half a mile away. It is where the giant sculpture of the girl's head is. Do you remember?"

Mum seemed amused: "So, let me get this right. There is a big sculpture of a girl's head at Madison Square...whilst Madison Square Garden is located here...which is a fair distance away from Madison Square?"

I then complicated matters further by saying: "Yes. Also, the arena is situated above Pennsylvania Station, which, of course, is in New York rather than Pennsylvania."

Mum was chuckling to herself as she replied: "I find this all very strange!"

We checked out of our hotel and took the train to New Jersey for our flight back to Toronto. Newark Liberty International Airport is one of the grimmest I have encountered. It is a place in which the staff seem to look at each passenger with contempt.

John's son, Derrick, had warned us about the frosty reception that we would receive: "Do not even try to make a joke or be friendly with them. They will arrest you!"

I had a snow globe that I had purchased at the Empire State Building seized from my hand luggage and their reaction made me feel like I had committed a serious criminal offence. Whilst I approve of the thorough approach to airport security, I am not sure that they have to be quite so unpleasant.

After making it through security without being detained, I was served an atrocious meal in Newark. I had made the mistake of thinking that a cheeseburger and fries would be a simple order to process. However, the understaffed fast food restaurant struggled to cope with the huge line of customers; all three of us.

The guy in front of me was furious with the amount of time that he was being made to wait, so he slammed his drink down in protest. The lid wasn't secured properly; therefore, the liquid content splashed everywhere. As you can imagine, this did not help to subdue his rage. A loud and aggressive rant soon followed.

The lady working behind the counter did not seem bothered and simply informed him that he would have to wait. The sole gentleman in charge of cooking the food casually flipped a couple of burgers. As the raw beef was lifted off the grill, the customer stormed off without his food. Any sane person would have taken this cue to follow suit. However, my socially awkward self did not know how to handle this situation. Therefore, I hesitated.

I was now at the front of the queue.

"What would you like to order?" the employee behind the counter asked.

The obvious disinterest and lack of customer service skills provided me with another excuse to leave. There was still time to walk away without placing an order.

"Cheeseburger and fries, please," was my meek response.

Once I unwrapped my burger from its packaging, I saw that I had either been given the severely undercooked one that was meant for the angry customer before me or an entirely new pink burger. As usual, I took the well-trodden path of least resistance by paying for my meal and sitting down at our table.

I stared at it for a while, until enough time had passed that would allow me to throw away my meal without causing a scene. I ended up buying more food from the Italian outlet that mum had chosen for her meal. This time, the food was edible.

We did not want to spend much longer in this dreadful airport but, of course, our flight was delayed by a couple of hours.

A fellow passenger summed up our collective frustration at being condemned to an extended stay in purgatory: "A two hour delay for an hour and a half flight."

Although the countless skyscrapers of New York do not particularly appeal to me, I could not help but feel warmth towards the city. It feels like the quintessential example of a metropolis. Perhaps this is due to the bombardment of footage of 'The Big Apple' that we have all been subjected to since childhood. This results in a feeling of nostalgia despite one having never visited the city before.

Eventually, we landed back in Toronto, where we crept into Auntie Becky's apartment and tried to avoid waking her. Fortunately, I can be quite light-footed when required, which has come from years of practice of trying to make my way past a neighbour without them stopping me for a chat. We accomplished our mission and got some much needed sleep before our long journey back to Manchester the next day.

# CHAPTER 11: THE HORROR OF A HOSTEL
## AND A PASSPORT FIASCO
### BARCELONA, SPAIN
### AUGUST 2011

We had not even made it to Barcelona before I realised that I had made a catastrophic mistake. I had used Expedia to book a package that included flights and a hotel but I had not sufficiently examined the details. It was only on the day before we were due to fly out to Spain, that I belatedly checked the location of our accommodation.

The hotel was listed as being situated in 'Tarragona, Barcelona' and I had naïvely assumed that this was in a neighbourhood of the city. In my defence, there is both a street and a metro station called Tarragona within the centre of Barcelona. On further inspection, it became apparent that the hotel was in the port city of Tarragona, which is over one hundred kilometres away from Barcelona.

I was now faced with the choice of either undertaking the one hour train to and from Barcelona each day or finding some alternative accommodation. Given that everything that I wanted to see was in Barcelona rather than Tarragona, I plumped for the latter.

The Tarragona hotel was non-refundable so this resulted in the farcical situation of paying for two lots of accommodation but only staying in one. A quick search online found that the only reasonably priced establishment at such short notice was a hostel. I had never previously considered staying in one before but I had little choice now.

This was the first trip that I had arranged with my friend Paul, and I already had to let him know that we were downgrading from the comfort of a hotel to the unknown quantity of a hostel.

"So we are going to stay in a hostel because you booked a hotel over a hundred kilometres away? And we're going to pay for both? Excellent!"

At least his text message indicated that he saw the funny side to it. This was quickly followed by another SMS: "Remember the film *Hostel*? Is that what awaits us?"

There was a certain level of concern that was intertwined with Paul's humorous comments. I was starting to feel rather apprehensive about it too. We were former Grammar school pupils who had grown up in comfortable surroundings but now we would have to stay in a hostel with a communal bathroom. I had only faced such horrors on the occasions that the Metrolink network was down and I had to use a replacement bus service instead.

*   *   *

We encountered an almost empty airport on arrival in Barcelona. This was not what I had expected to see in one of the most popular tourist destinations in Europe, so I began to worry that we had somehow ended up in the wrong city. Tarragona, perhaps. Even the tourist information stand had been abandoned.

A friend of a friend had suggested purchasing a five day travel card that would cover all of our journeys within the city centre during our stay. We followed this advice and boarded the bus that would take us towards the city centre. Our passes did not cover the express bus service but we were not in a hurry. It did, however, mean that we had to change our mode of transport to the underground metro once we had reached the last stop, Paral-lel. After that, it did not take long to reach our final destination of Diagonal, which was the closest stop to our hostel.

It was time to locate the place where we would be spending the next four nights. The tension was palpable. I felt an extra level of pressure, since it was my mistake that had led us to this point. We made our way to where the hostel was marked as being present on the map but we could not see any sign of ¿Qué Tal?

We carried on a bit further before we were approached by a middle aged local man. He began speaking in Spanish but we did not understand him.

He must have noticed our blank expressions because he then asked, "English?"

We nodded sheepishly.

"Ah, very good," he continued.

Paul gave me a nervous look before whispering, "*Hostel*."

He was only saying what I was thinking. Did the tone of excitement in the man's voice indicate that English people were regarded as premium stock for their sadistic murderous games?

"Where you need to go?" asked the man.

Paralysed by fear, I was unable to respond. Eventually, I pulled myself together and pointed to the section of the map on which I had highlighted our hostel. Perhaps it was for the best that I had not asked him verbally, as '¿Qué Tal?' roughly translates to 'How are you?' in English.

"Follow me," urged the Spanish stranger.

Paul and I looked at each other again, both with an expression that said: 'Here we go, this is the end. It was nice knowing you, mate.' He ushered us through an unmarked door, as we collectively took a deep breath.

It appeared that the man was just being helpful, as there was another man stood behind a reception desk that was waiting to greet us. Then again, everything looked as normal as this in the film that we had been referring to all day.

I cleared my throat, before asking: "Hi, can we check in, please?"

The hostel employee politely responded by saying: "Yes, of course Sir. I will just need your passports."

We turned around and thanked the man from the street, who was now leaving the premises. We were still not sure if we were thanking him for helping us find our accommodation or for luring us to a gruesome death. We were also uncertain as to whether we had handed our passports to a member of a criminal network that was currently arranging which client was going to torture and murder us.

He photocopied our documents before returning them to us and saying: "I will show you to your room."

As well as the prospect of being greeted by a psychopath with a chainsaw, we were also gripped by the fear of what condition our room would be in. Would there be hundreds of cockroaches, stained sheets and a leaking roof? As the hostel employee slowly turned the door handle, we prepared ourselves for something horrific. Fortunately, the room seemed to be just about acceptable and superficially clean enough that it did not induce a panic attack for either of us.

The receptionist left after he had informed us that we could ask for any assistance if it was required throughout the night.

I then alerted Paul to something rather disturbing: "If we open the wooden shutters behind you, we could see the reception area and the guy that we were just speaking to."

Paul quickly responded by saying, "Or vice versa."

We tried to put the thought of a stranger peering into our room to the back of our minds by having a look at the rest of our surroundings.

I switched on the huge fan that was secured to the ceiling and offered my initial assessment: "It does not look as nice as it appears in the pictures online."

Paul was more blunt with his verdict, as he simply stated that it was "awful." I tried to offer some positivity by mentioning how good the reviews were but this did not seem to help.

We looked out of the window and saw a stack of restaurant tables and chairs below.

"Perfect for anybody who wants to climb through our window," Paul mused.

I tried to be positive once more but it was becoming more difficult: "I don't think that anybody has any intention of breaking into this place. Maybe the tables and chairs are there for us to escape."

We unpacked our cases before noticing something strange; the fan felt like it was getting hotter. It was a simple propeller based contraption rather than an air conditioning unit, so the air being circulated should definitely have been cool. Upon closer inspection, I concluded that it was actually the power supply that was getting hot.

"A fan that feels like it is getting hotter the longer that it is in use and possibly puts our life in danger!" was my cheerful summary.

This reminded me of how scented tissues irritate my nose, causing me to sneeze. This results in a ridiculous situation in which the more I seek to alleviate the problem by blowing my nose in a tissue, the worse it gets.

We had not had anything to eat since lunchtime, therefore we decided to have a quick wander through the surrounding area and try to find somewhere to have a late night supper. We walked along Diagonal until we reached Passeig de Gràcia. I had read that this was one of the most famous streets in Barcelona and that two of Gaudí's most renowned creations can be found here.

"Do you mind if we have a quick look at some Gaudí buildings?" I asked Paul.

"Yeah, whatever. What are they?" he replied.

"They are a couple of extravagant buildings that people visit in order to admire the architecture," was my rather clumsy explanation.

It was not long before we were standing in front of Casa Milà. This apartment building was designed by Antoni Gaudí at the start of the twentieth century. He had already established a formidable reputation by this time, so it was no surprise that the building's owners, Pere Milà and his wife, Roser Segimón, turned to Gaudí.

Incidentally, Segimón was the widow of Josep Guardiola. I am referring to the colonist who made his wealth in South and Central America rather than the footballer who gained legendary status as a player and manager of F.C. Barcelona.

As is often the case, the building received a more critical response at the time of opening than it does today. It was nicknamed 'La Pedrera,' or 'The Stone Quarry,' due to its rugged shape. Over time, the unusual architecture, lack of straight lines and the eye-catching facade were celebrated by locals and tourists alike. The nickname persists but it is now used as a term of endearment.

"Not as nice as the apartment blocks in Wythenshawe," was Paul's assessment.

I assumed that he was kidding, which is usually a safe bet since it is difficult to recall many occasions in which he has been serious. We walked further along Passeig de Gràcia until we reached the next Gaudí building. Casa Batlló seemed prettier to me. Again, there are not many straight lines to be found in the design of this building but the facade is even more dazzling than Casa Milà.

The exterior of the building is covered by a colourful mosaic of broken ceramic tiles. The irregular shaped windows and balconies seemed to contradict the rules of architecture but the end result was spectacular. Nicknamed 'Casa dels Ossos,' or 'House of Bones,' it was unlike anything that I had ever laid my eyes upon.

"Seen better," was Paul's predictable verdict.

Equally foreseeable were our culinary choices during our stay in the city. Would we try any of the abundance of local Catalan or Spanish dishes? Of course not. We were a couple of uncultured and unworldly young British men who were wandering around in a foreign country. As expected, the Golden Arches of the McDonald's logo seemed to draw us in like lost sheep being herded into a capitalist pen.

The fact that we did not speak any Spanish probably made our decision easier, since the language of McDonald's seems to be universal. Although I mention Spanish, Catalan is the other co-official language of the region. Catalan culture, as well as the language, is important within Barcelona, with the issue of independence a hot topic of debate throughout the region. None of this crossed our minds though. Since it was quite late at night, we were just glad to finally sit down to eat.

As we devoured our burgers and fries, we were approached by a unkempt woman who was holding a piece of paper that was detailing her request for money. She placed this on our table and began speaking to us in Spanish. As Paul's wallet was within touching distance of the paper, he quickly grabbed it and placed it in his pocket. I had not seen Paul move so quickly since we had practically ran to avoid a former classmate in the local Tesco store.

She may well have been genuinely asking for money but it is possible that she was going to try and pinch his wallet. It seems a shame to assume the worst but it was probably sensible to be cautious, given that the theft of one half of our money supply on the first night was a risk not worth taking.

It was still very warm outside as we made our way back to our hostel. We were in need of showers to cool down but this meant that we would have to face our biggest challenge of the trip so far. Somehow, we would have to find the courage to face the terrifying prospect of using a communal shower. Neither of us were keen to go first, so there was a stand-off before I caved in. Fortunately, our room was one of the closet to the bathroom, so I did not have to travel too far.

This was a welcome relief considering the fact that I only had a towel to cover my modesty. Thankfully, my mind did not have enough time to generate a detailed nightmare scenario during my ten yard journey to the communal bathroom. If I had been required to travel any further, then I am sure that it could have conjured up images of being left stranded in the middle of the hostel with only a towel preventing myself from being completely exposed to all of the guests.

As I opened the door, I braced myself for the worst. Whilst it was not exactly sparklingly clean, it appeared to be just about acceptable. I felt relieved that I was able to lock the door behind me. I checked that I had indeed locked the door. I checked again. It was now safe enough to enter the shower. After the showering process was complete, I felt pleased with myself that I had managed to conquer this insurmountable task. The absence of a towel to stand on whilst I dried myself was a minor inconvenience. At least there was a hand towel.

I safely negotiated my passage back to our room and I informed Paul that it was his turn to face the music. I resisted the temptation to give a hellish description of the bathroom, given that this may have resulted in him abandoning the mission altogether.

A few minutes later, he returned with his verdict: "It was awful but better than I expected, I suppose."

We debated whether to turn on the heat-producing fan before agreeing that we should switch it on but only for a brief amount of time. There were two single beds in the room, which we pushed as far apart as the laws of physics would allow. Before switching off the lights, I informed Paul that we would have to get up at eight o'clock in the morning, as I had pencilled in a stadium tour of Camp Nou, in addition to some sightseeing around the city.

He seemed sceptical, so I reaffirmed my position: "I mean it. We are up at eight."

*     *     *

I woke up the following day to the sound of Paul's laughter.

"I thought we were getting up at eight?!" he cackled.

I felt so tired that I was barely able to respond.

"What time is it?" I asked.

This resulted in more laughter from Paul.

"It's twelve noon. I thought that we were getting up at eight! I've not been able to wake you for the last hour or so!"

It took me a few minutes to collect my thoughts and come to the realisation that we had wasted our first morning in Barcelona. Worse than that, it was time to face the communal bathroom again. To my horror, I saw that the hand towel that I had used the previous night was now doubling up as a bathroom floor towel. An even worse possibility was that this had always belonged on the floor and that it had been put on the hand rail in error. My hands suddenly felt less clean.

Despite our late start, we decided to press ahead with the stadium tour. We had discussed visiting Camp Nou for the previous couple of years; hence, the stadium tour and Monday night's match formed the central component of our trip. We were so thirsty that I bought a two litre bottle of Coca-Cola and Paul purchased the biggest bottle of orange juice that he could find.

We boarded the metro, which was not as busy as we had feared. Perhaps we had subconsciously been aware of the perils of using public transport during the rush hour, so our brains had cleverly shut down until it was a more appropriate hour to wake up and begin our day's activities. Or perhaps we were just lazy swines.

We disembarked at Maria Cristina station, which is only a short walk from Camp Nou. Although it was not a match day, I felt excited as we approached the iconic stadium. The concrete exterior looked rather dull and dated compared to some of the newer grounds across Europe but the sheer size of it was striking.

We made our way over to one of the ticket kiosks and asked how long it was until the next tour was scheduled to commence.

We were told: "You can go now. There is no guide. You are free to walk through the stadium at your leisure."

We handed over the required amount of Euros and entered the stadium that we had seen so many times on television. We began in the museum, which houses the plethora of trophies that the club has won since its inception in 1899. The Champions League trophies, La Liga titles and Copa del Rey silverware was proudly displayed alongside memorabilia relating to legendary players from the club's past and present.

Given that Paul and I spend much of our time talking about footballers from the 1990s, we were eager to alert each other every time that one of us spotted some playing kit that had been worn by the likes of Stoichkov, Koeman or Romario. Modern day greats like Messi, Xavi and Iniesta were also honoured in this way.

The museum was interesting but the stadium itself was what we had come to see. Our first view of the pitch and the 99,354 spectator seats was breathtaking. The uncovered stands seemed to reach into the sky, underlining the fact that it is has the largest capacity of any football stadium in Europe.

As a side note, the stadium with the largest capacity in the world can, rather surprisingly, be found in Pyongyang, North Korea. Although I am tempted to suggest that it is difficult to be sure of the accuracy of the official capacity of 114,000 due to the country's rather dubious relationship with the truth, it has apparently been independently verified.

Paul focused on the lack of protection from the elements: "If it rains we will get soaked!"

He was right but the weather was so hot that it was probably the sun that we should have been concerned about. Thankfully, Monday's match was due to kick off late in the evening, so the risk of being sunburnt was pretty low.

We were able to take in the view from another couple of vantage points, including from pitchside. Being able to stand next to the turf where so many historic matches had taken place was thrilling. A rope and a polite sign asking people to keep off the grass was enough to discourage us from running onto the famous turf but I am sure that there are often more daring visitors that quickly step onto the pitch. We joined the rest of the tourists by having our photo taken in the dugout.

"Back on the subs bench. Story of our lives," Paul joked.

In truth, this comment applied to myself more than Paul. After all, he was a former professional footballer who had previously been signed by Sheffield Wednesday, Rochdale and Bury.

We also got to walk down the tunnel where the players emerge from before every match. It must be an overwhelming feeling to walk onto the pitch in front of nearly one hundred thousand adoring fans. Interestingly, there is a small chapel by the tunnel that players are free to visit and say their prayers before or after matches. We did not get to see this but we took up the opportunity to have a look at the away team's dressing room and the press box.

Best of all, we were able to have our picture taken whilst holding the Champions League trophy that the club had just won for the fourth time. I had visions of dropping the trophy but we somehow managed to avoid succumbing to this fate. We would, of course, be charged a small fortune for this picture and we would have to walk through the huge merchandise store in order to exit the tour.

Paul took this opportunity to poke fun at the club: "Corporate money obsessed thieves. It's not on," he said as he clutched his copy of the photo that we had just paid for.

We met up with one of Paul's old university friends, who was now living in Barcelona. Gab and his girlfriend had kindly offered to cook us dinner back at their apartment. I always find this type of situation awkward. Gab was Paul's friend rather than mine, which meant that I would often find myself in the role of observer whilst they conversed. They spent hours reminiscing about their time studying international business in Manchester and talking about their old classmates. They were not being rude, it is just an inevitability of such a scenario.

After detailing how he had been approaching international companies about career opportunities and discussing how they had been to interviews where rival candidates had flown in from America, Gab turned his attention towards me.

"So what companies have you been looking at?" he asked.

We were obviously operating in different circles, as I had been plodding along in casual retail work and I had only recently started in a rather mundane office job.

"Chappers has been looking at Tesco and Asda. Stacking shelves!" Paul quipped.

In order to avoid further embarrassment, I was more than happy to return to my role of observer. Paul and I would laugh about that moment for years to come though.

Not content with the splendid hospitality he had shown, Gab treated us to a quick tour around the Gothic quarter. The narrow streets and charming buildings were full of character. The cathedral was impressive and appeared to be a focal point for local people to congregate. We thanked Gab for the generosity that he had shown and began our metro journey back to our hostel.

"What companies are you looking at?" Paul asked, as he laughed uncontrollably.

*   *   *

We managed to get out of bed at a more respectable time the following morning. It was a good job really, seeing as I had put together an ambitious itinerary for the day ahead. We would visit Parc Guell, Montjuïc and the beach at Barcelonetta. Paul was thrilled about the latter but he was slightly apprehensive about our other scheduled stops.

Both Parc Guell and Montjuic were vast areas that were likely to be heaving with tourists. They were also quite far away from each other, which meant that this would involve a few uncomfortable trips on the metro.

I made a suggestion: "The beach can be your reward for all of the sightseeing."

I am not sure whether this appeased Paul but we made our way to Diagonal metro station in any case.

According to the map that I had, Parc Guell was a few minutes' walk from Lesseps metro station. With another two litre bottle of Coca-Cola in my hand, we began our trek to the celebrated park. I spent a few minutes looking at the map and calculating the precise route that would take us there but this was a pointless exercise because virtually everybody that arrived at the station was heading to the same place.

Paul was already cursing the gruelling schedule: "A long uphill walk in this heat. And then another trek up Montjuïc. Perfect."

To be fair, it was really hot.

"Just think of the beach," I suggested.

Parc Guell is one of Gaudi's most revered creations. Having been impressed by some of the buildings that he had designed, I was looking forward to having a look around a large open space that he had been given creative licence to mould into his desired image. We headed straight for the most photographed spot in the park; a view of the two picturesque pavilions at the main entrance lay behind the serpentine bench that was covered by colourful ceramic tiles.

We sat down on the bench and patiently waited for a brief window in which we could take our photographs without having dozens of fellow tourists in shot. As well as being aesthetically pleasing, this was surprisingly comfortable. Apparently, Gaudí asked a workman to drop his trousers and sit on the prospective bench to ensure that he could create a mould that ergonomically fitted the shape of one's posterior. Whether this story is true or not, the comfort of the bench made our wait more pleasant than expected.

The pavilions reminded me of the house that Hansel and Gretel encountered in the well-known Brothers Grimm fairytale; except that these buildings were covered in ceramic tiles rather than cake and confectionery. We were relieved to walk around the less crowded areas of the park and have a look at the unusual vibrant design.

We saw the beautiful staircase with its iconic salamander that was again covered in a multitude of colourful ceramic tiles. This is an example of the inclusion of many artistic features in Gaudí's work that pay tribute to the natural world. The lack of straight lines that are present in the park, which we had also noticed at Casa Milà and Casa Batlló, are said to be down to his belief that straight lines are rarely present in the natural world, so they should not feature in his architecture either.

We also saw the impressive porticoes with their sloping supporting columns, as well as more ceramic tiles and animal designs that had been incorporated into the design of the park.

"Not bad. It was a bit better than Wythenshawe Park."

It sounded like Paul was warming to the sightseeing. "Let's get this Montjuïc out of the way so we can head to the beach."

Perhaps he was not.

We made our way past the souvenir sellers outside the park gates and resisted the temptation to purchase a mini ceramic salamander that had been made in China. Another metro journey took us to Plaça d'Espanya, where we were able to walk past the huge Venetian Towers that stand on either side of the avenue leading to the exhibition district and the many sites of Montjuïc. The imposing National Art Museum of Catalonia stands at the end of the avenue. I could have tortured Paul by insisting that we spend a few hours looking at the artwork but I took mercy on his soul.

We bought some more soft drinks from the terrace in front of the art museum and admired the elevated view of the avenue with the Venetian Towers .

As we began walking up Montjuïc, Paul asked the inevitable question: "So what is there to see up there, Chappers?"

I tried to tailor my answer to resemble something acceptable to Paul: "We will visit the stadium that was used in the 1992 Olympics and the former home of the football team, RCD Espanyol. There's also a fort at the top."

Paul grimaced, as he looked up and said: "That looks like a long trek up there. It better be worth it."

It was clearly going to be a long and tiring walk to the top, so we were relieved to reach our first scheduled stop. The Olympic Stadium looked rather dated, which was not particularly surprising, given that it was originally built in the 1920s. After Berlin was chosen ahead of Barcelona as the host city of the 1936 Olympics, a 'People's Olympiad' was planned in protest to the games being held in Nazi Germany.

Ironically, the event did not materialise due to the outbreak of the Spanish Civil War, which established the dominance of the Franco dictatorship across the country. The stadium was renovated and it finally hosted an Olympic Games over half a century later.

Paul smirked as he said: "Better than the Nou Camp. Best team in Barcelona used to play here."

It did not look like a stadium that had played host to the Olympics just over twenty years beforehand but the backstory to the failed attempt to hold the 1936 Olympics here added to my intrigue.

"Are we going straight up to the Fort now?" Paul asked.

I knew that my response would not go down well: "We are going to have a look around the Botanical Gardens on the way up."

Paul sighed, before replying: "Botanical Gardens! Seriously?! What's next on the agenda? An antiques fair?!"

I nodded before indicating that we should resume our quest to reach the summit. The route had become hard going now. Climbing this long and winding path up the hill under the intense heat was taking its toll on us.

We eventually reached the Botanical Gardens, where Paul was able to once again express his frustration: "After a long walk, we now get to walk around some fancy garden whilst we burn in the sun."

The gardens were not particularly spectacular but they were pleasant enough and our visit gave us a break from the uphill climb. I took enough photographs to justify our visit to Paul before leaving the grounds.

The walk to the top of the hill felt even more gruelling now. The heat was unbearable and the gradient seemed to be getting steeper by the minute. The fort still appeared to be a long way off. Paul stopped in his tracks and looked up at the cable car that was approaching the summit.

"Chappers. Why have we walked up this hill when we could have taken the cable car?"

I paused before providing my response: "You would have missed out on the Botanical Gardens if we had taken the cable car."

Paul shook his head and muttered: "Please tell me that we are going straight to the beach after this?"

I nodded before leading us to the summit and completing our expedition. The fort at the top of the hill, officially known as Castell de Montjuïc, was built in 1640. The history of the fort is a rather sombre one; it was formerly used as a prison and it was also the site of political executions. The cannons that we walked past were used to fire upon sections of the city's own population during the rebellions of the eighteenth and nineteenth centuries.

Paul was not concerned by any of this though. "At least we will get a good view of Barcelona," he reasoned.

Typically, the sky was becoming increasingly dull and cloudy. This often happens when I visit places at high elevation. I am not sure whether this is simply something that should be expected due to the nature of weather systems or if I am just unlucky in this regard.

"An eight hour trek up a mountain and we can't even see anything," Paul quipped.

Despite his exaggeration, I shared his frustration. Our reward had not matched our exertions. Nevertheless, we had a look around the fort and took some photographs. Or at least I did. The walk back down Montjuïc was slightly easier but it was still uncomfortable in the heat.

"Get me to that beach, Chappers," Paul pleaded.

Unfortunately, we had to get back on the stuffy metro in order to visit the beach. It was so uncomfortable that we decided to exit the train earlier than we had planned and complete the rest of the journey on foot. We disembarked at Marina. Surely with a name like this, it would be close to the beach? It turns out that the name of the station is rather deceptive because it is around two kilometres away from the waterfront in the Barceloneta district.

Paul was not impressed: "You're trying to kill us via heat exhaustion, aren't you?"

I tried to assure him that we were not that far away but I shared his pain and despair. The sight of sand felt heavenly. We had survived the challenge of roaming around Parc Guell, scaling Montjuïc, negotiating the metro system and walking an additional two kilometres. All whilst getting destroyed by the sizzling August sun. Paul proclaimed that he had "earned this."

A vendor approached us as we settled on a spot on the beach.

"Coke. Water. Three Euros," was his opening sales pitch.

We dismissed him without purchasing anything and relaxed in the sun. It was not long before we needed to cool down, so we made our way into the sea. This was a rather slow process as we were both wimps who struggled to cope with the cool water.

Paul was the first to summon the courage to eventually submerge himself in the sea. A couple of minutes later, I tentatively joined him. The refreshing dip in the sea was much needed after the gruelling schedule that I had put us through. We eventually returned to where we had left our belongings and let ourselves dry under the intense afternoon sun.

Our feeling of relaxation was interrupted every few minutes by various vendors offering us drinks, whom we duly sent packing on each occasion. Eventually we ran out of the drinks that we had brought with us to the beach. At least there were plenty of vendors knocking about.

Except that they had all vanished now.

It felt like we had been the victims of a cruel joke; there had been dozens of them pestering us for the last hour but the moment that we actually needed to buy some drinks, they were nowhere to be seen. We waited a few minutes but there was no sign of them returning. Had they been a figment of our imagination? Maybe our brains had melted in the intense heat.

I pointed to a row of shops that lined the beachfront and said: "Let's try and find some drinks there. There must be some in those shops."

Unbelievably, the fridges were empty in every single store. There were plenty of inflatable fish, paddle boards, buckets and spades but not a trace of any liquid refreshment. Had we missed our chance to purchase any drinks? Would we perish due to dehydration? We slumped back to our spot on the beach and resigned ourselves to our fate.

Then all of a sudden we heard a familiar voice over our shoulder: "Coke. Water. Six Euros."

It had become clear that we had been defeated by a more experienced and resolute competitor. After dismissing him and his rivals for the last hour, we were now completely at his mercy and he was making us pay for it. Pay double, in fact.

"Can we have one water, one Coke and a tube of Pringles, please?" I asked.

He nodded and handed over the goods. In return, I gave him twenty Euros. I waited for some change but he just shrugged his shoulders and looked at me with a blank expression. This veteran beach vendor had seen off bigger and better men than us. I knew that I was no match for him, so I sat back and watched him slink off with twenty Euros and a tidy profit.

After a relaxing few hours on the beach, it was time to leave. The sail shaped W Barcelona Hotel, provided an interesting backdrop for my final photographs of the beach. I imagine that this six star hotel was a far cry from ¿Qué Tal?

Our lack of confidence in being able to order a meal in Spanish may have contributed to our decision to eat at McDonald's again but this was more likely due to Paul and I being a couple of uncultured slobs. The evening mirrored our first night in Barcelona; fine dining in McDonald's, building up the courage to use the communal shower in our hostel and facing the dilemma of whether to turn on the heat-producing fan. And worrying about whether we would wake up with one of the hostel workers standing over us, watching us sleep.

"Did you enjoy today, Paul?" I asked.

He laughed, before replying: "I enjoyed the beach. Nobody else will have been daft enough to visit Parc Guell and Montjuïc on the same day though. Those beach sellers had the last laugh didn't they?!"

Just before turning out the lights, I remembered that a friend had told me that the Magic Fountain show of Montjuïc was the best thing to see in Barcelona at night. As this spectacular display of colourful lights, water and music was held on most nights, I told Paul that we would try and check it out after the match the following evening.

"Yeah, whatever," was Paul's enthusiastic response.

I had a quick look online and discovered that it was closed on Mondays and Tuesdays. Of course it was. We could have gone during the previous three nights but we had missed our chance.

*   *   *

We treated ourselves to another lie in before heading out to explore some of the most famous places in Barcelona. La Sagrada Família was only a short walk away from our hostel, therefore it was our first port of call. Our first sight of it confirmed what I had read online; this was Gaudí's unfinished masterpiece.

He had taken over the reins of this architectural project in 1882 and had dedicated the rest of his life to its creation. However, the building remains unfinished to this day. There have been many timelines put in place, with the latest projection being that it will be completed by 2026. This date will coincide with the one hundred year anniversary of his death. After being hit by a tram, it is said that the unassuming architect was mistaken for a homeless man during the identification process.

Another thing that I had read about the building was that it is constantly heaving with tourists. We joined a queue to enter what is regarded as the symbol of the city and we were told that it would take around thirty minutes. Apparently, that is quite good going for visiting La Sagrada Família.

Paul was not impressed: "After all of the walking yesterday, we now have to queue up all day for a cathedral. Great."

We were actually in a queue to visit a basilica rather than a cathedral but I thought that it was best not to correct him on this occasion. It is a common misconception that Sagrada Família is a cathedral but it does not hold that status. It is an easy mistake to make, as a church of this size and stature would normally be given that title. The city's cathedral is actually located in the Gothic Quarter; we had briefly admired the exterior of the building, without realising that it was a cathedral, during our walk through the area a couple of nights earlier.

Our time stood in the queue provided us with the opportunity to examine the stunning level of detail of the basilica. As with much of Gaudí's work, the building seems to have an organic element to it and it contains a large amount of symbolism.

Once we gained entrance, we discovered that the interior was just as impressive. The high ceilings gave it an open feel and the twisting columns resulted in an unusual look, without being clunky and taking up too much space. I often find that the churches that I visit during my travels can seem similar but this accusation could not be levelled at La Sagrada Familia.

I had been advised that the view from the high vantage points meant that it was worth purchasing a ticket for the lift that transported visitors to the top of the towers. Unfortunately, this meant hanging around for another forty minutes but I could think of worse places to kill time.

The view of Barcelona was indeed very good but the best aspect was being able to admire the detail of the upper part of the building from a distance that would have otherwise been impossible. I took some pictures of the Gargoyles looking out towards the city skyline before we made our way down the narrow staircase that led us back to street level.

"Where to next, Chappers?"

The obvious answer to Paul's question was La Rambla. The most famous street in the city is a busy and vibrant place that is lined with restaurants, kiosks and street artists. A short metro ride later, we were in the midst of it all. This largely pedestrianised thoroughfare was lined with trees and heaving with crowds of tourists, many of whom were watching the various independent performers in action. There was a small group gathered around a man who was painted in bronze and stood perfectly still.

Here was my opportunity to deliver the joke that had been wasted on Mum in Toronto but Paul beat me to the punch: "He's showing more movement than half of Man United's players!"

Other street acts involved performers providing the illusion that they were either levitating, appearing to stand on one leg all day or just dressed in an extremely uncomfortable robot outfit on a hot day. There were also people offering to draw caricatures for tourists, selling their unusual sculptures or juggling an array of fragile items. This helped to create a jovial atmosphere, which is always a welcome relief within a busy city.

We had a gentle stroll and explored the nearby points of interest, including the Gothic Quarter and the famous indoor market, which can be found just off La Rambla. Placa de Catalunya is situated at one end of the thoroughfare and a statue of Christopher Columbus stands proudly at the other.

You can usually find a monument dedicated to Columbus in most places in the world. People often make the mistake of thinking that he was Spanish, due to his transatlantic voyages of exploration undertaken in the name of the Catholic Monarchs of Spain. He was actually an Italian by birth. Mind you, his name does not sound particularly like a Spanish or Italian name, so I think that people can be forgiven for making this error.

The impact of his expeditions was felt around the world and he undoubtedly helped shape the course of history. Although his accomplishments have long been celebrated, there is a growing debate as to whether we should be glorifying them.

Countries in the Americas and the Caribbean basically became enslaved by the Western world, with violence often used to extinguish any resistance.

The Taíno were the indigenous people of several Caribbean islands such as the Dominican Republic, Haiti, Cuba and Puerto Rico. Following the arrival of Columbus and the Spanish contingent in 1492, the Taíno were killed in large numbers as the colonisation of the region took hold. Those that survived the violence succumbed to diseases, most notably Smallpox, that the Europeans brought over. The Taíno were believed to have been extinct by the end of the sixteenth century.

In recent years, there has been a focus on how the surviving Taíno married Spanish colonists, resulting in the continued existence of the race within many Caribbean people's D.N.A. composition. The Slave Trade that was in operation from the seventeenth until the nineteenth century, saw the mass importation of African slaves to the Caribbean. The majority of today's Caribbean population can trace their ancestry back to the African slaves that were brought over by European countries.

"That's a big statue isn't it Paul?" I asked.

"Yeah, massive. We have done enough sightseeing, now let's get some food and go to the Nou Camp," he replied.

We took the tram to Maria Cristina once again, where we searched for a place to eat near the stadium. Our decision to travel to the ground early paid off, as the metro, although still busy, was not as crowded as we had worried that it might be.

A joyful and exciting atmosphere was building as we walked towards the stadium. The restaurants were getting busy, which resulted in our instincts guiding us to the least crowded one. We did not even look at the menu before entering but surely they would be serving some Spanish dishes?

Our waiter confirmed the inevitable: "Welcome to our Italian restaurant and pizzeria."

We entered the stadium over an hour before kick-off, which meant that we were able to take photographs without thousands of people pushing past and obscuring the view. Paul had employed his usual trick of sneaking in an Oasis lid, due to the standard practice of the staff at football grounds being instructed to remove this whenever selling a drinks bottle. This was the equivalent to a boxer seeing a punch coming and plotting his counter strike in advance. It was a pleasure to witness a master at work.

I took photographs of the stadium from just about every conceivable angle before we settled into our seats. We were pleased that we had purchased fairly decent tickets in the middle tier, in line with the centre circle. I would have liked to have sat in the top corner of the stadium, in order to capture the perfect image of the entire stadium, with the city skyline in the background. We had great seats for actually watching the match itself though.

I felt someone tapping my shoulder, so fearing the worst, I turned around. I had anticipated that we were about to be informed that we were sat in the wrong seats but it turned out to be a fan of the opposition team. Normally, the fact that I was wearing an F.C. Barcelona shirt would have been cause for concern but the name on the back of my retro jersey was also one of the most legendary players in the history of this stranger's football team.

Diego Maradona had a brief stint playing for Barcelona during the early 1980s, before transferring to Napoli, which are the European team that he is most strongly associated with. He led the Italian club to the first two league titles in their history, in addition to an Italian cup and a UEFA cup. His exploits in Italy, along with spearheading Argentina's World Cup triumph in 1986, have resulted in him being regarded as one of the greatest players in the history of football.

"Maradona! Where did you get that shirt from?!" he asked me.

Fortunately, English was the go-to language for the majority of tourists when trying to communicate with people in another country. I informed him that I purchased it online from a company that sells retro football shirts from around the world.

"Cool! Can I take a picture of the back of your shirt whilst you look out at the pitch?" was the next question.

I obliged, before asking him to take the same photograph with my camera. This episode highlights how sport, despite its many evils, can provide shared memories for people all across the planet.

The football match that we were about to watch is held every year shortly before the start of the season. The Joan Gamper Trophy is contested annually by Barcelona and a guest team, in honour of the Swiss man who, along with a collection of individuals from Spain, Switzerland and Britain, founded the club in 1899.

Gamper also scored over one hundred goals as a player and later oversaw a successful era as club president. In 1925, he was accused of supporting Catalan nationalism after Barcelona fans jeered the Spanish national anthem, yet applauded "God Save the Queen." Following a battle with depression, he committed suicide in 1930.

The sun began to set as kick-off approached, which made the stadium even more pleasing on the eye. We were disappointed to have travelled all this way only to discover that Lionel Messi, the world's greatest player, was not in the starting line-up.

The rousing rendition of the Futbol Club Barcelona anthem lifted our spirits in time for the commencement of the match. It was obvious that supporting this club had a deeper meaning for these fans. The club motto is 'Més que un club,' which means 'more than a club.' This is a fitting phrase for F.C. Barcelona, given that there is a great deal of symbolism for much of the city's population.

Perhaps the defining moment in this regard was the murder of the Barcelona club president, Josep Sunyol, by Spanish nationalist soldiers after the outbreak of the Spanish Civil War. Due to his affiliation with a political party that supported Catalan independence, he became known as the 'martyr president.' Several of the club's players, along with those from Bilbao's Athletic Club, enlisted in the war effort against the nationalist military.

The club already had a strong association with Catalan identity prior to the Franco dictatorship but it was during this period that it took on even greater meaning. The Spanish authorities banned the club from using its current name and badge, due to the association with Catalan nationalism. The club was renamed Club de Fútbol Barcelona, in order to conform with the Spanish language. This remained the official name until the end of the dictatorship in the 1970s.

More significantly, the violent suppression of dissenting voices resulted in up to fifty thousand deaths in forced labour and concentration camps, in what is sometimes referred to as the 'Spanish Holocaust.' This is in addition to the hundreds of thousands that died during the civil war.

The true extent of the terror remains unknown, with well over a hundred thousand people unaccounted for. Thousands of unmarked mass graves are thought to contain the bodies of those murdered by Franco's men. Remarkably, Cambodia is the only country in the world with more 'disappeared' people than Spain.

Real Madrid were regarded as Franco's favoured team, with

Barcelona fans often complaining that their great rivals received preferential treatment, whilst the Catalan club faced severe restrictions. This only intensified the rivalry, resulting in matches between the two sides being regarded as amongst the most significant and hostile occasions in world football.

The legendary Johann Cruyff certainly endeared himself to Barcelona fans after signing for the club, by declaring that he could never have signed for Real Madrid due to their links with the fascist regime of Franco.

Although not at full capacity, there was a good atmosphere inside the stadium as the crowd proudly waved their flags and cheered on their heroes. In the end, Barcelona won 5-0, with Messi scoring twice after entering the action at the start of the second half.

My excitement was obvious as we left the stadium, following the conclusion of the match.

"I am glad that we finally got around to booking this trip. Twelve years ago, we watched a television broadcast of United winning a Champions League final here. Cruyff, Rivaldo, Ronaldinho and countless other legends have graced that pitch."

Paul pounced on this opportunity to use humour to mask our concern about the situation that we were about to face: "I bet Ronaldinho didn't have to get the metro home with ninety thousand people though!"

The stadium was too far away from our hostel to travel on foot and we lacked the assertiveness and basic social skills to flag down a taxi. Therefore, public transport was our only option. We took a deep breath before joining the stream of football fans that were walking down the stairs of the metro station. The temperature seemed to be increasing by the second, although I am not sure how much of this was down to our anxiety rather than the accumulative body heat of all the passengers.

The first train was a write-off, as there was no chance of even getting on it. The crowd had cleared a little by the time the next vehicle pulled up to the platform but we had no inclination to attempt the journey until the number of people had been reduced further.

Eventually, we plucked up the courage to board the third train that had entered the station. With a mass of people crammed into the carriages, I had not felt such a tight squeeze since the time that I had convinced myself that I could fit into a pair of jeans that had a waist size of thirty inches. After finally arriving back at our required station, we felt a wave of relief, in addition to a few sweaty bodies brushing against us as we left the train. Fresh air never felt so good. After that journey, ¿Qué Tal? did not seem quite so unpleasant.

We had a brief conversation about souvenirs before going to sleep.

"Are you going to buy any souvenirs, Paul?" I asked.

"No. You?" he replied.

"No."

That was pretty clear cut. To be fair, my parents and my brother already had a drawer full of useless souvenirs, so they did not need any more tat.

*   *   *

The following day, we took the bus to Barcelona-El Prat Josep Tarradellas Airport, which would be the scene of a very strange sequence of events. Upon arrival, we approached the Monarch Airline desk and checked in for our flight.

After handing our documents back to us, the airline employee noticed something about our booking, which she duly informed us about: "Sorry sir, you have only paid for carry-on baggage for your outbound journey. You'll have to pay extra to take your bag on.

This must have been buried somewhere in the smallprint of my Expedia booking confirmation.

"Fine, we'll pay for that. How much is it?" I asked.

The employee smiled, pointed to something behind my shoulder and informed us that: "Customers have to pay for extra items, such as baggage, at the kiosk over there. You can skip the line and see me upon your return."

We trudged over to the passenger service desk, where Paul used his credit card to pay for the right to take our bags on board with us. We then walked sheepishly back to the woman that had checked us in, cutting in front of a family of four that included an angry looking man.

"Hey! They're cutting in!" he complained.

The airline employee informed him that she had given us permission to do so. Feeling the hostile gaze of the man behind us, we showed her the receipt.

"No problem sir, I will send your luggage through now," she stated.

After walking about a hundred yards in the direction of the departure gates, Paul stopped in his tracks. He seemed to have a pained expression written on all over his face and he had gone noticeably quiet.

"Chappers, we're in trouble."

What could be the matter? I told myself that it must have been something trivial that Paul was joking about.

"Chappers...after I paid for the baggage, I put my passport in my luggage. That's long gone now."

I immediately resigned myself to the worst case scenario. Paul would obviously not be able to get through passport control without a passport and his bag had already begun its journey towards our aircraft. This would mean spending an extra night in Barcelona, which would result in me needing to inform my employers that I would not be able to make it to work the next day.

I had only been working for the data management company for three months, so would they terminate my temporary contract? I tried to ease such concerns by asking the rhetorical question, "Who needs a job anyway?"

We were back at the Monarch employee's desk for the third time in ten minutes.

Paul tried to explain his predicament to the lady that we had spoken to earlier: "Hi...I packed my passport in my case...then checked in the case. So I don't have my passport."

She looked confused, as she asked: "How have you managed to do that?"

We explained the sequence of events that had unfolded but she still seemed incredulous.

After an awkward minute of near silence, she cautiously and quietly advised us that: "The bags are on their way to the plane. Maybe passport control will let you through if you explain what happened?"

She seemed unsure about the advice that she had just given, which did not exactly fill us with confidence.

The security area was busy, so they opened up a new lane just as we arrived. This was perfect timing for us but added to the ever increasing frustration of the man that we had cut in front of at the check in desk. His family were at the back of one queue and we were now at the front of another, despite arriving after them.

He threw his arms up to gesture how unfair this was.

"Chappers, that guy is having as bad a time as I am!" Paul chuckled.

I suggested that: "With how things are going for him, the airline will tell him that there was a double booking and that his seat is no longer available but then he'll see you walk straight through and board the flight without a passport!"

We approached passport control as if we were on Interpol's most wanted list. I suggested that we should "act naturally and stay calm."

Paul laughed nervously and responded by saying that: "We would not be acting naturally if we stayed calm. We are never calm."

I imagined being hauled into a dark room and interrogated for hours upon end. Perhaps I would be tortured. And I was not even the one who had misplaced his passport. Heaven only knows what they would do to Paul.

The border force officer certainly looked like he was ready to deal with a terrorist threat. Or teach a lesson to a couple of suspicious characters who were spinning an unlikely tale about a missing passport.

Paul pre-empted the inevitable question: "My passport is in my case... which is being transported to the plane."

The officer looked unimpressed as he asked: "What do you mean? I don't see how this could be."

Paul gave a detailed account of what happened and after a few minutes of scepticism, the stern looking man seemed to have deemed this explanation to be truthful.

"Do you have a photocopy of your passport on your person?" the officer asked.

Paul reached rummaged inside the pockets of his shorts in vain, before vocalising his latest realisation: "No. That's in the case too!"

The officer tried his best to offer us an escape route by asking Paul if he had his driving licence or any form of identification on him.

Paul laughed, before responding: "It's all in the case!"

He was not even in a position to offer a bribe, as his wallet was also in his luggage. The officer paused, indicating that he was deciding what the best course of action should be.

His response was remarkable: "Just go through."

He flicked his head back, as if to say that he was going to pretend that this incident had never happened, before he continued: "You'll have to explain this at the gate. It's up to them if they let you fly."

We felt relieved, although slightly worried about the security standards at the airport. Thankfully, one of the airline employees at the gate was the woman who had checked us in. She must have cursed the sight of us as we recapped the story for her once more.

She seemed tired, which was reflected by her response: "Well, I must have seen your passport to check you in. I remember your story. Ok, you can fly."

Somehow, Paul had made it onto the flight without a passport or any other form of identification on his person. We took our seats on the plane and took a collective sigh of relief. At that point, the angry man and his family entered the aircraft and made their way over to their seats. They were sat in the row directly in front of us of course.

Almost immediately, I dropped some coins on the floor, which rolled forwards towards the angry man's feet. He returned them to me without saying anything. Feeling slightly nervous, I dropped one of the coins again.

"Sorry, mate," I said apologetically.

This time, he provided a verbal response as he returned the coin:

"You're trying to give this money away aren't you?!"

Thankfully, it appeared that he had calmed down somewhat. If this had happened half an hour beforehand, he may have caused the flight to be cancelled due to 'a police incident.' At least we would be back in Manchester in a few hours. We would have to try and explain ourselves to border patrol upon re-entering the United Kingdom but we felt better about the prospect of doing this in our home country.

Upon landing at Manchester Airport, we were faced with a dilemma. There were two queues at border patrol; one for passengers with an E.U. passport and another for passengers without an E.U. passport.

"Chappers, which queue do I join? I have an E.U. passport but I don't have it on me. Do I join the queue for people without an E.U. passport? Technically, that is true as I do not have an E. U. passport on me!"

After we reached the front of the queue, we attempted to explain the unlikely sequence of events.

The security officer seemed stunned: "I have never encountered such a situation before. I just don't understand how you were able to board the flight."

After a lengthy discussion with a colleague, he offered a novel solution: "I will let you retrieve your luggage and your passport if your friend stays here with me as an insurance policy."

Paul was the person without a passport, yet I was the one that would be held at border control.

"See you later Chappers!" Paul chuckled, as he left me behind.

Time seemed to stand still as I waited in silence for his return. I imagined that people were looking at me and speculating about what I must have done to warrant my detention.

The officer broke the silence with an understated comment: "Let's hope that your friend comes back."

Just when I started to wonder whether Paul would leave me at the mercy of the authorities, he returned with his passport in hand.

"Who needs a passport to travel, anyway? I may not bother bringing it next time," Paul joked.

I assumed that his comment was said with tongue very much in cheek. In any case, I felt that the trip had been a resounding success, despite the passport fiasco.

"We'll go to the Gamper match every year," I boldly proclaimed. Paul laughed as he replied: "Yeah and we're getting up at eight." Needless to say, we have not been back since.

# CHAPTER 12: SENSIBLE DECISIONS AND A MOMENT OF PANIC
## WASHINGTON D.C. AND HOUSTON, THE UNITED STATES OF AMERICA
## OCTOBER 2011

Dad and I were once again indulging our obsession with mixed martial arts. The week-long trip to the United States was a far from sensible adventure in many ways. I had recently returned to university in an attempt to gain another degree; this time one that had better prospects of directly leading to a career of some sort.

My Human Nutrition course was scheduled to begin during the first week of October; therefore, I took the smart decision of missing the entire first week in order to watch a couple of UFC shows in America. I persuaded myself, and more importantly my disapproving mother, that it was only an induction week and that I would not be missing out on anything substantial. In reality, it was another example of how my obsession was leading to irrational decisions. It hardly set the right tone for my return to higher education.

Another dubious decision was to book an outbound flight on the day of the first show. We had to fly from Manchester to Paris, and then on to Washington D.C. in time for the show that began at around five o'clock in the evening. We only had a couple of hours leeway, which meant that any hiccups along the way could have derailed the first part of our trip.

Fortunately, we landed at Washington Dulles International Airport at the scheduled time. Clearing U.S. immigration was as pleasant an experience as I had remembered. Our ESTAs were still valid from our previous trip to Las Vegas but I could not help but think that there would be a mix-up and that we would end up being detained for long enough to miss the first show.

"Your ESTA seems to be valid. I'll just have to take some biometric data. Place both of your thumbs on the scanner, then place the four fingers from your left hand on the scanner, followed by the same with your right hand. Then look into the camera," the immigration officer instructed.

I just about managed to hold it together long enough to follow these basic instructions.

"What is the purpose of your visit to the United States?" he asked.

This was a perfectly reasonable question but I often get nervous in this type of situation. I had absolutely nothing to hide but I felt on edge, as if I was an international terrorist that was about to get apprehended at the border.

"I am here for a couple of mixed martial arts shows," I mumbled.

Without showing a trace of emotion, the officer nodded his head.

"Where will you be staying?" he asked. My heart rate increased exponentially with each question.

"We will be staying in central Washington D.C. for three nights, then in Houston for another four" I stated.

The blank expression of the man in the booth was not giving much away before he began his next comment: "I see..."

Here we go. A night in the cells lay in store for me. Or perhaps I would be shipped off to Guantanamo Bay indefinitely.

"...welcome to the United States of America, Sir."

After our previous trip to Las Vegas, we were well prepared for the irritating culture of excessive tipping that is forced upon you in the United States. The taxi driver that took us from the airport to our hotel was the first individual to politely steal our money. We checked into the hotel, feeling relieved that at least we would not have to hand over another gratuity for the next few hours.

"Welcome. I can see that your room is all paid for, apart from the city tax. That will be another twenty dollars in cash, please."

We had been in America for an hour and we had already been robbed twice by smiling assassins. Of course, city taxes are commonplace throughout the world but we had already developed a siege mentality by this stage.

We dropped off our luggage in our room, before making our way to the Verizon Center for *UFC On Versus 6: Cruz vs. Johnson.* As it was close enough to travel there on foot and it was still daytime, we had no problem finding our intended destination. If we had lost our bearings, we could have just followed the droves of people dressed in hideous skull and crossbones inspired Tapout and Affliction t-shirts.

Once inside, we joined something that resembled a queue for a hotdog stand. After multiple people had barged their way to the front of the stand, it was finally our turn to purchase some hotdogs. As usual, I did not get a drink due to my desire to avoid sharing a public toilet with thousands of drunkards.

Following Demetrious Johnson's unsuccessful attempt to wrest the bantamweight title from Dominic Cruz's grasp, we left the arena. Our final challenge of the day was to find our hotel in the dark but this proved to be a very simple task in comparison to the earlier tests of keeping the smiles on our faces intact as we were mugged by the taxi driver and the hotel employee. Our room was basic but pleasant enough to provide a good night's sleep.

*   *   *

We woke up feeling refreshed and ready to explore the capital of the United States of America. Having consumed a bizarre and unhealthy breakfast combination of pancakes and bacon, we set off for the obvious starting point for our day of exploration.

The most famous and revered landmarks of Washington D.C. are found along the National Mall. The area commonly attributed to this National Park is flanked by the State Capitol and the Lincoln Memorial, although not all of this lies within the official boundaries. Illogically, we decided to start exploring the area from the Washington Monument, which is situated more or less in the centre of the Mall.

The Washington Monument was built in honour of George Washington, who was the first President of the United States. It did not have the most original design but it was still able to make a strong impression. With a height of over five hundred and fifty feet, it is the world's tallest obelisk. I am tempted to throw in a joke about the character Obelix, who featured in *The Adventures of Asterix* comics, but I just do not have the Gaul to do so.

As I began taking photographs, I noticed a sign that stated that the monument was closed due to the repair work that was being carried out following damage caused by an earthquake that had occurred less than two months beforehand. I had been completely unaware that there had been an earthquake in nearby Virginia in August that had sent shockwaves through Washington D.C. and beyond.

Dad seemed somewhat relieved: "I am glad we were not here for the earthquake. I had never considered the possibility of an earthquake here in Washington."

The closure did not particularly bother me, since I had not planned to visit the top of the monument in any case. What I was really looking forward to seeing was the Reflecting Pool that ran for over two thousand feet from the Washington Monument to the Lincoln Memorial. The pool was immortalised by the Civil Rights rally of 1963, in which Martin Luther King Jr. gave his "I have a dream" speech in front of around two hundred and fifty thousand people that had gathered alongside the body of water.

I had already planned the photographs that I wanted to take, which involved recreating some of the iconic images from the aforementioned rally, such as the view along the full length of the pool from the Lincoln Memorial. Before we reached the Reflecting Pool, we walked through the open space of the World War II Memorial. A fountain is situated in the centre, surrounded by fifty six pillars and a couple of triumphal arches.

As the name suggests, the memorial was built to honour the Americans who lost their lives during the Second World War, which numbered over four hundred thousand. Like most war memorials, it was a poignant reminder of the tragic loss of life that war brings, as well as the brave sacrifice made by so many.

The location of the memorial has proven to be a topic of debate within the United States since its opening in 2004, with some complaining about the loss of the once interrupted view of the Washington Monument from the Lincoln Memorial. I understood this viewpoint as I had wanted to capture the image that I have just described but I could hardly be upset about a memorial for those that lost their lives during the war.

I soon felt further disappointment; this time guilt free. As we approached the pool, it appeared to be under renovation. It was unclear whether it was just the section that I was nearest to that had been drained, so I still had a glimmer of hope to cling on to. This was promptly extinguished by the sign that informed us that the entire pool was closed.

Following the long walk to the Lincoln Memorial, I went through the motions of taking my photographs but my heart was no longer in it. Instead of being able to admire a beautiful pool that displayed the reflection of the Washington Monument, I was looking at the rather bleak sight of two thousand feet of mud or soil of some sort. It was becoming difficult to imagine the mass of people that had gathered there for protests, celebrations and open air concerts that have punctuated American history.

"You can use your imagination to picture what it would look like with water, Dave. It's still a nice view."

Dad's attempt to console me was unsuccessful. The photograph that I was most looking forward to taking in Washington D.C. had been ruined. This highlights a flaw that I share with many other travellers; having an image in mind for a photograph before you have even reached your destination is part of the process of essentially recreating other people's experiences.

The photograph that I wanted to take would have merely been an inferior version to the images that I had seen in history books and on television, yet I had obsessed over taking it. In practice, the best photographs are usually the ones that are more personal and unique to one's own experience. The same can be said about activities; we often concentrate on reliving other people's adventures rather than creating our own.

I quite literally put the disappointment behind me by turning around to face the Lincoln Memorial, which honours one of the United States of America's most celebrated presidents. Abraham Lincoln led the Union to victory in the American Civil War of 1861 to 1865 against the Confederate States of America, that had attempted to break away from the United States due to the recently elected Lincoln's opposition to slavery.

These southern states relied heavily on slaves to work in the cotton plantations and agricultural industry. Members of the Confederacy expressed their belief that black slaves should not be regarded as equals to their white masters. In a country which has a disturbing history of white supremacy, the Union's victory in the American Civil War, which claimed the lives of over six hundred thousand and led to the abolition of slavery, was a defining moment.

The Lincoln Memorial was architecturally inspired by Greek temples, with Doric columns a prominent feature of the exterior design. We ventured inside and found that, unsurprisingly, a giant statue of Abraham Lincoln was the dominant feature of the central chamber. Dad and I paused to consider the significance of the man whose image sat before us.

He is a rare example of a president that is fondly remembered by both sides of the political divide, yet his death also demonstrates the anger and violence that has long been attached to the politics of the United States. Out of the forty five presidents in the country's history, Lincoln was one of four that were assassinated whilst in office.

"You wouldn't want to be elected president in America then. You may be the most powerful person in the world but you will probably be assassinated!" Dad remarked.

This was obviously an exaggeration but in order to move the

conversation on, I nodded in agreement. The other chambers contained inscriptions of the Gettysburg address that Lincoln delivered during the Civil War and his second inauguration address. After reading his inspirational words, we left the memorial building in order to explore the rest of the National Mall. We stopped by the Vietnam Veterans Memorial, which was a rather different design to what one has come to expect from a war memorial.

There were two black granite walls that met at what was not quite a right angle. This is the type of detail that would normally bother me but it was an intended feature of the design, so that one wall pointed towards the Washington Monument and the other in the direction of the Lincoln Memorial. The names of over fifty eight thousand members of the U.S. Armed Forces that lost their lives during the Vietnam War are inscribed on the one hundred and forty panels that form the majority of the walls.

The aesthetics may not be to everybody's liking but the memorial certainly succeeds in illustrating the sheer scale of the loss of life. When walking along the seventy five metres of each wall, a sombre feeling is inevitable as you consider that each inscription represents a human being that was killed in yet another man-made conflict.

I enunciated my thoughts to Dad: "There are so many names. Seeing them all laid out like this makes you realise just how many people died. Many of them were younger than I am."

Dad nodded in agreement, before simply stating that, "War is a terrible thing."

There were two additional parts to the memorial, which acknowledge the contribution and suffering of those that are often overlooked. *The Three Soldiers* features men that comprised the major ethnic groups involved in the American war effort; European American, African American and Hispanic American.

The soldiers are positioned so that they appear to be looking in the direction of the walls that contain the names of their comrades that perished during the war. There has been debate over whether this detracts from the impact of the original memorial but I found that it added a human element to the statistical nature of the walls.

The Vietnam Women's Memorial honours the females, whom were mostly assigned as nurses, that risked their lives during the conflict in South East Asia. The memorial features statues of three uniformed women tending to a wounded soldier, which again helps visitors to build a human connection to the memorials. We then headed over to the other side of the Reflection Pool, where we inspected yet another memorial that served as a reminder of the human cost of war.

The Korean War Veterans Memorial includes a mural wall and a pool of remembrance but we were drawn to the most striking feature. There are nineteen stainless steel statues that resemble a platoon on patrol. The statues are situated amongst bushes, which symbolises the difficult terrain that the armed forces encountered. Over thirty six thousand Americans lost their lives in a war that was fought on the other side of the planet. The day's recurring theme of death caused by war was beginning to overwhelm us.

Dad offered his thoughts: "When will we learn? War after war has killed so many people."

I concurred, before glumly stating that: "There does not appear to be much sign of that happening The U.S. and its allies are still involved in the Iraq War."

We moved on from the topic of war and walked over to the inspirational, yet bittersweet, Martin Luther King Jr. Memorial. This featured the *Stone of Hope,* which has an image of the Civil Rights icon carved into granite. Dr. King was one of the most prominent figures in the Civil Rights Movement and he was awarded the 1964 Nobel Peace Prize for his efforts in the non-violent struggle for racial equality. Just four years later, he was assassinated prior to a planned march that had been organised as a form of protest against poverty and economic injustice.

He was posthumously awarded the Presidential Medal of Freedom and the Congressional Gold Medal but his real legacy was the impact of his role in the battle for equality. There has been much progress made since the 1960s but there is still a long way to go. It would certainly be interesting to hear his thoughts on the racially offensive remarks and policies of the current President of the United States.

From the Martin Luther King Jr. Memorial, we could see the Thomas Jefferson Memorial on the other side of the Tidal Basin. Constructed in honour of one of the founding fathers of the United States, the marble and granite building, which features numerous pillars and a shallow dome, appeared to resemble the Pantheon of Rome.

Our view of the Franklin D. Roosevelt Memorial was less clear, which was to be expected, given its open space design. The four 'outdoor rooms' represent the four terms that he served in office but we could not make out much detail from our vantage point. In acknowledgement of Roosevelt's paralytic illness that caused him to rely on the use of a wheelchair, the area was designed to be accessible for people with physical impairments.

As it was getting late, we decided to get some dinner rather than travel to the other side of the basin to visit the aforementioned memorials. Ben's Chilli Bowl has become synonymous with Washington

D.C. since it first opened its doors in 1958. Although it is a small, family owned food outlet, it has garnered a reputation that has attracted celebrities, and even Barack Obama, to sample its signature dishes, such as the chilli half-smoke.

This is not where we ate though. Instead, we dined at Nando's. We had never visited any of the multitude of restaurants from this global chain that began life in South Africa; therefore, at least we were trying something new. Washington D.C. was the first location for a Nando's restaurant in the United States; hence, we could make a rather weak claim that we were indeed dining at somewhere noteworthy within the nation's capital.

Although we were in a restaurant that can be found in five continents and we were in an English speaking country, we still managed to make this a confusing experience for ourselves. Firstly, we sat down at a table, expecting a waiter to take our order. After a few minutes, a member of staff came over to inform us that we were required to place our orders at the counter.

We trudged over and joined the queue, which only had one person in it prior to our arrival. Consequently, we did not have much time to figure out what we wanted to eat. Fortunately, the menu did not seem to be the most varied; we could have chicken or...chicken. It was soon my turn to place an order.

"Can I have quarter of a chicken breast?" I asked tentatively.

I could not hear the member of staff's response, due to how loud the noise level was within the restaurant. Therefore, I politely asked him to repeat what he had said. Again, I could not make out what he was saying. Reticent to ask him to deliver his response for a third time, I gambled by assuming that he was asking me a question that required a simple yes or no response.

Therefore, I just nodded and said, "Yes, please."

The Nando's employee looked at me like I was incredibly stupid, before shouting: "HOW HOT WOULD YOU LIKE YOUR MEAL?"

Suddenly, I felt as stupid as this man thought I was. Thankfully, I realised that he was asking me how spicy I would like my meal rather than what temperature I would like it served at.

I cannot even imagine what his reaction would have been if I had said: "Well I certainly don't want it cold! Around thirty four degrees would be preferable."

I asked him what the options were and he informed me that I had the choice of medium, hot, extra hot or something to do with herbs that I could not quite make out over the noise of the restaurant. I plumped for the option of hot.

"What sides would you like?" he then asked.

I started to panic again. Which two items could I quickly pick, so that I do not hold up the queue any longer?

"Fries and..." I mumbled as I scanned the menu for the first acceptable item.

"...corn on the cob."

I felt relieved but this was short lived.

I believe that he said: "Would you like Peri-salt on your fries?"

I once again resorted to nodding and hoping for the best.

"What would you like to drink?"

I gave the quickest answer that I could think of, which was, "Coke, please."

The barrage of questions was the precise reason why I avoid eating at Subway but I had not anticipated this scenario at Nando's. With the line of questioning complete, I felt like I had completed the latest level of a computer game.

I did not fancy Dad's chances but he resorted to the tried and trusted method of saying: "I'll have exactly the same as him."

Well played, sir. Well played.

Dad may have regretted saying that because he was clearly not enjoying how hot the flavouring was, nor the fact that his chips were covered in Peri-salt. Nevertheless, we both satisfied our hunger by finishing our meals. We had seen a fair amount of landmarks today but there was still more than enough left to keep us busy the following day.

We stopped by the White House on our way back to the hotel. Given that Barack Obama was not available for a chat, we took photographs by the gate instead. Darkness had now descended but the most famous building in Washington D.C. was still visible due to the external lighting. I took some photographs before suggesting that we return in the morning.

We were now faced with the task of locating our hotel, whilst travelling from a different direction in the dark. I was equipped with a map that I had picked up at the hotel but we just did not seem to be able to find our accommodation, despite knowing that we were agonisingly close to it.

Dad approached a police officer to ask for directions, which made me feel somewhat apprehensive, given that American police officers carry guns and that my dad has a habit of making jokes that could easily be misconstrued. Fortunately, Dad did not say anything that could be misinterpreted as a threat of violence, so the officer pointed out the route that we should take, rather than pointing his gun at us.

There were several occasions in which we said to one another that, "This must be it," or that: "Our hotel should be around this corner," but even after receiving the police officer's help, we could not find it.

This was despite the fact that our map was indicating that we were almost on top of our intended destination. Dad, who normally shows a steely determination in these scenarios, gave up.

"Let's just get a taxi. I know we're only a minute away but it is getting late," he glumly stated.

We approached a taxi and asked the driver to take us to our hotel.

He chuckled as he asked: "Are you sure? We are almost there already."

We explained that we were tired and had already spent too much time trying to find it.

The driver apologetically accepted: "OK, if you are sure. But it is just around the corner. I feel like I am robbing you for your fare."

This felt like a role reversal; here we were, a couple of tourists in America, almost forcing someone to take our money. He started his engine and set off towards our hotel. True to his word, it was indeed around the corner, about twenty yards away. We gave him five dollars and had the unusual feeling of being pleased to have grossly overpaid for something. We were just happy to be back at our hotel for the night.

\*　　\*　　\*

We returned to the White House the following morning, ready to explore more of the historic sites of the nation's capital. Our second visit to the home of the president was similar to the first. We walked around the perimeter of the grounds and took some photographs through the openings in the gate. Daylight provided a more familiar image of the White House this time, with the immaculate lawn now visible and the pristine building looking more striking against the blue sky.

"Do you know that African-American slaves formed a considerable part of the workforce that built the White House? And now the President is an African-American. That's quite a symbolic shift in American society," I proclaimed.

Dad gave a rather strange response: "And it is called the White House!"

I assured him that its name is not derived from the ethnicity of the occupiers but I guess Obama's ascension to the Oval Office confirms that.

We were unable to enter the White House because you are required to arrange this through your Member of Congress, or in the case of foreign visitors like ourselves, through the relevant embassy in Washington. It would have been interesting to go on a guided tour but visitors are not permitted to take photographs inside, so at least I could console myself with the knowledge that I would not have been able to capture any photographic evidence in any case.

The occupier of the White House held as much interest to me as the historic building itself. Barack Obama is an eloquent and gifted public speaker who was voted the most admired man in America for eleven consecutive years.

His political views were more in line with my own than the majority of the current crop of global leaders, who seem intent on dragging us back to the dark ages. Obama attempted to make health care more accessible to poorer members of the population, stimulated the Supreme Court into finally legalising same-sex marriage and he joined other world leaders in signing the 2015 Paris Agreement that sought to tackle climate change.

Obama also signed an agreement with Russia to reduce the number of nuclear weapons at each country's disposal, normalised relations with Cuba and was an advocate of gun control. It must be noted, however, that a considerable proportion of the U.S. population does not share this view, which is demonstrated by the election of his successor, who is his polar opposite.

We travelled on foot, once again passing the Washington Monument, before making our way down the side of the National Mall that we had not visited the previous day. We soon reached an area that was marked on my map as the Smithsonian Institution. My eyes, and subsequently my camera, were drawn to the red sandstone 'castle.'

It was the most aesthetically pleasing of the buildings in this area but it probably contains the least interesting, albeit fairly useful, material. It houses the administrative offices and information centre, whilst the other ten Smithsonian buildings located on the National Mall were museums and art galleries. Rather than subjecting Dad to an afternoon of staring at historical artefacts and paintings, we moved on to Capitol Hill.

The Capitol Reflecting Pool lies at the end of the National Mall. We stopped here to take some photographs and admire the view of the United States Capitol that we could see behind the body of water. After a pleasant few minutes, we reluctantly left the ducks of the pool behind us and walked towards the Capitol building.

It had a somewhat similar appearance to the White House, with the same immaculate finish and European style of design. The building in front of us was completed in 1800 and it is the home of the United States Congress. It has been the battleground for American politics for over two hundred years and it has become increasingly polarised in recent times.

Posing for photographs on the steps was as far as we ventured before moving on to another arena of political debate. The Supreme Court of the United States is the highest court in the American judiciary system. Consequently, it has been the site of many landmark decisions that have had a profound effect on the lives of the citizens of the country with the third largest population in the world.

Both sides of the political divide have accused the Supreme Court of bias throughout the years. This is not particularly surprising, as American politics has seemingly become as fanatical as the world of sport, with supporters of the red and blue teams clashing in a similar manner to tribal warfare.

"It looks like the Lincoln Memorial," was Dad's simple assessment of the Supreme Court building.

I did not entirely agree with this but I could see his point. In a similar fashion to the memorial that we had visited the previous day, the Supreme Court building had a resemblance to a Greek temple. The huge columns and white marble exterior provide an image of grandeur rather than extravagance, which was fitting for a court of this magnitude. There appeared to be some renovation work taking place but this did not diminish the impressiveness of the building.

There is a large paved area in front of the court and a couple of statues either side of the steps leading to the main entrance.

Dad flippantly remarked: "What do you reckon they are? Greek or Roman Gods? That's usually a safe bet."

I had no idea at the time but it turns out that the female figure on the left side of the steps is the 'Contemplation of Justice,' whilst the male figure on the opposite side is the 'Guardian of Law.'

The nearby Library of Congress is regarded as the national library of the United States and claims to be the largest in the word. In fact, the library is spread across three buildings. The Thomas Jefferson Building is the oldest of the three and it was the one that we thought was the grandest. It is linked to the John Adams Building and the James Madison Memorial Building via underground passageways.

It was one of many historic sites that we had visited but had not entered. In truth, Dad would have had little interest in exploring the historic library so it would have felt a little inconsiderate to have made him spend an hour or two there. We actually could have done with using the internet facilities but we headed back in the direction of our hotel to visit a public library instead.

There was a UFC Fan Expo taking place during our upcoming trip to Houston but I had left the meet and greet schedule at home. Once inside the library, I asked if I could use one of the public computers. Seeing as we were in the United States, of course we had to pay a fee for this service. I found the appropriate website and scribbled down as much information as I could before the time that we had paid for elapsed. Begrudgingly, we paid another fee to resume our internet access and finished recording all of the information that we required.

We still had some time to visit some tourist attractions before the day had drawn to a close but we ended up stumbling upon a fake version of the Oval Office within a souvenir shop. This was obviously a tacky gimmick that was designed to take as much money from tourists as possible but we could not help but feel amused by it.

Given that we had not seen the real thing, we decided that we may as well join the queue to have our photograph taken in this mock office.

Dad suggested that: "We can tell people that we had a tour around the real White House," and he genuinely seemed to be considering this possibility.

I played the role of party pooper by pointing out how it would be obvious to everyone that this cheap set up was not the real thing. We had our photograph taken in the 'Oval Office,' with Dad sat at the President's desk signing a document, whilst I leaned in to study it. With the way the world is going, I sometimes wish that I really did have the power to authorise new laws.

"Mr. President, would you like to have your photo taken whilst stood at the podium addressing the press?"

I assumed that the store worker was referring to my dad rather than Barack Obama. We took it in turns to pose for photos before paying the fee. As our experience came to a close, we did not feel quite so presidential whilst handing over a handful of dollars for this tourist trap.

We had a flight to catch the next day, so we called it a day and headed back to the hotel, stopping off for some fast food on the way. We were soon back in our hotel room, in our pyjamas, watching several consecutive episodes of the U.S. version of *The Office*. It brought back memories of our rock 'n' roll nights in Las Vegas.

I asked Dad what he thought of Washington D.C.

"It's certainly different to Las Vegas," was his reply.

"Las Vegas is the ultimate fantasy land but here is more serious. You will have liked all of the history though," he concluded.

I nodded in agreement and stated how the places that I had visited in the United States all had a very different feel to them.

The United States of America is the fourth largest country in the world, so it is not surprising that there are many different cultures and traditions throughout this vast land. To put it into perspective, the U.S. is only slightly smaller than the entire continent of Europe. Although governed by a central government in Washington, each state can almost be seen as an independent country.

They all have their own laws and many public services are run at state level. The European Union operates in a similar way; each country is self-governed but adheres to certain regulations implemented across the collective. As conservatives and liberals battle it out to shape the future of the country, it is more apparent than ever that there is not just one American Identity; there are many.

*　　*　　*

The following afternoon, we were back at Washington Dulles International Airport, ready for our onward journey to Houston.

Dad asked: "What is there to see in Houston? Ranches and cowboys?"

It was an understandable question, as any mention of Texas in popular culture will more than likely involve the very things that my dad had asked about. In truth, I had researched whether it was feasible to visit the sand hills, desert valleys, mountains and rivers from Houston but I had discovered that the state of Texas is larger than the entire country of France. This would make it very difficult to venture too far from Houston, which is the fourth largest city in the United States.

I informed Dad of the disappointing news: "I think that it is just a big city. I have read that there is a man-made water wall though."

Dad took it in his stride: "Well, we're only here for the UFC anyway."

As we made our way through the security area, we encountered something most unexpected; a U.S. airport worker that seemed friendly and jovial.

A female security officer had noticed my biceps and chest bulging out of my undersized T-shirt, prompting her to remark: "Excuse me, Sir...I'm going to have to see your abs."

I was so used to the strict nature of U.S. airports that I instinctively reached down to lift up my top. She smiled to indicate that she was only joking, which was probably best for all concerned. She would only have been thoroughly disappointed with my slightly podgy belly that had been increasing in size with each day spent in America.

"I want to see my abs too," would have been the response of an individual with a razor sharp wit, which I most certainly was not.

The arrival experience at George Bush Intercontinental Airport was fairly straightforward, since we had travelled on a domestic flight. The taxi journey to the Athens Hotel and Suites was also unproblematic, which made me wary that everything was running too smoothly and that something unpleasant was bound to occur sooner or later.

We were greeted by a rather abrasive hotel worker, who not only gave the impression that she could be capable of killing us in cold blood but that she would probably enjoy it as well.

"Your room is ready. I'll lead you there now," she unenthusiastically stated.

Despite her lack of 'southern hospitality,' everything was still going well. Then we entered our room. I had chosen this pokey little hotel because it was located in the shadow of the Toyota Center, which was set to host *UFC 136: Edgar vs. Maynard III* at the weekend. After seeing the online pictures, I had low expectations. I was hardly expecting a palace.

The old fashioned furniture and decor was in keeping with what I had imagined beforehand. The carpets and bedding looked like they had seen better days but it was of an acceptable standard. There was just one problem. With the word 'one' being the key word here. There was only one bed and I did not fancy spooning Dad for the next five nights.

I pointed out the fact that I had booked a twin room but the employee simply shrugged her shoulders and said: "We're full. I'm afraid that there are no other rooms available."

I looked at her in a manner that implied that there was surely an alternative that she could suggest but she failed to respond.

I then verbally communicated this by asking: "Is there any type of bed that could be brought into the room?"

She said that she would see what she could do and left the room. I did not hold high hopes. My low expectations were justified as she returned with an inflatable bed of sorts. It looked more like a sad abandoned lilo that one may see floating in a swimming pool. It was tired and worn but at least there were no visible stains that indicated the presence of bodily fluids.

With that mattered sorted, the employee gave us our room key and promptly made her exit. A short time later, we headed out for our early evening food. There was just one more thing that we needed to do before satisfying our hunger. Dad had taken a mixture of cash and travellers cheques with him on our American trip and he had almost run out of the former.

There was now a man called Philip stood behind the reception. His friendly and welcoming demeanour was in complete contrast to his colleague. We asked him about the travellers cheques and he said that if we were stuck, there was a money centre about a mile or so down the road.

Given that I had not seen a travellers cheque for over a decade, I was sceptical about whether they were still widely accepted. Dad assured me

that they were. We walked towards the nearest shop in order to change or
spend them.

"Sorry, we don't accept them," was the inevitable response.

Dad suggested trying McDonald's, with the reasoning behind this
being that they were a global franchise. We approached the teenage
worker behind the till and asked him if travellers cheques were accepted.

With a dumbfounded look on his face, his reply confirmed what I had
expected: "Travellers cheque. What's one of them?"

Dad explained but the teenager again stated that he had never heard of
this method of payment.

We tried our luck in several other stores before deciding to head
towards the money centre that Philip had suggested. I was becoming
wary that we were embarking on a long trek through downtown Houston
with a bunch of cheques in our possession. My nerves were heightened
by several groups of aggressive looking youths congregated on the steps
of some of the buildings that we passed.

In reality, there was no need to worry. Even if they had tried to mug
us, they would not have known what travellers cheque were and they
would not have been able to spend them in any case. We finally reached
the money centre but we were once again told that they do not accept
them. With the money centre not being able to help us, our chances of
finding somewhere that accepted the cheques did not appear to be great.

As we trudged back to the hotel, Dad suggested trying a tiny store that
we passed. I said that there was little point trying this place if the money
centre and the shops belonging to global brands did not accept the
cheques. Nevertheless, Dad entered the store and was rewarded for his
persistence. Surprisingly, this small independent store was more than
happy to take them as a form of payment. We bought some soft drinks
and snacks with a couple of the cheques and received enough cash in
return to cover our modest needs for the rest of the trip.

"I told you. Travellers cheques are still good," Dad proudly
proclaimed.

I chuckled to myself, before replying: "Yeah, if you fancy a two mile
walk before every purchase, then travellers cheques are the best form of
payment."

We returned to McDonald's, which prompted Dad to make another
questionable assertion: "For a nice meal, you can't beat a McDonald's."

Whilst I was tempted to reply that one most certainly could find a
better place to eat, I just went along with it in order to quickly satisfy my
hunger. Unfortunately, the teenager that we had spoken to earlier was no
longer manning the tills. Thus, we were denied a triumphant return, in
which we could have presented him with the cash to pay for our meal,

along with a tale about how we had cashed in the travellers cheques elsewhere.

After devouring my meal, I walked towards the toilet but found that it was locked. I asked an employee if I could have the code for the door but I was given a physical key instead. This seemed just as old fashioned as using a travellers cheque to make a payment but the real concern was the amount of germs that were more than likely making a home on the surface of the key.

I made use of the facilities before discreetly handing the key over to Dad to use, as if it could unlock a safety deposit box containing millions of dollars. Once it was time to leave, we returned the key and headed back towards our hotel.

My first night's sleep on the inflatable bed was not the best. Every time that I made a slight movement, the bed made a horrible squeaking sound. At first, I was concerned about disturbing Dad but I need not have worried, as he was soon snoring as loudly as humanly possible.

As it turned out, I was the only one that was being irritated by the noise of the inflatable bed. To the extent that I was unable to fall asleep for hours. It was hardly the most comfortable bed but I must have fallen asleep at some point, as I eventually opened my eyes and saw daylight.

*   *   *

After having a basic but satisfactory breakfast consisting of cornflakes, we arranged for a taxi to take us to the San Jacinto Monument. This was located at the site of one of the most important battles of the Texas Revolution. In a situation that contrasts sharply with today's reality, Mexico was the colonial power ruling over Texas during the 1820s and 1830s.

This was a result of Mexico gaining independence from Spain, which like many other European countries, had gained a foothold in America. Back then, it was Mexico that was holding debates over the number of immigrants that they should allow in from the United States, with Texas seeing an influx of English speaking settlers.

The Texans successfully rebelled against the Mexican regime during the Texas Revolution of 1835-36 and declared the Republic of Texas to be an independent sovereign nation. The Battle of San Jacinto, in which the Mexicans were defeated, was the decisive moment in this episode of Texan history, paving the way for independence.

General Santa Anna, who had successfully fought for Mexican independence from Spain, signed the peace treaty that stated that Mexico would leave the region. A decade later, Texas was annexed by the United

States of America. Another couple of decades further on, Texas was one of the states that formed the confederacy, which unsuccessfully attempted to break away from the United States during the Civil War.

Our first sight of the San Jacinto Monument reminded us of the first landmark that we had visited in Washington D.C. the previous weekend. Like the Washington Monument, it was a column that was over five hundred feet tall and was situated by a reflecting pool. The octagonal column is the world's tallest war monument and is situated by the Houston Ship Canal.

We examined the base of the monument, which provided some historical background on each side. It was interesting to read about events that differed greatly from today's world. I had not expected to be looking at inscriptions that described how Texans suffered under the Mexican regime until they were defeated by Texan citizens and immigrant soldiers.

We then tilted our heads and looked up towards the top of the monument, upon which rested a two hundred and twenty ton star. This was the most fitting symbol for the battle, as the Lone Star was featured on the national flag that was adopted by the Republic of Texas, which eventually became the state flag following its annexation by the United States.

Dad seemed impressed by the size of the star: "Let's hope that the star doesn't fall off and land on us. We would not stand a chance. It's huge."

I thanked Dad for creating such an unpleasant scenario, before looking up anxiously and considering this highly unlikely possibility.

With a sense of relief that we had avoided being killed in the most horrific yet comical manner, we took the elevator up to the observation deck. The view was pleasant enough, with the Houston Ship Canal and the *USS Texas* (BB-35) battleship visible from our vantage point. We admired the view for a few minutes before making our way back down to the base of the monument.

We walked along the side of the reflecting pool, which lived up to its name by displaying the reflection of the San Jacinto Monument on its surface, on our way to the *USS Texas*. This was a legendary battleship that had served in both world wars, before being converted into a museum and heralded as a national landmark.

I am unable to recall exactly why Dad and I did not board the battleship but I strongly suspect that it was because we were a couple of cheapskates who were reluctant to pay the entrance fee.

Nevertheless, we admired the ship from close quarters, as I pondered the significance of the vessel: "It is quite something to think that this battleship was used in World War I, nearly a hundred years ago, and also played a part in the Normandy Landings on D-Day during World War II. It also saw action in North Africa and the Pacific, so it has an impressive history."

Dad nodded in agreement, before responding: "It's not as big as I thought it would be. It's still imposing though. Imagine seeing that travelling down the Manchester Ship Canal."

We returned to our taxi and asked our driver, who had waited for us whilst we had explored the battleground, to take us to the Galleria shopping centre. I had little interest in the shopping centre itself but I had been intrigued by the existence of a man-made waterwall that was located nearby.

I had read about this on a 'top ten things to see in Houston' list but the driver had no idea about what I was talking about.

"Waterwall? I've lived in Houston all my life and I ain't never heard of no waterwall," he firmly stated.

Triple negatives aside, I was surprised that he had not heard of something that was on a list of must-see attractions in Houston.

Our driver genuinely seemed puzzled by what I had said: "A waterwall. Water.....wall."

A few minutes later, he continued to mumble to himself, seemingly trying to figure out what this mysterious attraction was: "A wall made out of water. Water. Wall."

The driver was not any wiser by the time we had reached The Galleria. As there did not appear to be any signs to direct us to the waterwall, we had a look for any exits that could lead to an open space in which a waterwall could be located. After a few unsuccessful attempts, we finally found what we were looking for.

I had not felt so underwhelmed since Manchester United had replaced Cristiano Ronaldo with Antonio Valencia and Gabriel Obertan. The Gerald D. Hines Waterwall Park is situated opposite an office building called the Williams Tower. It was built in the 1980s to compliment the tower, rather than to serve as a local attraction. The horseshoe shaped structure has apparently become a much loved feature of the Houston landscape but I could not find any evidence of this during our brief time in the city.

It is sixty four feet tall, to symbolically match the sixty four stories of the tower. However, I thought that the waterwall looked small and insignificant in comparison to the tower. The running water was pleasant enough but it felt more like a place for office workers to sit during their lunch break, rather than something that would appeal to overseas tourists.

After posing for the obligatory photographs in front of the waterwall, we made our way back inside The Galleria. We wandered around the unimaginative shops and consumed an early evening meal of barbecued chicken and fries, before heading back to the hotel. We had a different taxi now; therefore, we were unable to enlighten our original driver about what we had seen. I often wonder whether he is still driving around and muttering to himself about a mysterious waterwall.

*   *   *

We had one more day to kill before the UFC Fan Expo began but we did not have anything left on our sightseeing itinerary. At this point, I deeply regretted my decision to stay only three nights in Washington, which was full of historic buildings and attractions, but spend five nights in Houston, where there did not seem to be much of interest.

We did not do too much of note during our second full day in Houston. We had asked Philip, the helpful hotel employee, about places that we could visit but most of his suggestions, such as visiting the island city of Galveston, involved travelling long distances and spending more money than we wanted to.

The list of 'must-see attractions in Houston' included some rather bizarre entries. The Beer Can House, which is adorned with an estimated fifty thousand beer cans and other paraphernalia, is apparently one of the city's most loved folk art houses.

As quirky and interesting as it sounded, it did seem like the people that compiled the list were in need of some items to fill some of the top ten spots. Likewise, the National Museum of Funeral History seemed an odd choice for the list. Perhaps the unusual nature of these attractions warranted a visit but we passed up the opportunity.

I am probably being harsh on Houston, as there seems to be a few places of interest within the surrounding area. The Lyndon B. Johnson Space Center is home to NASA's training and research centres, as well as its flight control centre. Interestingly, "Houston, we have a problem," has become one of the most famous examples of an inaccurate quote, thanks to the movie, *Apollo 13*.

The real Jim Lovell actually said: "Houston, we've had a problem." In any case, the phrase has been adopted by popular culture, in reference to the discovery of an unforeseen problem. Again, if I had planned our itinerary better, we may have arranged a trip to the Visitor Center. There is also a network of underground tunnels and a Major League Baseball stadium but our experience of Houston left the impression of a rather bland city.

*   *   *

The last couple of days of the trip revolved around mixed martial arts. The UFC Fan Expo was held over two days at the George R. Brown Convention Center, which involved lots of queueing up to meet fighters and watching MMA demonstrations. By this point, I was well aware of how I did not necessarily enjoy the awkward interaction with the competitors but that this satisfied my hunger to collect something, photographs in this case, that was connected to the sport that I followed.

Over the course of the two day expo, we met the likes of Vitor Belfort, Rashad Evans, Don Frye, Forrest Griffin, Daniel Cormier and Bas Rutten. The expo was certainly an extremely efficient way of building my MMA photo collection, as I could make several additions per hour. I think Dad relished having a chat with the fighters but my disdain for making smalltalk, in any circumstance, remained as strong as ever.

Along with eighteen thousand others, we attended *UFC 136: Edgar vs. Maynard III* at the Toyota Center on Saturday night, which saw Frankie Edgar emerge victorious from the final act of his trilogy with Gray Maynard. My enjoyment of watching these live MMA shows was starting to wane. After all, one could get a better view on television, without being surrounded by thousands of drunkards.

The shows were also very long affairs, each lasting about seven hours. That's a long time to avoid using a public toilet. As my interest in the sport had not yet completely diminished, this would not be my last event that I attended

It was following the conclusion of the show, that we felt the benefit of booking a hotel so close to the arena. Only having to walk for a few minutes to our accommodation was a most welcome relief. The Athens Hotel and Suites did not seem so bad at this point.

\*     \*     \*

The following day, it was time to leave the United States. Our Expedia confirmation printout simply stated that our return flight was from 'Houston.' We had arrived at George Bush Intercontinental Airport, so it stood to reason that we would be departing from the same place.

We queried this with Philip at the hotel, who assured us that we would almost certainly be departing from the same airport that we had arrived at.

"You are catching a connecting international flight, so you'll be flying from the big international airport. I'm sure of it."

Nowadays, I would check this information online prior to departure but back then I was happy to go along with the advice of a friendly hotel worker.

Dad and I had arrived about two hours prior to take off and we were feeling quite pleased with ourselves that we had set aside so much time to navigate our way through the airport. We made our way over to a self-service check-in kiosk and began what we hoped would be a straightforward process.

I scanned our passports but the system display informed us that it was unable to locate our booking. I entered our booking reference instead but the result was the same. An airline employee came over to help, in a manner similar to the numerous occasions in which a supermarket employee has provided assistance after the self-service checkout machine has failed to recognise an item.

"She will be able to sort it, just like in the supermarkets," I told myself.

The helpful employee tried the same methods that I had employed but she was also unable to retrieve our booking. She asked to see our paperwork, so we handed it over.

"Oh…" she began ominously.

"… I can see why we are unable to find your booking."

She went on explain that there was just one problem; we were at the wrong airport. In our defence, it was a fairly easy mistake to make. Unfortunately, we were scheduled to leave Houston from the William P. Hobby Airport. This was a much smaller airport that handled domestic flights, such as the first leg of our journey.

"The two airports are located at opposite ends of the city. Sorry but I don't think that you can get there in time," was her grim assessment.

"OK, we will do everything in our power to make the flight," Dad insisted.

This resulted in her simply saying, "Good luck."

It felt like we were in a scene from the film *Taken,* with Dad playing the role of Liam Neeson and the airline employee having informed us that our mission of leaving America was doomed. Admittedly, our scenario was slightly less dramatic and had much less at stake.

Houston is the fourth largest city in the United States of America. Our chances of travelling across this metropolis, through busy afternoon traffic, and having enough time to check in, go through security and locate our gate, seemed pretty slim.

We leapt into the first taxi that we saw and explained our situation to the driver. We were expecting him to put his foot down and take off in the reckless manner that one may see in an episode of *Wacky Races.*

Instead, we were taken aback by his calm response: "I'm just going to finish my sandwich."

Our fate was now in the hands of this man. Unfortunately, it was clear that he felt that his sandwich was the most important thing that was in his hands. My coping strategy in a situation such as this is to immediately concede defeat and try to calculate the ramifications. If we missed our flight, and therefore our connecting flight from Atlanta, we would have to stay another night in Houston. A short notice flight would cost an additional few hundred pounds each and we would have to pay for another night's accommodation.

This was obviously a bad thing but we were lucky enough to be in a financial position in which we could take the hit. The bigger concern was informing my mother that we would be arriving back a day later, therefore missing the first proper day of my new university course.

Eventually, the driver finished his sandwich and casually began the fifty kilometre journey. Heavy rain added to the sense of impending doom. I continued my calculations during the course of the journey. Dad suggested that we may just about make it in time. I am not sure if he genuinely believed that but I replied that we had no chance and that we would have to make arrangements to stay another night.

My negative words were followed by more silence and tension as we watched our driver navigate his way through the city without a care in the world. We reached the William P. Hobby Airport around half an hour before our scheduled take off, which I reasoned would surely not be enough time to check in, go through security and find our gate.

Dad paid the driver the fare. We were due ten dollars in change but Dad said that he could just give five back.

This prompted the driver to finally show signs of life, as he replied: "I don't know. There was a lot of rain. Five dollars, I don't know."

We let him keep the ten, grabbed our cases, and ran inside, expecting the worst. It soon became apparent that this domestic airport was much smaller than the international one that we had arrived at. It resembled a bus station more than an airport.

We approached the check-in desk and I sheepishly asked: "Is it too late to check in for the Atlanta flight?"

The man behind the desk smiled and said: "Of course not. Relax, take your time, the flight is not due to leave for another thirty minutes."

If this had been the George Bush Intercontinental Airport, we would have been laughed at and told that we were already too late. With our boarding passes now in hand, we headed towards the security section, still unsure of whether to believe the calming words of the man behind the check-in counter. Unlike most other airports, there was not a queue in sight.

We quickly made our way through and located our gate. Within minutes of arriving at the airport, we had checked in, gone through security and made our way to the gate. I could not believe that we had made it.

Almost immediately, we were greeted with an announcement that our flight had been delayed by half an hour. We almost felt cheated; all of that rushing around and panic was for nothing. Our reward for overcoming all of the odds to get here on time was to have to wait an additional thirty minutes.

Dad laughed as he said: "It was never in doubt. I told you that we would make it."

225

# CHAPTER 13: A CHRISTMAS MIRACLE: NO SPORT INVOLVED!
## BRUSSELS, BELGIUM
## DECEMBER 2011

Something very strange and unexpected happened in December 2011; I booked an overseas trip that did not involve a mixed martial arts show or a football match! Indeed, there was not even a hint of a sport-related motive for arranging the trip. This was a huge moment in my evolution from a person who travelled to watch sports events in different countries, to someone who simply travelled for the love of travelling.

Mum was my travel partner for this long weekend break, which I felt a little awkward about, considering that I had recently decided to abandon my Human Nutrition university course in favour of returning to full time work with my former employers at the data management company. Looking back, I believe that I made the correct decision, because I would not have been able to travel so extensively in the following years if I had remained at university.

I knew that Mum would be disappointed that I was making the wrong choice for my career prospects. Like a true coward, I decided to keep this information from her until I had navigated my way through the trip to the Belgian capital. And Christmas. And New Year. And any other excuse that I could find to delay delivering the news that I knew would thoroughly disappoint her.

Following our arrival at Brussels Airport quite late in the evening, we took a taxi to our hotel in order to get a door to door service. The only problem was that our driver took us to the wrong door. In his defence, there are many Ibis hotels in Brussels; at least he got the right chain of hotel. When we informed him of this, he did not seem particularly helpful.

He simply pointed and told us that: "It is over there somewhere. I am unable to drive there due to the road design."

Thankfully, our hotel was only a few minutes away on foot. After checking in, we made our way up to our room and quickly inspected our accommodation for the next three nights. I was impressed by the cleanliness and the efficient use of space.

Mum echoed my sentiments: "It is clever how they have crammed so much into a small space, without making you feel uncomfortable."

It was late, so we just shared a tube of Pringles for supper. This particular brand of potato based snack has become a regular staple of my diet whilst on overseas trips, which is more to do with the robust tube that they are stored in rather than the taste of the crisps. It does mean that I have an extra thing to worry about whilst making my way through airport security though, as I always wonder whether the tube will appear suspicious on the X-ray machines. I have not yet been interrogated about carrying a tube of Pringles, so my concerns have most likely been misplaced.

\*    \*    \*

We woke up feeling refreshed after a good sleep and we then built up our energy supplies for the day with a substantial continental breakfast. Grand Place was the obvious location from which to launch our day of sightseeing.

The main square of the city, known as Grote Markt in Dutch, was a few minutes' walk from our hotel. This provided me with ample time to explain to Mum that there are three official languages in Belgium.

"Generally speaking, the north of the country speak Dutch, the South speak French and a small percentage of people in the east speak German."

Mum considered this for a moment, before posing the inevitable questions: "Why are the signs here in French and Dutch? Does that mean that we are in the north or south?"

I tried to appear confident as I informed her that: "Brussels is a designated bilingual region that is just about in the north. Besides, people have moved from the different regions over the years and most people speak multiple languages."

Judging by her next comment, I think that Mum accepted my explanation: "We have multiple dialects in China too. Mandarin, Cantonese, etc."

A maze of narrow cobbled streets led to a sudden opening that contrasted starkly with the route that we had taken. We were now stood in the middle of a huge public square that was surrounded by imposing important looking buildings. I examined my guide book in order to figure out what each building was.

The fifteenth century Town Hall is the most prominent building belonging to the square. I thought that it was aesthetically pleasing but I was keen to seek Mum's opinion.

"That's the Town Hall. I think that it looks nice. What do you think?" I asked.

She seemed impressed, stating that it was: "Pretty and grand. This is usually the case with Town Halls."

Mum was right but I felt that this Town Hall was particularly charming. Perhaps this was down to its picturesque setting on the perimeter of this beautiful square, which is surely one of Europe's finest.

What I did not notice on first inspection is that the building is asymmetrical. The sections on either side of the tower were built separately; hence, they are not identical. Their length varies slightly, meaning that the tower is not in the exact centre of the building. This is the kind of detail that I usually obsess about until I am pushed to the brink of insanity.

An old myth around Brussels states that this is exactly what happened to the building's architect, who committed suicide by leaping to his death from the belfry, after realising that he had made such an error. However, it is now thought that there were multiple architects involved in the project and, as I said earlier, the two sides were built separately. Perhaps they were never intended to be identical. Regardless of the inaccuracy of the myth, I deemed it best to simply admire the grandeur of the building rather than focusing on its asymmetric construction.

Mum turned and pointed towards the second most eye-catching building surrounding the square and asked, "What is that building?"

I checked my guide book to make sure that the information that I was about to give out was accurate: "In French, this is known as the King's House."

I then asked a leading question that was designed to guide the conversation in a direction that would allow me to talk about the building's history: "Why do you think it is called that?"

Mum gave the logical answer that: "It is the home of the King of Belgium."

As expected, this provided me with the opportunity to inform her that the name is rather misleading.

"As a symbol of his power, the Duke of Brabant ordered the

construction of an extravagant building opposite the Town Hall. It was built on the site of former cloth and bread markets, which is why the Dutch name for the building translates as 'Bread House.' There has never been a King that lived here. It now houses the Brussels City Museum."

Mum looked bemused, which was confirmed by her response: "So this building is known as the King's House in French but no King has ever lived here. And it is known as the Bread House in Dutch but it was not used to sell bread. Very strange!"

Regardless of the name of the building, it was undeniably very striking and would have been fit for a king. The ornate facade, reconstructed after being badly damaged by the French bombardment at the end of the seventeenth century, is an example of the Gothic Revival style of architecture. The arches, galleries and spires all formed part of a visually impressive building that the Duke would most likely have approved of.

I suspect that he would also have been most pleased with another structure on the square. The House of the Dukes of Brabant is adorned with busts that honour the various people that have held that particular title. This actually refers to seven guild houses that are located behind the opulent facade that we were now looking at.

They were not the only guild houses that lined the square. These tall and narrow buildings seemed to be forced together, lacking any resemblance of uniformity. I was unsure of the story behind each one but I instantly approved of the appearance of these individualistic houses that seemed full of character and intrigue.

The Grand Place has had an interesting history, with the centrally located square becoming a focal point for both positive and negative events throughout the ages. As I mentioned earlier, the French bombarded the city in 1695, destroying much of the square in the process. It was rebuilt but it was then extensively damaged once again during the Brabant Revolution, that established the short-lived United Belgian States at the end of the eighteenth century.

To complete the summary of the darker elements of its history, the square was the site of the burning of Protestant martyrs during the Inquisition and it was the location for the beheadings of a couple of Counts who dared to speak out against the regime of King Phillip II. The Town Hall also served as a makeshift hospital during the First World War.

On a lighter note, the square has been the site of a marketplace since the eleventh century, with its importance increasing over the years. Grand Place also plays host to a 'Flower Carpet' every two years. This tradition, which began in 1971, involves a million colourful begonias being arranged into a pattern that runs seventy seven metres of the square's one hundred and ten metre length.

Since it was December rather than August, the 'Flower Carpet' was nowhere to be seen. Instead, there was a huge Christmas tree in the centre of the square, surrounded by a series of poles that resembled street lights. I was not sure why they were there but I would find out later on.

There were a few stalls set up in the remaining space but they appeared to be more geared towards the Christmas Markets that would become busier during the evening time. We had a quick browse at the stalls selling souvenir drawings of the square and various ornaments, before concluding that the markets would be far more atmospheric once business had picked up later on.

The next item on our agenda was a visit to Manneken Pis, which was just a couple of minutes' walk away.

The interesting Dutch name of this statue prompted Mum to ask me: "What does Mannekin Pis mean?"

There was not much I could say to make it sound more sophisticated than it was, so I simply replied: "It is a statue of a small boy urinating."

Mum laughed and asked: "Why is this a tourist attraction?"

I relayed the information that I had read in my guidebook: "This twenty four inch sculpture initially served as a drinking fountain but it soon became one of the most cherished possessions of the city. It is supposed to demonstrate the sense of humour of the city."

Mum laughed again, which I took as a sign that it was having its intended effect.

The diminutive statue, originally installed in the early seventeenth century but replaced by a newer model in 1965, has been the subject of numerous attempts of thievery but has remained an enduring symbol of the city. During the twentieth century, it became customary to dress the boy in a variety of outfits.

This tradition has increased in frequency over the years, with 2016 seeing as many as nine hundred and fifty costume changes. That is almost as many changes of attire as Sarah Jessica Parker makes when hosting an awards show. It would seem that we were in the minority of visitors that saw the naked statue but I preferred that to the prospect of seeing him dressed up as Dracula or something else ridiculous.

Something else that borders on the absurd are the myths that exist around the inspiration for the statue. The most famous one is that the troops of the twelfth century Duke Godfrey III of Leuven, who was just two years old, hung a basket containing their baby leader from a tree during a battle against a rival army. The little boy then proceeded to urinate on the enemy, resulting in their defeat.

Other legends feature a variety of bizarre scenarios that ultimately end with a young boy urinating on something for a positive outcome. According to one story, a boy saved the city by urinating on the fuse of explosives that were going to be used by foreign attackers, and in another, the boy's urine put out a fire, thus saving the King's castle.

Prior to visiting Brussels, I had never heard of so many heroic and glorious ways in which urine could be used.

"Which story do you believe, David?" Mum asked.

I tried to figure out if she was being serious, before I answered: "None of them. Do you actually think that any of the legends ae true?"

Mum laughed again, before replying: "I'm not sure if any of them are true but I do like the one about him peeing on the other army!"

Both the statue and the myths about its origin seemed to have tickled Mum. On a more serious note, it was only recently discovered that a fault with the statue was causing up to two and a half thousand litres of clean drinking water to be Manneken Pis'd into the city's sewers. Thankfully, the fault has now been repaired, as people were starting to get Pis'd off about this.

We decided to head towards the Royal Palace. The centrally located streets that we had to pass were lined with rows of market stalls that caught our attention.

Mum stated that: "The stalls look prettier here, all lined up. It looks more festive."

I agreed with her sentiment and I was happy to stop and have a look at the variety of Christmas themed gifts on offer. In addition to the wood carvings, paintings and Santa figurines for sale, there was a wide selection of festive food and drink available to purchase. Things were not yet in full swing but it was possible to buy hot chocolate, waffles and gingerbread. We again decided that it would be best to return in the evening, in order to sample the festivities in all of their glory.

The Royal Palace, or the Palais Royal de Bruxelles, is located in the Upper Town, where the ruling class once presided over the commoners of the Lower Town. We climbed the open staircase leading up to the Mont des Arts, stopping to admire the view over the Lower Town. The spire of the Town Hall stood tall over the other buildings, whilst a statue of a man on a horse, apparently depicting King Albert I, appeared to be taking in the same view.

The staircase probably looks prettier during the summer but it looked a bit dreary on this dull winter's day. The area that is known as the Mont des Arts was the brainchild of King Leopold II, who had decided to create an arts quarter here, although much of it was built after his death in 1909.

Mum seemed somewhat underwhelmed: "So this is the Royal Palace? It does not look all that special. It's big and fairly pleasant but it looks like it could be a museum rather than a palace. The big Christmas tree at the front looks OK though."

Although this was perhaps a little harsh, I could see what she meant. The facade of this Neoclassical building is longer than Buckingham Palace but it does not look anywhere near as grand.

I offered some additional information, which helped to explain its understated appearance: "Although it is the official palace of the King and Queen of Belgium, they do not live here."

Mum nodded as she said: "Ahh, that makes more sense. It would probably be more extravagant if they actually lived here."

We took it in turns to take photographs of each other in front of the palace before a kind stranger offered to take a picture of us together. As he fumbled around trying to find the ideal angle and relevant button to press, we stood shivering in the cold. Our woollen hats offered some protection from the cold but we were in danger of becoming damp due to the rain that had begun to drizzle.

As the stranger lined up the photograph, I could not help but wonder if he would be tempted to run off with my camera like in the film *National Lampoon's European Vacation.* If the man began instructing us to step back in order to make the perfect photograph, I would become even more concerned.

As it turns out, my camera was returned to me with a nice photo of the two of us. This would prove to be the only such picture of the trip, given that selfie sticks were not yet as popular as they are today and I am most certainly not the type of person to ask a stranger to take a photo for me.

I was unaware that the archaeological site of the Coudenberg Palace was next to the Royal Palace. It began life as a castle in the twelfth century, before being used as a Palace by various Dukes until it was destroyed by a fire in 1731. The site of the former palace was built over and largely forgotten about until the archaeological site was recently opened to the public. An underground tour of a former Palace sounds interesting to me but I was completely unaware of its existence at the time of our visit.

For some reason, I was also ignorant of the fact that there was a Gothic cathedral nearby. If I had visited Brussels in 2004, perhaps I would have been eager to join the crowds that had gathered to observe the family of falcons that had made their home on the rooftop. They were known to acrobatically fly around the gargoyles, which certainly impressed spectators. Another notable building that we did not visit was the Palace of the Nation, which houses the Belgian Federal Parliament.

The palace and the parliament building were only separated by Brussels Park but we headed further East instead. It was another set of parliamentary buildings that I was interested in; those belonging to the European Parliament. It seemed an essential part of any visit to the city. After all, Brussels conjures up three images for many people: Brussel sprouts, 'The Muscles from Brussels' Jean-Claude Van Damme and the European Union.

*     *     *

It took us less than ten minutes to reach the collection of buildings known as Espace Leopold, which houses this legislative chamber of the European Union. Strasbourg is the official home of the European Parliament but Brussels plays host to a sizeable proportion of the meetings due to its proximity to the other E.U. institutions, such as the European Commission and the European Council.

Unlike most parliamentary buildings, the structures in front of us all had a modern appearance, reflecting the fact that they were mostly opened in the 1990s. The most prominent, eye-catching building is named after Paul-Henri Spaak, who was a former Belgian Prime Minister and a key figure in the formation of the European Economic Community. The building houses the hemicycle, which is a familiar sight on our television screens because this is the arena for political debates and addresses. The shape of the building seemed unusual to us, as it appeared to consist of a series of cylinder shaped glass and steel sections that were fixed together.

Another major European Union building in this area is named after Altiero Spinelli, who was an Italian politician and a founding member of the European Federalist Movement. This building contains the offices of MEPs and political groups, which was not a surprise to me, given its immaculate appearance and numerous shiny glass panels.

Mum asked: "Which of these buildings is the headquarters of the European Union?"

I knew that I would struggle to answer questions about the absurdly complex make up of the various E.U. institutions, considering that I barely understood them myself.

However, I tried my best to explain: "Well, this one houses the offices of European MPs and the one with the cylinder dome is where the debating chamber is. However, legislation is proposed in the European Commission."

My answer did not seem to provide any clarity, therefore Mum looked even more puzzled than before.

"So is that one the parliament building?" she asked.

I paused, before attempting to provide a simplified explanation: "It is where you will find the chamber of the parliament that you have seen on TV. But this building is only part of the European Parliament complex. As are those two over there. Although, the official home of the European Parliament is in Strasbourg."

Mum laughed, before replying: "Strasbourg! It's so complicated. I'll never understand."

I reassured her by stating that: "Most people struggle to understand it. I am not even sure that I do."

I decided to dodge any further discussion about the organisational structure of the European Union by suggesting that we should head back towards the Lower Town. Although I was attempting to avoid the other E.U. buildings, we may well have walked past a multitude of them without knowing it. As I mentioned earlier, there are several different E.U. institutions based in Brussels. Remarkably, around half of the occupied office space in the city is taken up by these institutions, with most located in the European Quarter that we were passing through.

After our visit to some of the European Parliament buildings, I can understand the frustration that some people have with the complicated nature of the set up. It can seem overly bureaucratic but I remain a fan of the European Union, at least in principle. In addition to more efficient economic trade between member states, the union provides solidarity between European nations and ensures that the fundamental principles of human rights and environmental protections are underpinned by E.U. law.

As there has been a spike in hostility towards the European Union, most notably demonstrated by Brexit, I think that it is important to examine the reasons why certain people express such anger towards it and what their objectives are for dismantling it. The E.U. is far from perfect, and the desire to be self-governed is understandable but I am often left perplexed by the particular reasons why people oppose it.

Many of the dissenting voices often display an aggressive nationalistic tone and vent their fury at the regulations that are set in place to ensure that the rights of humans, animals and the environment are respected. The year after our visit, the European Union was awarded the Nobel Peace Prize for contributing to, in the words of the awarding body: "The advancement of peace and reconciliation, democracy and human rights in Europe."

Indeed, the several decades that have followed the Second World War have seen a concerted effort to unify Europe and to avoid conflict.

Whether you are inside the European Union or not, surely you would want these protections in place? But then again, the agenda of the far-right directly opposes these things, given that they hope to improve their own circumstances at the expense of the more vulnerable sections of society.

We left the world of politics behind and made our way back towards the Lower Town, making a detour to visit the Palais de Justice. This colossal building houses the most important court in the Belgian justice system. From its inception, it has never been popular with the locals.

This is not surprising, considering that around three thousand homes were knocked down in order to make way for the construction of what is thought to be the largest building erected in the nineteenth century. Understandably, this caused a lot of anger, with the word 'architect' transformed into an insult within Brussels.

I was expecting to see one of the grandest neoclassical buildings in Europe but we were instead left looking at a mass of ugly scaffolding. This will not be a surprise to anyone who has visited the Palais de Justice, given that the ongoing renovation and seemingly permanent scaffolding has become the source of derision and humour in equal measure.

Work to repair the crumbling building began over thirty years ago but a variety of disputes and mismanagement has resulted in the most ridiculous delays. A couple of years after our visit, it was reported that the scaffolding itself required renovation.

Whether this was a tongue-in-cheek suggestion or not, the integrity of the structure has been brought into question by the introduction of additional scaffolding over the years. The building has been branded as the 'Palace of Scaffolding' and a common joke is that it appears to have been put behind bars for its past crimes. Nearly a decade on from our visit, a definitive completion date has still not been provided, with anything from the late 2020s until 2040 being offered as the most likely scenario.

One thing that I have regretted about many of my trips abroad has been my failure to explore the inside of some of the important buildings that I have visited. On some occasions, this has been due to having to pay an entrance fee or having a tight schedule to stick to. In this case, my hand was forced by Mum's need to use the toilet.

The interior of the building, which was free to enter, looked much more impressive than the exterior, although it was also in need of renovation. An abundance of statues, columns and marble gave the impression of grandeur that I had expected to have seen from the outside. I am not sure whether the toilets were as extravagant but despite being in a court building, I had no inclination to ask Mum for her verdict.

We arrived back in the Lower Town in time for evening dinner. We opted for a small restaurant with a homely feel to it and a mixture of local and international dishes on the menu. Previously, I would have chosen something like a burger and chips, in order to eliminate the risk of an unpleasant meal.

Perhaps in keeping with the spirit of my first non-sporting based trip but more likely due to some of the traditional offerings appearing to be relatively safe choices, I plumped for one of the most popular meals in Belgium. A traditional beef and beer stew, with a side serving of chips. Or frites, as they are known here.

Frites are an integral part of Belgian culinary history and we found that they are available to purchase throughout Brussels. They are often eaten with mayonnaise or with a stew like the one that I had ordered. For the purist, they are served with mussels, creating the de-facto national dish known as 'moules frites.'

There has been a long standing dispute between the Belgians and the French regarding the origin of this potato based food. The common usage of the term 'French fries' is the source of irritation amongst proud Belgians. In any case, Belgian frites are considered the superior version by the natives, who highlight the way that they are fried twice during the cooking process.

Mum ordered moules frites and we both decided to try some of the beer that Belgium is famed for. Our combined total of two beers probably meant that it was the trip that had seen the most consumption of alcohol to date. Oh, how wild we were back then. Mum offered me some of her mussels but I was not yet brave enough to try any molluscs. This would have to wait until my next trip to Belgium.

I thoroughly enjoyed my stew, frites and dark beer. This was certainly a step in the right direction in terms of my willingness to sample local food during my adventures around the globe. As for Mum, she enjoyed her meal, although unsurprisingly, she stated that it was "a little too salty."

After dinner, we went for a stroll around the narrow streets within the heart of the city. The Christmas markets were now in full swing, which meant that the area was packed with both tourists and locals. Whilst this looked much more festive and atmospheric than it did during the daytime, the lack of space was very frustrating. It was inevitable that we would be bumped into every few seconds and it was difficult to fight our way to the front of the stalls that we were interested in.

If it was possible to recreate this atmosphere without being buffeted from pillar to post it would be perfect but as this was extremely unlikely, we made the most of the situation that we found ourselves in. We were in the midst of what is regularly voted as one of the best Christmas markets in Europe, so we decided that we may as well make the most of it.

From one of the market stalls, we sampled some chocolate, which is another food offering that Belgium is renowned for.

"That was nice, wasn't it? What did you think?" I asked Mum.

She provided a positive reply, by saying: "It was very good quality chocolate."

Given that Mum's seal of approval is not an easy thing to obtain, I decided to purchase some more chocolate to take back with us.

We were soon back in Grand Place, where it became clear why there were poles with lights surrounding the Christmas tree. This was the scene of a spectacular light show that was performed every half an hour. Mum and I were enchanted by this unexpected visual display. Lights were projected onto the Town Hall, creating different patterns as music was played.

We enjoyed seeing the variety of colours and shapes being shown in such a beautiful setting. I was particularly fond of the plethora of stars that was being created on the most famous building in Brussels, which was the perfect accompaniment to the Christmas tree. We were charmed to such an extent that we returned half an hour later to watch another show. And several more times during our stay in the Belgian capital.

\*     \*     \*

We had another good sleep and breakfast, which prepared us for our final day of sightseeing. Our itinerary would take us away from the city centre, in order to explore an area containing a number of well known sites. A straightforward journey on the metro took us to Heysel, which is where the football ground best remembered for the tragedy of 1985 is located, along with the Mini-Europe amusement park and the Atomium. We started by taking the obligatory photographs of the latter.

The Atomium, like the Eiffel Tower in Paris and the Space Needle in Seattle, was built as the showpiece of a World Expo and it remains a symbol of the city. In this case, it was the 1958 edition. It was certainly an unusual building, as it was designed to resemble an enlarged version of a unit cell of an iron crystal.

Mum looked quizzically at this bizarre structure before asking me: "Is that a functional building? Are there rooms inside that you can walk about in?"

I can certainly see why she asked that question. We were essentially looking at nine stainless steel spheres that were connected by a series of tubes.

"Yes, Mum, it was built to showcase exhibitions and it is still used for that purpose today, I am guessing that most of the exhibition space is in the spheres."

The unusual shape did make me wonder how practical the building could be though. After entering the Atomium, its functionality started to become clearer. The connecting tube that runs vertically through the centre of the structure contains a lift, whilst the angled tubes feature, as we found out, extremely long escalators. Only one of the spheres at the top is accessible to the public, with a restaurant being located inside.

One of the spheres houses a permanent exhibition about the creation of the Atomium, whilst temporary exhibitions can be held in another. I am unable to recall whether any particular exhibition was being held in the additional space but we found the information about the inception of the Atomium to be fairly interesting.

It was supposed to highlight the potential for the use of atomic energy in a positive way but it received a fairly negative critical response. However, it soon became a cherished landmark of the city. To such an extent that the plan to dismantle it after just a few months was scrapped and it was decided that the Atomium would remain as a permanent fixture within Brussels.

We took the lift to the top sphere to take in panoramic views of the area. Although most of the historic sites of the city were too far away to admire, we still enjoyed looking down over the surrounding land. We could see Mini-Europe, which looked even smaller from our elevated position.

The King Baudouin Stadium, formerly known as Heysel Stadium, was also visible from our vantage point. Unfortunately, this will always be remembered as the scene of one of football's most infamous disasters. It was here that thirty nine supporters of the Italian club Juventus died shortly before the commencement of the 1985 European Cup final against Liverpool. A combination of violence between rival fans, the poor condition of the stadium, inadequate security provisions and the questionable decisions regarding ticket allocation, resulted in the tragic events that unfolded.

A section of Liverpool supporters surged passed the temporary fencing and outnumbered police officers that separated them from what was officially a neutral area but, in reality, had been occupied by Juventus fans. The supporters at the front of this section were crushed against a concrete retaining wall, resulting in the deaths of thirty two Italians, four Belgians, two French nationals and one person from Northern Ireland.

Incidentally, the cause of death is often incorrectly attributed to the subsequent collapse of the wall. Despite the disastrous incident, which also saw over six hundred people injured, the authorities decided that the match should go ahead as planned, due to fears that a cancellation would trigger more violence. Juventus won the match 1-0 but given the events of that evening, the result hardly seems important.

Fourteen Liverpool supporters were eventually convicted of manslaughter and a number of officials, including the police captain that was responsible for the relevant section of the stadium, and the former general secretary of the Belgian Football Association, were also successfully prosecuted for their part in the tragedy. English football clubs were banned from European competition for five years, with Liverpool excluded for an additional year.

Unfortunately, the disaster exacerbated the perceived connection between English football fans and hooliganism. Perhaps this played some part in the way that Liverpool fans were mistreated following the Hillsborough disaster four years later.

After leaving the Atomium, we entered Mini-Europe. Like the name suggests, this park is full of miniature replicas of European landmarks, built to a scale of 1:25. Although this was a gimmicky place that possibly appealed to children more than adults, Mum and I were impressed by the level of detail that had gone into creating these miniature buildings and landmarks.

"It's lovely. We can pretend that we are visiting all of the monuments of Europe. Don't you think so, David?" Mum asked.

A mischievous person may have commented that there is a degree of symbolism with a park full of European attractions being run by the authorities in Brussels.

I simply settled for a polite, "Yes, I think so too."

Whilst I would not go so far as to say that it was like visiting the relevant sites featured in the park, it was certainly possible to imagine how magnificent the real full-size versions would look in their original settings.

It was a strange feeling to walk through Europe and stand taller than historic landmarks such as the Eiffel Tower and the Leaning Tower of Pisa. I am used to being the shortest person in the room, so this was an unusual scenario for me. After visiting the tiny Manneken Pis statue the previous day, our trip to the Belgian capital was starting to make me feel like a giant.

Feeling like a beast, part of me was tempted to trample all over the replica landmarks and embark on a spree of destruction, as if I was a character in the 1980s computer game *Rampage*. Obviously, I am far too sensible to do that. Which is for the best, given how valuable some of the models were. For example, the replica of Grand Place cost around three hundred and fifty thousand Euros to make. It was ridiculous to think that a miniature model of a square was more valuable than many people's homes.

Whilst the faithful duplication of Europe's finest buildings was impressive, it was the small detail that accompanied them that we found to be truly charming. The miniature train that regularly made its way past Big Ben and the Houses of Parliament at Westminster was adorable. The sight of miniscule bulldozers knocking down the graffiti-laden Berlin Wall in front of the Brandenburg Gate was surprisingly uplifting.

If one of the purposes of the park was to encourage people to take an interest in some of the lesser known landmarks in Europe, then this appeared to be working. For example, I had never heard of the Adolphe Bridge in Luxembourg but I now had a visual image of this beautiful piece of architecture.

Feeling peckish, we picked up some frites from the canteen before leaving. I soon regretted the decision to eat in the canteen, which was packed with schoolchildren that were on an educational visit. Given that one of the best things about going away on a trip abroad is being able to escape the hordes of schoolchildren that I encounter on public transport during my daily commute, I was not exactly thrilled to have to navigate our way past them, merely in order to purchase a cone of frites.

Following another enjoyable portion of Belgian Frites, we left Mini-Europe and plotted our next move. As there was not any sign of a Mini-Asia or Mini-South America to explore, plans of global domination had to be put to one side.

Instead, we once again boarded the metro and headed towards Merode, in order to visit Parc du Cinquantenaire. Upon arrival, we were instantly impressed by the grandeur of the park. The monuments within the grounds were created for the National Exhibition of 1880 that commemorated the fiftieth anniversary of Belgian independence.

Its centrepiece is a triumphal arch, which had replaced the original version fifteen years after the exhibition. This may not be the most unique monument that one will ever see but the U-shaped arcade that surrounded it created an aesthetically pleasing image.

Mum suggested that it was like the Arc de Triomphe. I disagreed, stating that it looked more like the Brandenburg Gate, due to the quadriga statue on top of the multiple arches. In reality, it differs greatly from both, so neither of us were triumphant in front of the arch.

We took a few photographs from different vantage points as we strolled around the grounds. There is more to the park than the arch, with the oldest mosque in Brussels and three museums located within the surrounding area. As we were tired, we decided to wrap up our sightseeing for the trip and head back to the city centre, where we could wander through the Christmas markets and have our final evening meal.

We explored some of the other areas of the markets that we had not seen the previous night. This included an ice rink, which looked pretty against the backdrop of the Christmas decorations and stalls. I was too risk averse and afraid of people laughing at me to make use of the rink though. My memories of ice skating when I was younger involve me clinging on to the boards that surround the rink as if my life depended on it.

I did not fancy torturing myself with that experience again and I would not want to subject anyone to that unseemly sight. Besides, my brother had broken his arm the previous year and had informed me, multiple times, that ice skating is one of the most common activities leading to broken bones.

I remember being intrigued by a stall that sold churros. The fried dough-based snack reminded me of a type of Chinese food that I had eaten plenty of during my childhood. The Chinese version is usually served with congee, so I was surprised to see this Spanish variant being dipped into chocolate sauce.

Although we did not purchase any churros, it does highlight how Christmas markets provide people with an opportunity to sample foods and goods from other countries and cultures. Here we were, a mother and son of Chinese and British origin, standing in front of a stall selling a traditional Spanish snack in a market in Belgium. Continuing the international theme, we decided to have dinner at a Chinese restaurant near our hotel.

Before retiring to our hotel for the night, we could not resist the temptation to watch the light show at Grand Place for the final time. It was the most fitting end to a lovely few days in Brussels shortly before Christmas. Mum and I reminisce about the light show more than the historic landmarks within the city. This is not a reflection on the landmarks themselves but a result of the magical impression left by the show.

It was the highlight of a successful first trip that was, for once, not built around a sporting event. More importantly, I had made it through the entire trip without Mum detecting a scent of my plan to quit my university course. I even managed to get through Christmas and New Year without telling her. In the end, it was like most things in life; after weeks of building it up to be a bigger issue than it was, she was understanding and supportive.

241

As I reflected on my final trip of the year, it was now crystal clear that my obsession with sport had been superseded by my love of travel, which was now my true passion.

# CHAPTER 14: THANK YOU
## CLOSING WORDS FROM THE UNITED KINGDOM
## DECEMBER 2019

The process of writing this book has been interesting and thoroughly enjoyable. I have had to delve deep into my memory banks, which has caused me to realise how much I have changed as a person over the course of the last decade. That is part of life; after all, our experiences shape who we are.

Indeed, I am undoubtedly a different person to the one that started writing this book all those months ago. And I am sure that I will be different, although almost certainly still socially awkward, by the time that I release the next one.

The process of compiling the previous couple of hundred pages has allowed me to reflect on my time spent travelling to different places around the world. I am truly blessed to have been able to visit so many wonderful places and create such fantastic memories; even if I have made a fool of myself in the process.

I am grateful for having such loving parents, who have both played their part in my transformation from an borderline recluse to an introverted global explorer. They have also been good sports by allowing me to write about our comical mishaps, as have all of the other people that feature.

My wonderful wife, Carol, has also shown remarkable patience to have put up with my distracted mind and the many hours that I have spent adding new material when I was supposed to be feigning interest in the latest episode of *Emmerdale*.

The train operating companies of the North-West of England also deserve a mention for the invaluable contribution that they have made to the creation of this book. The vast majority of it has been written whilst either on one of their overcrowded trains or waiting at the station for one of their delayed vehicles to arrive. Without such a slow and unreliable service, I am not sure where I would have found the time required to complete the book.

Putting pen to paper, or in my case thumbs to touchscreen, I have made use of the time more effectively than when I used to spend the entirety of my commute playing the mobile version of *Football Manager*. Just do not tell the loyal fans of Colchester United, who were enjoying their rapid rise towards the Premier League until I abandoned their cause.

If the readers that have made it to the end of the book have taken even a miniscule fraction of the level of enjoyment from my misadventures that I have, then I will be most pleased. In any case, you should have enough material to make fun of me for years to come.

*　*　*

If, for some unexpected reason, you have enjoyed reading the book, the best way to show your approval would be to leave a review on the Amazon website. This can make a big difference for a small-time independent author like me. You can also tell your friends that they should read a book about a strange man that went on a few holidays with his mum and dad.

More information can be found on my website - www.theadventuresofanintrovert.com, which features a wider range of my photographs, a regularly updated blog and news updates regarding other books that I am set to release. I thank you in advance for the much-appreciated support.

Other books by the same author include:

*Tales of an Unsociable Traveller: The Road from Wigan Pier to Tsukiji Fish Market*

Printed in Great Britain
by Amazon

74253498R00151